MW00643295

Dennis O'Driscoll · Collected Poems

Dennis O'Driscoll was born in Thurles, Co. Tipperary in 1954. His publications include nine collections of poetry, a book of essays, two collections of literary quotations and the much admired *Stepping Stones*, interviews with Seamus Heaney (2008). He received a Lannan Literary Award in 1999. Before his untimely death during the Christmas holiday, 2012, he had completed *A Michael Hamburger Reader*, his homage to another fellow poet which is published simultaneously with this book, and a second collection of essays, *The Outnumbered Poet*. He received numerous honours and awards both in Ireland and the USA. He worked for almost forty years in Ireland's Revenue and Customs service.

By Dennis O'Driscoll

DENNIS O'DRISCOLL

Collected Poems

CARCANET

First published in Great Britain in 2017 by

Carcanet Press Limited
Alliance House
Cross Street
Manchester M2 7AQ
www.carcanet.co.uk

We welcome your feedback: info@carcanet.co.uk

A CIP catalogue record for this book is available
from the British Library, ISBN 978 1 78410 511 2

The publisher acknowledges financial assistance
from Arts Council England

Designed and set in Monotype Ehrhardt by Anvil
Printed and bound in England by SRP Ltd, Exeter

PUBLISHER'S NOTE

THIS book follows the plan which Dennis O'Driscoll drew up for his *Collected Poems* in May 2010, after he had completed the last collection of poems that he was to oversee, *Dear Life*. He died in December 2012 leaving 33 uncollected poems. Whether he had intended the *Collected Poems* to be his next book is not known.

His selection adds back to the choice he made for his *New and Selected Poems*, published in 2004, a number of poems from earlier books: 2 from *Kist*, 6 from *Hidden Extras*, 17 from *Long Story Short*, 13 from *Quality Time*, 6 from *Weather Permitting* and 12 from *Exemplary Damages*. He chose the two later collections, *Reality Check* and *Dear Life*, in full and proposed the addition of his post-*Dear Life* poems. These were published posthumously in 2014 as *Update* and are all included here.

He revised a number of poems for this collection and asked that the versions given here should be considered definitive and adopted for any future printings – and that his omissions be regarded as permanent exclusions.

ACKNOWLEDGEMENTS

Poems in this collection are from the following: *Kist* (Dolmen Press, 1982), *Hidden Extras* (Anvil Press and Dedalus Press, Dublin, 1987), *Long Story Short* (Anvil Press and Dedalus Press, Dublin, 1993), *Quality Time* (Anvil Press, 1997), *Weather Permitting* (Anvil Press, 1999), *Exemplary Damages* (Anvil Press, 2002), *New and Selected Poems* (Anvil Press, 2004), *Reality Check* (Anvil Press and Copper Canyon Press, 2007), *Dear Life* (Anvil Press and Copper Canyon Press, 2012) and *Update* (Anvil Press and Copper Canyon Press, 2014). 'The Bottom Line' was originally published in a limited edition booklet (Dedalus Editions No. 5, 1994).

CONTENTS

from Kist (1982)

from Hidden Extras (1987)

from Long Story Short (1993)

The Bottom Line (1994)

from Quality Time (1997)

9

from Weather Permitting (1999)

from Exemplary Damages (2002)

Foreseeable Futures (2004)
[from *New and Selected Poems*]

Reality Check (2007)

Dear Life (2012)

Update (2014)

From
Kist
(1982)

WISH

In a children's book, I read how wishbones
could be used as legs for model men.

Then, each taking a leg,
we pulled and broke.

The one who got a leg and groin
also got a wish.

KIST

On this lovers' morning, our hearts chime.
Later, the slow death knell of hers
and a coffin door slamming
in her last chill breath.

Preparing me for your
death, strands of silver,
coffin-handle bright,
thread your oak-brown hair.

And, as I pace behind the hearse,
my own face in its glass
takes on the wrinkled grain
of coffin wood.

(14 February 1975)

SIBLINGS

I am writing at exactly the moment
you sent me the message of his death
precisely this time last year.

Returning home from school to an empty house,
you learn the vulnerability of those
who know how thin the barrier of flesh is,

that looking forward becomes looking back
until there is nothing either way but death.
It is quiet in the office as I write,

hiding this paper under a file,
heat rising from radiators, someone whistling,
someone listing soccer scores.

We have spent a year without him – his thoughts
scattered, his burden of organs eased.
This is just another working day here:

queries, letters, tea-breaks, forms.
Any minute now some telephone will ring
but I do not dread its news, as then.

I concentrate upon this moment, cup it in my hands,
to understand what you have lost in these
past years as home became an orphanage

and the carpet in the hall was soiled
with the clay of their two burials,
your world refracted by a lens of tears.

TRACES

I

time sieves us into dust
our residue is gall-stone, bone
flesh offers no protection
elbow and back wear through its fabric

II

beneath the surface of our lives
skin deep is buried death
(like underwear we carry skeletons
folded neatly in our trunks)

III

its name is signed
between lines of forehead
in calligraphy of ribs
shakily on wet cardiogram, last will

IV

even from the brain's padded cells
life eventually escapes
bones like scaffolding mark sites
where flesh walls stood

PORLOCK

this is the best poem I have never written
it is composed of all the stunning lines I thought up
but lacked the time or place or paper to jot down

this is a poem of distractions, interruptions, clamouring telephones
this is a poem that reveals how incompatible with verse my life is
this is a home for mentally lapsed poems

this is the lost property office of poetry
this is my poem without a hero, conceived but never born
this is a prisoner of consciousness, a victim of intelligence leaks

this is the poem that cannot learn itself by heart
this is the poem that has not found its individual voice
this is the poem that has forgotten its own name

this is my most unmemorable creation
these are my most disposable lines
this is the poem that dispenses with words

WINGS

like tumbling masonry pigeons topple from a building
magpies flock for gold to where sun gilds a tree

the heron paddles with its skirts rolled up
lapwings at their air base wear a crew cut

thrushes pluck a field's loose threads
kettle swans simmer on electric rings

a team of wild geese rows across the evening cheering
and an exhibitionist bat opens a mackintosh

the hawk plays darts, the swallows skate
the drunken cuckoo hiccups one last time

then night's television screen of stars is switched on
a murder story with the owl's loud screams

PRAYER

Streets flood, thunder erupts,
wind-bent sycamore
is peeled of orange leaves.

Autumn's spreading rust,
our fire glows;
and I imagine refuge:

toiling together, reap and sow,
chancel chipped by rain,
vellum pages, plainsong,

smoothing snow of prayer.
If I could find a God
then I would believe,

bowing before its wind, its power.
I need to pursue music,
thunder, fire,

until they lead me
to this God
whom, already, I adore.

MIRACLES

I *Cana*

Making a chalice
of the glass
he wounded water,

keeping his blood,
his good wine,
until last.

II *Desert*

Loaves were multiplied
so that the poor
would eat their fill.

Beneath bread's crusted dome,
freshly each day,
he chose to come.

III *Calvary*

An icicle,
his frozen body drips.

Our wrongs rust
his forgiving palms.

His death, a red sunset,
brings the next day fair.

FLATLAND

Take-away foods, small late-night stores,
record dealers, posters for Folk Mass.
Coke and fried chicken make an ideal meal here,
unpacked in a bedsit, knocked back near a one-bar fire.

Down bicycle-cluttered corridor, by coinbox telephone,
special-offer leaflets, buff uncollected post,
weekends open optimistically beforehand
like sands of package holiday brochures.

Falling plaster bares ceiling laths, like piano keys
stripped of their ivory; fireplaces are blocked.
Revolving record wheels, slow music after pubs,
will transport lovers into a seagull-velvet dawn,

into stale cigarette smoke, lingering tastes of beer;
outside, ivy-bearded trees conceal the rubbish bins;
milk cartons roll through long-haired lawns;
the hall door buttoned with bells.

In neat gardens on the next street, wickerwork branches
will be baskets plump with fruit yet.
Couples yawn and part. Sunday now,
the heavy hours weigh down the watch's scales

to 4 o'clock, sports programmes on the radio,
as evening's cigarette-butt is stubbed out,
leaving an ashen sky which only
a working Monday will illuminate.

SOMEONE

someone is dressing up for death today, a change of skirt or tie
eating a final feast of buttered sliced pan, tea
scarcely having noticed the erection that was his last
shaving his face to marble for the icy laying out
spraying with deodorant her coarse armpit grass
someone today is leaving home on business
saluting, terminally, the neighbours who will join in the cortege
someone is paring his nails for the last time, a precious moment
someone's waist will not be marked with elastic in the future
someone is putting out milkbottles for a day that will not come
someone's fresh breath is about to be taken clean away
someone is writing a cheque that will be rejected as 'drawer deceased'
someone is circling posthumous dates on a calendar
someone is listening to an irrelevant weather forecast
someone is making rash promises to friends
someone's coffin is being sanded, laminated, shined
who feels this morning quite as well as ever
someone if asked would find nothing remarkable in today's date
perfume and goodbyes her final will and testament
someone today is seeing the world for the last time
as innocently as he had seen it first

From
Hidden Extras
(1987)

FIRST IMPRESSIONS

Open the hall door and let the year's
first sunlight in, picking its way through
coal seams of darkness: a gleaming copper
hot-water pipe; a bale of wheaten straw.

Hard green supermarket pears mellow on
the window-sill, one blackbird still gives preferential
treatment to our cul-de-sac, only a powdery,
eye-shadow cloud now smudging the sun.

Bad pennies, earth's small change,
dandelions are scattered everywhere.
Oval buds begin to hatch. And the sun
slips in through the front door,

restoring our storm-battered house,
converting it into a holiday home.

MIDDLE-CLASS BLUES

He has everything.
A beautiful young wife.
A comfortable home.
A secure job.
A velvet three-piece suite.
A metallic-silver car.
A mahogany cocktail cabinet.
A rugby trophy.
A remote-controlled music centre.
A set of golf clubs under the hallstand.
A fair-haired daughter learning to walk.

What he is afraid of most
and what keeps him tossing some nights
on the electric underblanket,
listening to the antique clock
clicking with disapproval from the landing,
are the stories that begin:
He had everything.
A beautiful young wife.
A comfortable home.
A secure job.
Then one day.

HERE AND NOW

There's a mirror that has seen me for the last time
— JORGE LUIS BORGES

There are poems I could write only in present tense
that I will never be in a position to again:
about looking into a mirror and seeing not one grey hair
or sitting with you in an unburgled living room,
the terminal diseases still dormant in our cells.

There is the poem of this very moment,
sunset streaking the horizon like a circus poster,
a v-neck of geese homing from stubble,
thistle fleece rising like soap bubbles,
a wasp in jockey colours racing the dark.

There is the poem of this unrecorded second,
so nondescript, so tame, so plain:
the smack of a gardener's spade, a distracting hum,
radio jingles leaching through a parked car;
and now a milkman's helper is distributing bills.

Somewhere else, locked in our past tense, beyond grasp,
first lovers thrill to mutual discoveries:
beginnings we too recall, pristine invigorating dawns
fresh as if earth's architect just left,
cloud's mortar setting above building-rubble hills.

And elsewhere, too, a world of frenzy: commodity markets,
blackberry riot police, crises of age and youth.
The unwrinkled glass that holds me in the balance
between past and future is a river I must cross,
floating out of depth towards its unreflective side.

READER'S DIGEST FAMILY MEDICAL ADVISER

'An A–Z Guide to Everyday Ailments'

Everyday asthma and brain tumour.
Everyday chilblains, cancers, coronaries.
Everyday depression and epilepsy.
Everyday falls and gallstones.
Everyday Hodgkin's disease and insomnia.
Everyday jaundice, keratosis, leukaemia.
Everyday multiple sclerosis, nephritis, ovarian cyst.
Everyday polio, pneumonia, quinsy, rheumatic pain.
Everyday syphilis, threadworm, ulcer, varicose vein.

Six hundred and twenty-four pages long.
Three columns wide.
One size fits all.

TWO SILENCES

I

his morning calls over, my father drives outside the town
he parks beside a rusty gate tied with baling twine
shy daisies eye me from a lush coat of green
we unpack lunch with the windows down
the sandwiches my mother made taste creamy and fresh
we dine in perfect silence
I smell the dark vapour from his coffee flask
and drink tickling lemonade from a chipped cup
there are slices of chocolate swiss-roll for dessert
and a banana ripening into cheetah spots
a breeze brings goosebumps to the barks
of trees that toss their heads of leaves back
to form chintzy lampshades for the sun
we take our ease, breadcrumbs hardening in our laps

II

my father was turning away from life exiled in pain
harder to locate with each hospital visit
drumming sonatas of impatience on a bedside locker
shuffling among dressing-gowned wraiths
whose slippers had worn the corridor linoleum to a blur:
after he was granted access to his day-clothes
I searched the gloomy wood-panelled billiard-room
and the tacky shop of evening papers, Get Well cards
a summer shower was drooping at the time I found him
on a remote bench beneath a patulous tree
ground staff clattered past with rake and barrow
in the recreation hall the chaplain would be tuning the TV
out at sea the mail boat was dissolving into mist
as I came near he turned the other way

DISTURBING MY MOTHER

In the ten years since our last direct exchange,
I have not dared to interrupt your rest.
It is so long since we were one family,
talking together in one inviolable room.

Our silence now is like a Sunday afternoon at home:
you taking your weekly break, dozing by the fire,
the newspaper sliding down your knees,
your face palsied by twitching flames.

A decade ago, your grating final breath
– a rasping gate – admitted death
and we set off on our own, your offspring,
a hunted, howling, endangered flock.

On the anniversary of your assimilation into pain,
I am referred to the same hospital for an x-ray.
Another family weeps at the entrance awning,
appalled at the indifference sweeping past.

'You're finished', the radiographer announces,
instructs me to put back my clothes and leave.
My future prospects show up clearly:
a ghost free of flesh, uniting you and me.

I await the medical results as I once waited
for exam reports during tense summer holidays,
going over the symptoms in my head like maths,
to calculate whether I pass or fail.

Back home, everything seems possible: sun amplifies
the silence, heats the garden seat, imprints on brick
the perfect image of this sycamore in which a bird, pumped
full of song, suppresses knowledge of life's hidden extras.

SIBLINGS REVISITED

I   *Declan at Twenty*

Only a few years ago, it was Jennings schoolboy stories
that I brought you. Now, I pack avant-garde books:
Tom Mallin, Alan Burns, a B. S Johnson play.

'There isn't enough enthusiasm in the world', you tell me.
And yours is revealed, petitioning for the release of prisoners,
contributing a series entitled 'Freedom' to *The Tipperary Star*,
reading African novelists, surveying a heron's nest,
displaying your unframed paintings along the bedroom wall.
In one corner, where a cliff of rock magazines used to rise,
back issues of *New Statesman* pile – the town's sole subscriber.
Of late, you have taken to playing the trumpet,
scorning sheet music in favour of the improvised tune.

You were maturing, swelling with cells, as parental death loomed,
called twice from the classroom for grim news.
I hint at the advantages of further studies sometimes.
Without success. And out of your seasonal job, of bog work,
you pay for essentials: subscriptions, membership fees, jazz LPs.
On blustery days, I wonder if the wind is with or against you
as you cycle there, along unsheltered miles . . .

Play me, improvise on the trumpet, the rhythm of your new life.
Blast me the notes of your freedom.
Show me how to extend past experience to joy.

II   *Eithne at Eighteen*

The local paper carries your photograph this week,
at work collating parish registers of baptisms and marriages.
But death is the category you first kept records of.

I remember you waiting in the spacious hospital lobby,
too young to visit our mother's cancer ward

though old enough to know the worst.
Then growing up to watch our father's graph
decline so rapidly towards the grave;
to buy school clothes with an executor's cheque.

Flush with saved earnings from your temporary job now,
you can afford to join me in the city for a day trip,
greeting me with the smile of the unvanquished,
trying on endless styles in department store cubicles.

You edge your way into the world with relish,
needing only a little support at this stage,
wanting only to channel your ardency
into one of the scores of jobs you patiently apply for
while vast untapped talent drains down the dole queues.

Enjoy the long evenings of these first post-school days.
Sleep well in our parents' ample bed.
That smile you surrender generously
has been achieved against the greatest odds.

DISARMAMENT

your first grey hairs
are picked off readily enough
and harmony restored

that metal sheen proliferates
and you risk baldness
as you eliminate invaders

STILLBORN

What we are lamenting
Is what has not been
And what will not have seen
This mild May morning.

What we are lamenting
Is unsuckled air
And what was brought to bear
This mild May morning.

What we are lamenting
Is our flesh and blood, this child
That has not laughed or cried
This mild May morning.

What we are lamenting
Is the life we crave
Snatched from the cradle to the grave
This mild May morning.

NORMALLY SPEAKING

To assume everything has meaning.
To return at evening
feeling you have earned a rest
and put your feet up
before a glowing TV set and fire.
To have your favourite shows.
To be married to a local
whom your parents absolutely adore.
To be satisfied with what you have,
the neighbours, the current hemline,
the dual immersion, the government doing its best.
To keep to an average size
and buy clothes off the rack.
To bear the kind of face
that can be made-up to prettiness.
To head contentedly for work
knowing how bored you'd be at home.
To book holidays to where bodies blend,
tanned like sandgrains.
To be given to little excesses:
Christmas hangovers, spike high heels,
chocolate éclair binges, lightened hair.
To postpone children until the house extension
can be afforded and the car paid off.
To see the world through double glazing
and find nothing wrong.
To expect to go on living like this
and to look straight forward. No regrets.
To get up each day neither in wonder nor in fear,
meeting people on the bus you recognise
and who accept you, without question, for what you are.

WHAT SHE DOES NOT KNOW IS

That she is a widow.
That these are the last untinged memories of her life.
That he is slumped in his seat at a lay-by.
That a policeman is trying to revive him.
That the knife and fork she has set are merely decorative.
That the steak beside the pan will go to waste.
That he has lost his appetite.
That the house she is tidying is for sale.
That the holiday snap will be used for his memorial card.
That he will not be subjected to direct light again.
That she will spend all night brewing tears.
That it is not his car she will soon hear slowing down outside.

DUMB CREATURES

autistic turtles are rent from their husks
the Himalayan musk's anus is raided for cosmetics
boiling pots of jellyfish spill over into oil

the rhino's horn is ground as aphrodisiac
tanned snakeskin tempts the Eden-seeking tourists
lizard wallets clasp their cash, elephant legs make trash cans

oryx and leopard blaze out of guns' telescopic sights
wildflowers draw their petal blinds tight
toadspawn is drained from ponds, corncrakes harvested

and butchered human skulls heap up like coral souvenirs
or the tiers of sterile eggs left unhatched by sea birds
on the beaches of atomic-test atolls

SERVING TIME

Fulfilling the forecast on the breakfast radio,
pods of hail were shelled on window ledges.
A wind that would whittle headstones
down to bones still rages as this poem
comes to you live from the second floor.
I take my place in the commentary box.

Here we all congregate at public hatch and desk:
the skinny spectacled clerk
with the Tupperware-packed lunch;
the new recruit, earnest in rolled-up sleeves;
the *True Romance* and thriller readers;
the lazy supervisor trying to command respect.

To work is to pray, but days stretch
long and monotonous as eternity
in my cell, where I toil without hope,
having groped from darkness summoned by bells:
the alarm clock's halo luminous, the plainsong
of birds unbinding, note by note, the night.

Look around this narrow retreat:
you cannot miss my two steel presses,
one seething with memos, the other hoarding forms;
and a cabinet with deckled piles of correspondence
from banks, corporations, accountancy firms.
I am undisputed Lord of the Files.

You may contact me here on weekdays
except during vacations and lunch.
Telephone queries, staff consultations
interrupt this script, as horns, hydraulic sneers,
sirens whimpering like hurt dogs
reach me from the piercing street.

It is not much of a life, serving time,
applying directives or laws,
and therefore not much of a poem,
though revelation strikes occasionally:
a glimmer of wisdom shimmering on my coatstand,
an inkling of transcendence in a momentary hush.

Search my desk with me: stamps and staples,
official envelopes, twine, press cuttings,
address books, antacid tablets, foreign coins.
What was it I set out to find?
A pair of shoelaces? The spare house key?
The secrets of the universe?

Look out across the two small apertures:
you can watch the backs of other blocks,
equal in dreariness. One cube of glass

reflects sky, songless birds, slipping sun;
and I can make out clustered heads,
eggs incubating within the metal combs.

Will they ever metamorphose and float away?
Open the window a little before it steams.
Look. Gulls dipping for tea-break crusts
evoke deserted shores, skuas, kittiwakes,
wings clipping uneven hems of waves,
chestnut streams charging untamed.

Although I plod routinely on,
greeting familiar faces in the same place,
espying the same familiar strangers in the streets,
changes do occur, marked by collections, whip-rounds.
The amended staff-sheet instructs us to delete
the name of one colleague, killed cycling from work.

As these last words are relayed to you,
my watch's nervous tic advances on half-five.
I exit past the check-in clock where red blobs glow
like tail-lights in the traffic home
or votive lamps we lit as children
praying for a favourable exam result, a steady job.

OFFICE PHOTOGRAPH

for Margaret O'Sullivan

There will be no reunion for this class of people:
some are dead already; one immured in a convent;
others ill, retired, transferred, settled abroad.

But, for the duration of this photograph,
a fresh, foot-stamping morning reigns
(a few wear overcoats) and in the foreground

a wiry tree is barbed with buds.
Behind us, sun disperses shadows
of venetian blinds, like prison bars, on desks

and projects the film of dust specks
fidgeting on our stacked backlog of files.
We stare – clear-eyed, smiling – into a pensionable future.

Dressed in our best and at companionable ease,
we stand oblivious of how such scenes
will flash before us, summoning features

out of memory's frame, blurred by moving time;
and how this tableau, so tranquil in spring light,
so fixed in a known hour and place,

will develop into a focal point of change
as news comes of some name we match, then,
to a placid, frank, unwary face.

MAN GOING TO THE OFFICE

(a painting by Fernando Botero)

They all rush to the windows as he leaves.

Wife, child, sister-in-law and servant wave,
though they might also be dismissing him, pushing him away,
wiping him out of their lives with imaginary dusters,
holding palms out for their share of his alms.
Now that his business-suited back is turned, they can relax:
mother pours another coffee, crocheted with cream,
and flicks through glossy magazines, winnowing crumbs of toast;
the open window ideal for sunbathing or keeping track of neighbours;
the afternoon free for an unmolested nap, when sister gardens
and the infant's pudgy mouth is hushed with jelly beans.

As he bustles back through the front door at night, muttering,
he will find an immaculate cloth set, a hot meal ready.
Laying his bowler crown aside, dabbing his regal moustache,
he will sit, enthroned, at the head of the rectangular table
permitting the poodle, a foppish courtier, to lick his feet,
throwing it rinds of meat and bread.
And the ladies-in-waiting will pamper him,
bridling their impatience or stifling scorn,
careful not to exasperate him like clients
or provoke, like inefficient secretaries, a fit of spleen.

AT THE TOP

In overheated rooms, hung with rustic prints,
they sling jackets off and their sweatlines show.
A dozen identical concrete floors below,
their reserved parking spaces are mapped out.

These are the indispensable men of the world
who know the cost-effectiveness of everything,
set sales targets, launch new lines, flamboyantly
sign redundancy notices and dividend cheques.

At rush-hour, kaleidoscopes of company cars
clash in the tailbacks of suburban carriageways.
Some stay late, poring over bad debts,
loosening the noose of a tie around

a forceful neck, contemplating a change
of advertising agency or adding final
touches to the rationalisation plan.
Wars, shortages, strikes all have their uses.

Even futures can be traded in.
The past is something to be grappled with
when pre-tax profits need to be compared.
Fortune shines on them like bonus issues of shares.

A LIFE STUDY

Here is a woman on a bus
half-way through a book
entitled simply *Life*.

I squint, but cannot decipher
who the author is
or what it is about.

She seems to be enjoying it
or is too absorbed at least
to look out at shoppers

wrapped up in their thoughts.
How is *Life* classified?
Fantasy, allegory, myth?

Is she dying to know
the kind of ending it will have?
The book slams unexpectedly.

She gets off at the next stop.

CONCEPTION

scum of humanity
seed of pain

multiple warheads
arms racing to stake their claim

the triumphant achieve spina bifida
or ambition malnutrition or fame

and hundreds of millions of sprigs
are disseminated in vain

a lost civilisation
a bedclothes stain

SPOILED CHILD

my child recedes inside me
and need never puzzle where it came from
or lose a football in the dusty laurel bushes
or sneak change from my jacket to buy sweets

my child will not engage in active military service
or make excuses about its school report
or look up from a picture book, dribbling a pink smile
or qualify for free glasses or school lunch

my child will not become a prodigy of musicianship or crime
and will evince no appetite for hamburgers or drugs
and will suffer neither orgasm nor kidney stones
reduced neither to a statistic nor a sacrifice

my child will not play space games with its cousins
or sit adrift on a grandparent's choppy lap
or slit its wrists or erect a loving headstone on my grave
or store a secret name for frogs or treetops

my child will not be a comfort to my old age
my child will not be cheated or promoted or denied
my child will trail me, like a guardian angel, all my life
its blemishes, its beauty, its shortcomings and promise

forever unsullied and unfulfilled

KILLYKEEN

Such glowing of grass
and plopping of fish
and lapping of water
and sauntering of cattle
and loosening of leaves
mottled as petrified rock . . .

The late year rallies
for another few days,
musters forces
of bees and midges
and weightless butterflies
for the last pre-winter raids.

Watch that seabird
skim like a dandelion puff
above the lake,
the shiny pate of which
is barely creased.
Peace, I suppose,

is the word for this,
for so much buzzing and beating
and screeching and splashing
as we fix on a line of nettle-dense
pines, the lake slaking
a thirst we carried –

a parched earthenware jar –
through the citified year.
A hare among ferns at dawn.
Now a heron hunched against sunset.
I toss a stone into the water
to see how deep it goes.

DAY AND NIGHT

I

wrapped in a sheer white negligee
      you are a fog-bound landscape
familiar but seen in a new light
      transformed by seamless mist
tantalising, trimmed with tufts of cloud
      I know that after the fog lifts
the climate will turn sultry
      I can detect a sun-like breast
already radiating through the chiffon dawn

II

in hot darkness, the transistor on
      a five-note raga plays
five senses that ascend the scale of longing:
      until the gasps of music peter out
and a taut night is plucked limp
      we are out of meaning's reach
your vellum blotted with invisible ink
      my head at rest
between your breasts' parentheses

CONTRACTS

after Paul Celan

I   *Irisch*

Grant me ingress
to your sleep
to count sheep,
licence to traverse
your dream slopes,
the turbary rights
of your heart's peat,
in perpetuity.

II   *Du Warst*

You were my only loophole
in the repressive act of death:

my last escape clause.

TIME-SHARING

In our time together, we are
travelling in the heated car, a violin
concerto uncoiling from the radio,
hills streaming with winter cold,
year-end fields threadbare
from wear and tear of cattle, burnt
meringue of snow on mountain tops.

We blurt past farms and cottages:
those whose era we share
are glaring from net curtains
at a morning chill for milking
or for setting off to factories in the town,
their segments of road deserted.
It is like a childhood journey

of sleep and open-eyed surprise,
of hermetically sealed life
in the eternal present
before the final destination is reached.
We hold hands on the gear stick
and, at this moment,
fear for nothing except the future.

THURLES

after Zbigniew Herbert

A childhood too boring for words
is lost without a fragment in that town.
And, so, I have held my tongue about its gutturals;
its sky slated consistently with cloud;
its mossy roofs restraining excesses of rain.

One house watches out for me though.
I know where its colander is kept and the special
knack required to use its tin-opener
and the exact key in which the kitchen door,
scuffed by a ring-board, creaks:

things I cannot depict in dictionary terms,
through heartless words that fail to resonate.
Others are suppressed in embarrassment or pain
(all families have passed their own equivalents
to the Official Secrets Act).

Yet everything there translates into feeling:
the plates the dead have eaten from before us,
the layers of wallpaper that still pattern memory,
the hairline crack in marble that was my fault,
the rose-arched garden explored down to its last stone.

Back in the city, I resort to standard words again.
Unable to identify possessions by their first names,
I call them only by their surnames
– by their brand names –
and will never discover their real names.

INFIDELITY

What O'Driscoll needs is what Leopold Bloom frankly adores:
the 'ample, bedwarmed flesh' of Molly Bloom. For he lacks
credence in the body, its sweetness and plenty.

            — AIDAN MATHEWS, *The Irish Times*

they are letting us down, the bedwarmed women
being let down themselves into beds of clay
that swallowed Molly Bloom and Milly Bloom
those who fed our grandfathers' fantasies and our own
those who combed the library shelves for historical romances

those whose shining eyes solicited the darker sides of streets
those who were the fertile ground where ancestral seeds fell
those who held their flesh at arm's length
and those with gyrating bodies bandaged in tight jeans
only bony fingers left to caress your thinning scalp

gone those posing for sepia photographs and cheap videos
all the old loves that haunted your marriage becoming ghosts
all let down by their flesh, bra cups emptied, basques unbound
all those around whose necks possessive hands coiled
those doing nature's work or God's, lay sisters or unmarried mums

serene behind the mortician's make-up
they will be stripped of every fleshy asset
and after their brief orbit of the globe
silent as the ovum's mysterious rotations
will be brought gently down to earth

HOME AFFAIRS

Death is moving into newly-constructed suburbs,
through semi-detached houses, identical twins.
Black limos will transport widows who have come as brides . . .

Readymix trucks drum up concrete support
where the foundations of our married lives are laid.
We will slice the keyhole loaf of bread together here.

This evening, a rainbow unfolded its colour chart
and I imagined these dwellings once painted, tamed:
the knock of radiators in a dry-lined sitting room;

whispers and bickerings filtered through air vents;
the small-hour lulls only troubled sleepers know
or babysitters waiting for the owners to reach home.

                 *

Dashed housefronts gleam like popcorn, a mirage
seen from what will be the main road through estates,
bearing working couples, fuel deliveries or crowded bus,
pavements reserved for skateboards, shopping trolleys, prams.

We are strolling on its asphalt arc, a desert airstrip
covering ancient cow-tracks, smoothing paths,
a digger's tyre marks – arrowheads – along its verge.
All we will reap from now on in this raw settlement

are plastic piping, gypsum board and brick.
New fridges and washing machines will rust
in mountains of indestructible sediment,
our baths end up as drinking troughs.

                 *

With a poker for sword, a fireguard for shield,
you provoke the blazing fangs to fume and spit.
Will they know peace who sit quietly in their own rooms?
I trace the braille goosebumps of your body
and begin to lip-read as the night intensifies.

*

It is an ordinary morning without pain.
Sun's spotlight stares from a dishevelled sky,
ruffled with clouds like a safety curtain.
Summer is in heat again: gooseberry scrotums swell,
hard blackberry knuckles will soon ooze with blood.

The window swings out on to a butterfly-light breeze,
a heady aura of sweet peas, rose fumes, poppy seasoning.
Cut lawns exude fresh hay; grasshopper blades whirr;
resinous smells of wood pervade the tool shed.
No bad news breaks today, no urgent summons,

no pacing outside intensive care units.
The sun blossoms in its foliage of cloud
and we fortify ourselves with its light, our house's silence,
against the troubles, worries, turmoil
other mornings will, irrevocably, bring.

BREVIARY

Storm

a vein of lightning slits the sky
discharges a haemorrhage of rain

*

Idolatry

the strawberry is a sacred heart
a tooth here is a foot in heaven

*

Hospital

between pre-natal and mortuary
the research unit

*

Manna

a yolk of moon
shell speckled with stars

*

Night Watch

to get to sleep
he started to count sheep
but they too were
being led to the slaughter

*

The Father

after William Carlos Williams

so much depends
upon the sound
of his red car

coming at night
around the final bend
toward home

scattering white chickens
and shattering glazed puddles
of rain

From
Long Story Short
(1993)

COUNTRY ROADS

Black and white
marble whirls
of light and cloud
mark the end
of another November day.
Now the car
is pressing forward,
a stray cat, bright-eyed,
peering through the dark.

How desolate
the route looks
from the wind-rocked
driving seat.
On the stereo
the Solemn Vespers join
with the fading horizon
to map out
the world to come.

COUPLES

The frail economies
those cars contain.

Small hatchbacks
bought on term loans.

She is pregnant
with their first.

His boss has hinted
at lay-offs.

They part with a kiss
outside her office.

Maybe his orders
will improve.

Maybe she will
be made permanent.

ALCHEMY

Over many years
I have toiled
to create
Essence of Life
as bath cubes and perfume
on a commercial basis.

But no matter
how much laughter
or even love I add
to the tear ducts and spleen,
I cannot purge
some acrid residues.

To support my children
– who eat everything sweet
they lay their hands on –
I may cut my losses soon
and sell it all off
as an insect repellent

or an anaphrodisiac.

THE DEATH OF A BEEKEEPER

after reading the novel by Lars Gustafsson

Dusk strikes early this far north.
Silver days. Then dark
no house light perforates.

I will not talk of illness.
I will take the dog out walking
to the summer huts

and know I am alive
by the swarms of breath condensing,
tracks left behind me in the snow.

Iced marsh and lake
whichever way I go...
I startle elks

a weekender will shoot
when this pale landscape thaws,
gives up its ghost.

Something gnaws my flesh,
like mice behind
a skirting board.

I am a healthy distance
from the hospital,
doctors homing in

on microscopic sections,
masked and gloved,
combing through my cells.

The plaster ceiling
of the sky caves in
and snow cascades,

packs my hut in styrofoam
as though for despatch
(URGENT: PERISHABLE GOODS)

to a more temperate zone.
Soft flakes, white corpuscles,
will ease my pain.

Under Alpine roofs,
the bees are stacked
in viscous sleep,

their sun god hibernates
beneath the frozen lake.
My dog no longer

recognises me by smell;
I am changed.
Snow pollinates the ground,

simplifies the shapes of things.
Then snow blots out
all record of the snow.

MISTAKEN IDENTITY

Could I begin by asking what you were thinking of as the gunman approached?

Nothing very precise, actually. I was vaguely annoyed at pet owners. It's not fair to those who walk the streets. I'm nearly sure I had a flash of memory also – something reminded me of the nest under the yew at my grandmother's. We found a clutch of warm, fawn eggs one summer there.

A woman, too, I think, a belt tied loosely round her waist?

Yes, that's right. She proved to be a key witness.

I've just recalled the way the hens would tap their legs like tuning forks, then hold their drawling notes long into the afternoon. My grandmother was always making things – knitting or crochet. Or baking. Peach flans, seed cakes, raspberry meringues.

What kind of fear did you experience as the killer was about to strike?

I was a bit behind in my work. A few times in the last month or so a pain had flared down my left thigh. Fear that the eldest would go near the quarry again, that the new video might be robbed during our holiday.

Can you describe how you felt after you learned the news?

It was a kind of reverse dream. You know how when you dream that you've done something with someone (or *to* someone, as it often is) you expect them to remember the experience too. I once flew under the waves with the kids, viewing candy-striped fish from the cockpit . . .

This time, it is they who have the details; I can't remember any of it – the shot, the emulsion of blood, the surgeon, the dizzy lowering into the clay, the statement about mistaken identity.

What would you like one more sight of?

The family, of course. My record rack. A girl in tennis dress. A sky aerated with stars. Swallows in summer that pedal uphill, then freewheel down. A blackbird on my front lawn charming worms. Sparks of moonlight kindling a tree. More ordinary things – the Sunday lunch as it is served, the steaming gold of roast potatoes and chicken skin. The shirts folded after ironing. A running bath.

Any regrets?

That we are as similar in death as life, clustered here under the same headstones. But, to tell the truth, I never wanted to stand out. I would hate to have seen those newspaper reports with my name in them and the neighbours no doubt saying how quiet I was and the bishop praying for my soul and the police confirming I had no subversive connections.

Anything else you miss?

The smell of life given off by the earth that I have no nose for here. Those transparent moments at bedtime nothing had prepared me to expect. The sports results.

Finally, do you forgive your killer?

I accept death as I accepted life – as something to get on with.

3 A.M.

I'll give him a minute longer
before I break the news.
Another minute of innocence and rest.
He is in the thicket of dreams
he will still be struggling with
as he stirs himself to take my call
wondering who in Christ's name
this could be.
           One more minute, then,
to let him sleep through what
he's just about to wake to.

COLORADO

They are crying, the sisters. It is time to part. Now they must
revert to adult roles. Their parents turn aside, too pained to speak.
Mortality is what they feel, draining their fortitude, hot tears.
Where, if ever, will they meet next? The mountain air is tinged
with the uncertainty of this, like white-limbed aspens brushed
by wind.

And to reverse the sorrow they would have to return home,
the children behaving as children again, the parents re-enacting
parenthood. They would need to be conceived and born and
weaned once more, taken by the hand to school.

It is life they weep for, therefore – time, distance, change – while a
luggage-laden car slips down the incline, joins the traffic flow and
bypasses the canyon, water cutting hard rock to the bone.

WAY OF LIFE

The longest queues.
The cheapest cuts.

The high season beaches.
The rush hour delays.

The densely populated quarters.
The comprehensive schools.

The public ward for babies.
The public house for celebration.

The special offers.
The soccer turnstiles.

When admission was reduced.
When group rates were available.

During lunchtime or weekend.
During Sunday or bank holiday.

At weddings, parks, parades.
At Christmas markets, January sales.

Wherever people gathered.
When crowds took to the streets.

FRUIT SALAD

I   *Peach*

There's not much point in trying
to cultivate a sultry peach of words.
Just pass me one to stroke, to eat,
or paint it from a glowing palette;
colours dart from apricot to apple,
flames licking velvet hide.
Hold its downy, yielding roundness,
fondle its lightly clothed contours,
taste its golden mean, its sweetness,
before it starts to shrink and shrivel,
starts to wrinkle like a passion fruit.

II   *Strawberry*

Strawberries with whipped cream,
a sunset ripple on your plate . . .
A cordate locket, a precious stone;
cut one and expose the marbled core.
The wholesome rubicundity of outdoors,
not the hothouse plastic of tomatoes;
compact, meaty, flecked with seeds,
the bracts a garnish (parsley on beef,
verdant ferns in a bouquet of roses).
A July day provides the ideal accompaniment,
lazy as the cream dripping from the whisk.

III   *Pear*

Most easily hurt of fruits,
bruising under a matt coat of skin,
smooth as bath soap inside;
halved, a perfectly stringed lute.
It hangs in a shaft of autumn light

timeless as a bronze cathedral bell
or disturbs the peace and drops
– a hand grenade, pin still intact,
a toppling shell of glycerine.
We take refuge from our troubles in its syrup,
wasps burrowing through heady pulp.

IV   *Apple*

All apples lead back to that first temptation:
trees behind the thatched farmhouse,
forbidden fruit, a warts–and–all beauty,
pupating in pink silk blossom
then fired and glazed in summer,
brushed by a red admiral's wings,
wine–dipped like nectarines or green
as nettles stinging with tart knowledge.
Bite the way back to a primal silence,
your rhythmic crunch shutting out
the world, digesting its hard truths.

V   *Fruit Shop*

Orange skins baked to a crust
(fluffy whiteness underneath);
raspberries like bleeding gums;
melons whose haunches
are tested for ripeness...
I buy bananas racked like chops
and apricots, one blemished
with a spot (which I'll slice off,
cheddar flesh wholesome again).
I pinch a bulbous, plum-size grape.
Lemons tumble from an opened crate.

AN URUGUAYAN BAGATELLE

on looking into a travel guide

I find it heartening to know
That, should I take flight to Montevideo,
There will be an abundance of hotels,
Salt Atlantic winds, barbecue smells.
If I care to taste the local beef
The variety of cuts will strain belief
And language: no single word like 'steak'
Does justice to the specialities they bake,
Then serve with gravy, rice or mash.
Tips are recommended (use Diners Club or cash).
This guide makes little of the open lands
Rolling from Brazil to coastal sands:
Purple prairies, countless cattle,
Sheep ranches, few Indians (their battles
Bravely lost), big cats decimated.
A beach-loving population, estimated
At three million. Roseate spoonbills on the wing,
Zorzals in the jacaranda sing . . .

Then progress to gambling or whores,
Both legal if pursued indoors.
Teatro Solís nights, the price of gems or leather,
Zum Zum disco club, when to find good weather;
The gaucho statue, parks and shopping streets,
The World Cup stadium (70,000 seats).
But nothing of crime or neighbours' fights,
Idle Sunday pastimes, rural courtship rites,
Of colonels, cloudscapes, office workers' pay,
Tupamaro threats or what the children play.
To check this book, attempt my own rebuttal,
I'd need a PLUNA jet, the airport shuttle.
Its street-map names only those avenues
With tourist promise – I'd quickly lose
My way in anonymous, dull squares:

It is like the pattern of a life, all cares
Blanked out on holiday, the pleasures stressed,
Long plain miles of tedium suppressed.

1989

Beijing students on their black bikes;
shoals wavering through river-wide squares,
merging and separating in the sun,
fish that test the purity of a habitat . . .

They remind me of school-going cyclists
in my childhood, chains clenching teeth
for the final assault on Liberty Square.
(That was Thurles in the late sixties,
Mao's book colouring the thoughts
of a few red-headed pupils.)

Tiananmen Square was cleared by guns.
On Wenceslas Square, the crowds
cheered as the guard changed,
bringing relief to banned philosophers
moonlighting as night-watchmen
who had waited for the day to dawn.

All was quiet on Liberty Square
in this year of revolutions,
just some lads in drunken dispute
tripping from the Chinese take-away
or my young brother and his friends
urged by a policeman to move on,
not to disturb the peace
of sleepy residents
with talk of world events.

CULT OF PERSONALITY

Authors' photographs were removed from the covers of their books
for fear of encouraging – God forbid – a personality cult.

— MIRCEA DINESCU

1. Elena Ceauşescu was a scientist. Learned papers appeared under her name. Her experiments took human, social, architectural forms.

2. Nicolae, her husband, was a cobbler. His collected works would have insulated a Bucharest apartment against eavesdroppers or cold. He published 17 books the year before he died.

3. Supplies of surplus paper were released for other approved publications. But their authors could not show their faces. The first family was not to be upstaged by good looks or intelligent features or expressions betraying their country, underlined by hunger or anger or fear. Faces were political statements.

4. The photograph that stays in mind is of the old couple – anyone's grandparents – in overcoats and scarves. He is hectoring the military court, flailing as if at a railway official who cannot make trains run on time.

5. Then the firing squad. The bodies abandoned like ragdolls. Time to read books in heated rooms, authors photographed on covers (hands hide double chins; fingers tap keyboards that don't require the sanction of the police).

6. There are authors everywhere who, given the half-chance, would monopolise all available paper for their books; who would love the billboards at airports to display their words, the refashioned main thoroughfares to carry their names. Negative reviews are amassed like hit lists. Rave reviews are ghost-written by themselves. Writing is their power struggle.

7. Samuel Beckett shied from publicity, hated to be photo-graphed, shunned media attention. His obituary in *The Times* was printed alongside Nicolae Ceauşescu's. Beckett's photo was the larger of the two.

THE BEST YEARS

I'd had all kinds of infections, my bladder still wasn't working
properly, giving me a lot of pain, my neck pain was going on, but
because I was starting to be able to move things a bit more easily
than I could before, I really did think I was on the mend, that
everything was going to be all right, that the tumour was going
away, that it had probably gone, and that I'd be walking.

— CLIVE JERMAIN, 1965–1988

I

the misery of a common cold
        its dreariness
streaming blood-and-water eyes
        coarse throat
blocked nose running raw
        cracked voice
chapped lips, eardrums smarting
        when you blow
chill shivers make an icicle
        of the spine
dull thunder in your temples
        the heaviness before rain
drained of all ambition
        except bed
drowsing above wet
        tissue cloud
as the world sets
        beneath your snivelling contempt
(hot drinks, crisp sheets, magazines)

III

the misery of a common cold
        its dreariness
or repeated exposure to a dose
        of tiresome flu

as minor by-products
     of cancer drugs
a teenage vocabulary
     that comprehends
terms like 'radiotherapy'
     and learns
through nausea and fatigue
     precisely what they mean
and that from the inside
     can define
catheter, manual evacuation
     neuralgic pain
or a slow-developing astrocytoma
     in the spine
(nibbling the stem of the brain)

III

you want to keep on breathing
     cling to life
as closely as your metal rod
     does to your spine
to filter air through
     an infection's silt
to tidy what's left
     of sweat-matted hair
still coaxing sleep when discos
     close and revellers hit the streets
(Valium crushed in ice-cream
     brings occasional relief)
to maintain belief in God, give thanks
     for twenty years
and for your writings – agonising
     though it is to type –
heaters, blankets, friends
     bombard you with warmth
(but a further cold is coming on)

TAKING LIFE

We live the given life,
follow the gossip of world news,
learn to eat stewed sheep and cows,
tilt the soup-bowl backwards,
use the rear-view mirror
to check impending threats.
Whatever appetites transpire
– boiled sweets, reproduction,
race meetings – we indulge
or sacrifice to God,
our food supply sustained
by charge-card orders
or own-brand bargains
in suburban shopping malls.
We accept the hierarchies
at work, defer to the boss,
moods changeable as climate.
The revelations that occur
are taken more or less on trust,
the flow of menstrual blood,
the red nose blowing cold,
the fear of old age and taxmen,
the deliberations of the bathroom,
having adapted since birth
to illness and disappointment,
growing into the inherited role,
typecast by face and accent,
dressing as convention specifies
to chair a board meeting
or sign on for the dole.

Always within inches of extinction,
we see our lives through
to the bitter end.
Sunday, we read the papers,

mend a daughter's bike;
Monday, sell detergent products
or set the washer to 'long spin'.
We purge ourselves of gloom,
shake off morbid thoughts,
like the eclipsed moon
wiggling free of the stubbly
shadow of the earth,
make the best of things,
enjoy a little fame
– name in the local paper,
championship of darts or golf –
and bring up the children
to be mannerly, adaptable.
This is the life.
There is no mystery about it.
It is what we are living now,
fitting a truck horn to the car
or sitting on a bar-stool
arguing the toss with friends
or amending standing orders
through a show of hands,
our monuments all around us
– churches, prisons, flats,
buildings that scrape
the surface of the skies.

JOB

What is it
that my gloomy father
gets so worked up about,
white sheets
rumpled into a lather?

And why is my mother
yielding to his whim?
And why do I
(marked for life)
rush breathlessly to win?

Could they not have turned over
or taken more care
to leave me
in my element,
exhaled with their air?

RESIDUARY ESTATES

I

After the nausea
of chemotherapy,
after the vomit
and the sores,
bald patients rest
on pillows stuffed
with long hair
from Treblinka,

78

sleep off
the side-effects
of God and man.

II

Cancerous cells are immortal
laboratory tests suggest.

Is this the everlasting life
my mother now enjoys

that she had prayed for:
the life beyond the grave?

III *After Bertolt Brecht*

wasted by illness
left for dead

flowers rooted
in her soiled body

to weigh so little
she must have taken

enormous pains

IV

the calm between storms
is the silence in which
the dead are not named
until relatives are informed

HIM

I

let me keep this pair
of partly-worn shoes
so I can wear them
to the end of the journey
they were intended to complete

I will aim them
where they were meant to go
I will follow in his footsteps
before his tracks are covered over
and his route cut off

II

we bought so much ham
for funeral sandwiches

did we really think
the whole town shared our loss

the surplus meat began to stink
long before our appetites returned

III

the last bar of his soap
became a transparent ghost
and finally slipped my grasp

BODY TIME

I

They drag you screaming
from the hot bath
of the womb
and dry your spattered hide.

II

The outside world
you enter is less stable.
You must adjust the temperature
with gloves, lovers, smokeless fuel.

III

Now you wallow in a bath
that turns cool – pull the plug
and wait a dreamy minute,
water sloughing like a skin.

IV

And listen to the sound
your life makes
flowing down the waste-pipe,
the stifled noises as it drains away.

MISUNDERSTANDING AND MUZAK

You are in the Super Valu supermarket
expecting to meet me at 6.15.

I am in the Extra Valu supermarket
expecting to meet you at 6.15.

Danny Boy is calling you down special-offer aisles.
Johann Strauss is waltzing me down special-offer aisles.

I weigh mushrooms and broccoli and beans.
You weigh beans and mushrooms and broccoli.

It is 6.45. No sign of you.
It is 6.45. No sign of me.

You may have had a puncture.
I may have been held up at work.

It is 6.55. You may have been murdered.
It is 6.55. I may have been flattened by a truck.

Danny Boy starts crooning all over you again.
Johann Strauss starts dancing all over me again.

Everything that's needed for our Sunday lunch
is heaped up in my trolley, your trolley.

We hope to meet somewhere, to eat it.

ROADS NOT TAKEN

How tantalising they are,
those roads you glimpse
from car or train,
bisected by a crest
of grass perhaps,
keeping their
destinations quiet.

You remember a brimming
sea on the horizon
or an arch of trees
in reveries of light;
then a bend that cut
your vision off
abruptly.

Some day you must return
to find out how they end.

THE NOTEBOOK VERSION

Flicking through my notebook,
I come across 'black butterflies
in the honeycomb heart of asters'.
Too grandiloquent, I think, too rich;
or, to cite another page,
'rich as the rain
treacling down lush leaves;
rich as summer pudding.'

Here, I jotted down
the title of a book I'd seen:
Infections of Fetus and Newborn Infant.
Imagine landing, head first, in a ward
where such a text is necessary.

Then scraps in need of inspiration's
heat to weld them into place:
'There isn't much glamour
in the breadman's life.'
'The sadness stations reek of
like disinfectant and stale smoke.'

Too much of the world
eludes the grasp of art;
there are no poems
index-linked to suffering.
The notebook turns
emotive at this point:
'A day approaches when
pen, ink and alphabet
will be destroyed . . .'

Hence the endstopped cautions:
'You must write better.
Your poems have no future.
They are only as good as they are now.
This is the time they stand the test of.'

IN OFFICE

We are marching for work:
people fresh from dream bedrooms,
people whose flesh begins to slip
like old linoleum loosening on a floor,
people with head colds and lovebites,
girls startlingly immaculate,
pores probed with cleanser,
showered hair still wet;
people subordinating their tastes and talents
to the demands of office,
the uniform grind of files.

We forego identity and drive
for the security of such places,
a foyer guard by the spotlit tapestry;
soft furnishings; a constant heat;
gossip with the copier's undulations;
crushes on new recruits; booze-ups
after back-pay from disputes . . .
We are wasting our lives
earning a living, underwriting new life,
grateful at a time of unemployment
to have jobs, hating what we do.

Work is the nightmare from which we yearn to wake,
the slow hours between tea-breaks
vetting claims, scrutinising invoices.
We are the people at the other end
of telephone extensions when you ring,
the ones who put a good face on the firm,
responding to enquiries, parrying complaints,
the ones without the luck to have inherited
long-laned retreats, fixed-income bonds,
who yield to lunchtime temptations,
buy clothes and gadgets, keep retail spending high.

We age in the mirrors of office lavatories,
watch seeds of rain broadcast their flecks
along the screen of tinted glass, a pane
that stands between us and the freedom
which we struggle towards
and will resign ourselves to
when the clock comes round.

MIDNIGHT OIL

Sprinklings of light
in the downtown high-rise.

There are mistakes
which must be rectified
before tomorrow,
awkward contracts to finalise.

More than ever now
the building is a crossword,
dark squares starting
to outnumber clues.

And, as in a late-night
room transmitting
fluorescent signals
of a sick-bed vigil,

the struggle which takes place
is, to the pained occupant
of the swivel chair,
a matter of profit or loss

– in other words, life or death.

LOOKING FORWARD

I

We have already advanced
to the stage where we can
convene seminars on cost/yield ratio
and child sexual abuse.
We have reached the point
where genetic engineering can create
a tender, tasty, waste-free sow,
a rindless cut above the rest.
It certainly is not the experts' fault
if minds, like power supplies, break down
under the strain of our pace of life
or if bodies are stifled by the human crush
– tears like oil welling from rock –
or if hunger sears as soils erode:
remember the humblest shanty town
is still the corrugated product
of great skill and ingenuity.
Desert missile tests or rocket launches
may, on rare occasions, prove disastrous;
but we are capable of learning from mistakes
and will get things right the next time.
The alienated are just slow developers,
suffering the growing pains of evolution.
Out of the dung heap of chemical spills,
a thornless mutant rose will sprout,
its scent as fragrant as a new deodorant spray.

II

It's a great age to be alive.
Look at the girls flitting past:
styles were never more enticing,
the denier of nylon never more fine.
And watch the men, so gentle
in their linen suits, their lemon sweaters,
wheeling the baby buggy to a crèche.

Our freedom is unprecedented:
to lose faith in the church,
to choose six lottery numbers and win,
to zoom in close on the adult video,
weather better thanks to global warming
(naked crowds swarming to the beach
turn mole-brown on a sunny spit).

This epoch can accommodate so many tastes:
water skiing, sado-masochism, cottage pie...
Lose no time in enjoying earthly goods,
for tomorrow (in a manner of speaking,
at least) we die, although drugs may yet
be found to keep us long-lasting as plastic,
durable as nuclear waste in concrete tombs.

III

*The modern order was not guaranteed by basic laws
(natural selection, mechanical superiority in anatomical
design), or even by lower-level generalities of ecology or
evolutionary theory. The modern order is largely a product
of contingency.*

— STEPHEN JAY GOULD

Chantilly lace and lycra.
Haiku and Norse sagas.
Tow bars and rotary blades.
All here by chance.

False teeth and puncture kits.
Apricot jelly and fax machines.
Laxative pills and Gregorian chant.
All here accidentally.

The stories of your life,
awkward scenes you rescreen
in the bedroom's dark
have no universal moment:

you are on your own
when long-lashed showers,
pebble-dash of hail
hammer on the glass like truth.

Only by eliminating nature,
wiping clean the slate,
will you prove your place
at evolution's peak,

leaving pools of genes
to regroup, a cold
starlit soup on which
a skin begins to form.

POULAPHOUCA RESERVOIR

Where ivy grows on a house, the family gets worn out.

— THE POULAPHOUCA SURVEY

1. The name 'Poulaphouca' means the hole of the spirit. Quern-stones by the submerged cottages will be ground in the mills of God, fine as the distinction between Father, Son and Holy Spirit.

2. *The Shell Guide to Ireland* calls it 'the great lake of the Liffey hydro-electric works'.

3. Life goes on in that Atlantis. Ivy grows on houses. Haws redden in autumn. Roses are pruned back. Thatch is replenished. Bridal veils float like surf on the clear-skinned water. Turf fires blaze in the lake at sunset.

4. The Field at the Bottom of the Lane is at the bottom of the lake. The Field Under the Well is under water. A school of fish chases in the School House Field. The Coarse Little Field, The Field at the Back of the House, The Inside Field are flooded permanently. Garnaranny, Farnafowluch, Carnasil-logue, Coolyemoon are spoken of in bubbles.

5. During summers of drought, you can see outlines of houses. Their owners' names linger at the tip of the lake's tongue. Chimneys poke above the water like the blowholes of hunted whales.

ROSE WINDOWS

The road is uphill.
Heathers, ferns.
A mica sheen.
Bracken stirrings, streams.

The train whinnies
into the distance
as you take
a tentative step.

*

Row your boat home
in the sulphurous dusk,
the matt lake lined
with corridors of pine.
Fish rings, shingle,
skidding waves.

*

You wake within range of two cuckoos
– their voices bubbling through algal green –
to find creation has begun:
a blue silkscreen of hills
is printed through a mesh of haze
and everything is new
under the emblazoned sun.

*

An open door admits
the summery smells,
sounds of peaty streams;
hedges blossom with small bells;

thin-sliced, wing-wrapped butterflies
alight on the buddleia bush.

*

The tangerine cottage door,
a colour warm as a hearth fire.
Spring rakes out crocus flames.
A coal–black cat squats
by the frosted window-pane.
A scarf of smoke is tucked
inside the chimney.

*

Gravel heaps
– purpose forgotten –
now host flowers.

Bindweed and nettle
vie for domination.
Ivy scales a telegraph pole.

It's no one's job
to curb
the blackberries.

*

At dusk along
a byroad,
the peppery scent
of tight whitethorn
ephemerally perfect
as you pass
in a collapsing big top
of striped light,
beams streaming

like canal water
through lock gates
of cloud.

*

Strolling beyond the cottage
on your own, breathing peat smoke,
kicking a stone, hayricks
like a tribal village . . .
Row upon row of water glazes strands:
wind–grooved waves stir life
where ochre starfish splay
and lull you with shanty rhythms
to the seabed flickerings of sleep.

*

The last evening, watch
the town lights twinkle
across the bay, like notes
playing a slow air
you might entitle
The Touchstone or The Turning Tide
when you go inside to pack.

*

Squeeze out
all the segments
of this orange day
before it disappears
into the sunset.

SIBLINGS UNITED

for Eithne at 21

Not a care tonight
about which of the family
is out late, sharing the roads
with reckless drivers
or who is short of money,
feeling out of sorts.
We are all here, survivors,
converging at your twenty-first.
You are no longer a child
and I am no longer required
to act as trustee
of our father's will.

United, we declare your independence.
I drink to your health
along with workmates
(you have a full-time job now,
plan a fortnight in France)
or I chat to a slim cousin
remembered with fat legs
propelling a toy scooter,
uncles last seen at a funeral.
We pose for photographs,
slip arms round waists
like life belts . . .

You cut through your name,
dripped in sugar icing
on the home-made cake,
expose the darker
layers underneath.
A close-dancing family
tonight, we celebrate
that you have come of age:

ardent, happy, relaxed
in your floral party dress,
showing no after-effects
of your years of grief.

LONG STORY SHORT

A mane of grass matted the centre of the lane.
Ivy vaulted famine-built stone walls.

The topiary had begun to outgrow
its own shapes, geese and lions running wild.

Flowers bloomed in fair-isle patterns;
like Bali temples, pine trees loomed.

My steps echoed against the battlements
where a dead calf, suppurating in the heat,

made a banquet for the tethered guard dog
(flews soaked in lukewarm blood).

Larval ripples surfaced on the pool
of the calf's eye, flies' static crackled.

The day held its breath. Insects fizzed in
tubs of mossy water. Squawk of crows.

I had walked to the pillared boathouse
when the cattle grid rattled, the barking began.

MAGDALA

Young Women Face High Cancer Risk from Pill
— NEWSPAPER HEADLINE

who lay down
     their lives for love
who swallow the host
     daily communicants
who are betrayed
     by men with crowing cocks

girls in seedy rooms
     mothers in tower blocks
lithe polished secretaries
     obeying the commands
carved in tablets of bone
     sacrificing all they have

let us atone
     this is her bleeding body
she has revealed to you
     and offered up
kneel and adore
     before you nail

your passion to her
     wide-open embrace
though you live in sin
     her grace will redeem you
skin miraculously pure
     perfume anointing your flesh

NO MAN'S LAND

when the sexes surrender
the weapons of their battle
and step arm in arm
along the precarious peace line
when they lie down together
like lion and lamb
setting enmities aside
for the sake of a natural alliance
> what words soar
> on the warm breeze
> of a whisper
> what mysteries are solved
> what promises waft
> from perfumed rooms
> what loyalties are pledged
> with lace and polished nails
> what treaties are sealed
> by tongues and teeth
> through cindery winter nights
and what pay and prospects
does the future hold
what school-to-shop trajectories of days
what anorak-and-tracksuit routines
walking a neutered dog

OPERATION

I removed slates
tight as muscle fibre,
opened a flap of skull.
There was a fungal whiff,
sprinklings of wood
like bone dust
on the vascular wires.

Fresh views had not
been aired in this
cramped space for years,
a fine grey matter smeared
the brittle beams,
dotted lines left
signs of worms.

No wonder the roof
had sagged abstractedly:
the house was brain-dead
though its heart
continued to beat
regularly as feet
clambering up the stairs.

TEMPUS FUGIT

X to III by the school clock.
The pendulum paces its cage.
Now I know what time means:
at III, I will be older by ten minutes,
this moment will have passed.

A singsong teacher lists
the industries of Wales.
The fly Glossy Gleeson freed
from a red Elastoplast tin
scales the chalky blackboard . . .

I never saw my friends again
once we had walked out together,
backwards, on our last day, slipping
through the wrought iron gates
– all that remains of the school.

If we chanced to meet
what would there be to say?
What would we have in common
(crow's-feet; grey hairs landing
like some migratory birds)?

READING PRIMO LEVI ON THE TRAIN

We breach the ordered peace
of our atrocity-free mornings
forsaking the solitary confinement of sleep
for transportation by commuter train
to where labour pays debts owed
to building society and bank.

We bear food parcels
– salad rolls and fruit –
our working lunches.
A woman cradles a package
– slop bucket or lampshade?
Hair clings to our heads still.
Chains hang from slender necks.
So many of us to kick, to kill,
so much flesh to torture and despise
beneath the modish cuts
of suit and skirt, so many tales
to force abruptly to an end,
so many souls expected home at dusk
to spirit away in cattle trucks...

The train clatters on.
Whatever this day holds
we will live to see it through,
march back down gravel drives,
their cindered, osteal sounds,
watch stars like gold-filled teeth
chatter with us in the cold.

REMEMBERING MARINA TSVETAEVA

Hair straight as a witch's, face foretelling its future,
you walked these Paris streets with your chubby son
(did you starve yourself to keep him fed?).
But I still prized our months of ecstasy in Prague,
the silken skin surviving under a threadbare shift,
green eyes shining out of the darkness where
you prowled – slim and frisky as a tigress –
our passion squeezed through every pore.

You were wild and volatile, an endangered species,
yielding your quivering pelt on the mountain floor.
I can hardly look your poems in the eye these days,
they hang our old emotions out like underclothes.
The Julian calendar's certainties had been abolished,
Crimean afternoons around the stewing samovar
– you used to declaim your verses then, weave your spell,
Godlike as a spider in its web of entrapped flies.

The trials of repatriation summoned years ahead:
your husband would be shot, your daughter detained;
the rope you'd knot your life with would be spun.
This story is a film the audience leaves early.
They know how it will turn out; no surprises,
no reprieve, happiness never the twist your fate secretes.
What you'll learn is that the body you create and cook with
must be lumbered from sticky sick-bed to prison gates;

that love goes unrequited; that blows, like poems,
come in cycles; that truth persecutes.
Do not return to Moscow, Marina. Do not return.
Petals drip from my cherry tree, casting an arc
of blossoms, a pink splash animating spring grass
that makes me wish we could link arms again and, among
these monumental boulevards, exchange our plans
with the surreptitious fervour of lovers or of spies.

EXPERIMENTAL ANIMALS

after Miroslav Holub

It's much cushier when it's raining rabbits
than cats and dogs. The animals for experiment
should not betray too much intelligence.
It grows unnerving to watch their actions mimic yours;
terror and horror you can empathise with.

But, for real heartbreak, take a newborn pig.
Fantastically ugly; possessing nothing
and desiring nothing except its swig of milk;
legs warping under all that weight
of uselessness, stupidity and snout.

When I must kill a piglet, I hesitate a while.
For about five or six seconds.
In the name of all the beauty of the world.
In the name of all the sadness of the world.
'What's keeping you?', someone bursts in then.

Or I burst in on myself.

ARBOR VITAE

I

Rooks change
the personalities of trees,
nesting in their brains:

lesions in a winter dawn
as red skies
x-ray nerves and stems.

II

The brain furrowed
with concentration, worry
is starting to unwind.

The hair shaved
for the operation
grows back posthumously.

III

I think of him at times
when my limbs tingle
with pins and needles
then go dead.

CASE STUDIES

I

It is easier to prove the existence
of leukaemia than of God

and so I pan for God
in the marrow of bald children

who trust in Him with passive smiles
above their Disney World pyjama tops,

faces magnified to corpuscles of dots
in yellowing newspaper photographs.

II

Add to the accidents you've
read about or known,

and multiply by all the victims
named in phone-calls to expectant parents,

the crushing death of this young woman
whose body was reduced to slush

as the bus she ran for registered
her minute impact with its wheels.

IV

Dawn blinks into existence
like an intravenous drip.

The water trolley rattles,
constellations of beads

clouded in condensation.
Beside one bed, a draught of urine:

red vintage wine
decanted for analysis.

IV

Her chances dim under theatre lights
as she hangs on to life

by a slim surgical thread.
Past childhood rashes, teenage acne,

the illnesses of old age strike home,
planted – like bulbs of ova – before birth.

A riddling which, her world
turned upside down, death solves.

THE TRAIN

She is suffering on the quiet. When she confides in the doctor, he finds nothing much the matter and reassures her. Eventually, of course, she is referred for tests. Meanwhile, she puts a brave face on her pain, smiles a strained smile for the Christmas photograph, keeps everything as normal for us as she can.

She leaves Thurles station for a hospital in Dublin and, looking back, freezes into a premonitory pillar of salt tears. She sees the cathedral into which she will be elevated; the primary schools two of her children attend; hairdressers and grocery shops. The town in all its shabby glory. A Biblical kingdom pondered from a mountain-top.

Her train eats into the landscape, passes life by.

I used to place old pennies on those tracks for wheels to flatten. They came out warped and limp like Dali clocks. As if, in the ensuing silence, time stood still.

BACK ROADS

I

soon after the Volkswagen bounces out
of Granny's cobbled yard
our father starts to say the rosary
announcing the mysteries as he drives
(the family will not stay together nonetheless)
Declan's cot straddles our grazed knees
on a back seat draped with tartan
I pretend to be asleep
a lemon slice of moon sprays its eerie light
on our seven faces (Eithne is not yet born)
he sounds the horn as we pass Tobins' house
(no point now, Jimmy and Kay are dead)
bedroom lights distinguish cottages
frost doodles on car windows outside crossroad pubs
cats' eyes and potholes, insect blizzards, sugar beet
our parents malign some relative or other
a cloud smothers the moon, all goes black
the sorrowful mysteries hover round the car

II

The road back is impassable.
I lie, a quilted astronaut, in a strange bed,
Our Lady weightless on the wall,
her head in painted clouds.

The adults natter around the range,
eating sandwiches of cooked meat
red as my uncle's weathered face,
as feast dates on his Mill Hill calendar.

I start to sleepwalk into space.
The damp-snouted pump is guarding the farm,

curved handle a tense watchdog's tail;
hens snuggle in deep-litter roosts.

I am launched into the eye of sleep.

III

My father ran the family museum.
Our first buckled shoes,
spoke-fingered men I drew,
messy attempts to write,

school essays marked with grades,
were deposited in his archive,
dated and labelled meticulously
as bell-shrine or torc.

Nothing of that booty has survived,
not a snippet of hair, not a pair
of gloves secured elastically
to the sleeves of a gabardine coat.

He didn't even notice it was
plundered, cleared out to make space.
He had adopted another role,
curator of my mother's past.

The honeymoon Ford, so prominent
in the photo album, seemed
a prototype of the last car he drove,
with her memorial card laid out

beside him on the passenger seat.

IV

There are twists
on this journey
I had not expected,
unsignposted turns.
I am lost
in the landscape
of my childhood,
a muggy climate
of tonsillitis
and Sunday drives.
Every move I make
takes me to a house
or bridge or mill
that seems familiar.
Milk churns congregate
at farm gates,
men with tweed caps
cycle from a match,
blue-smocked wives
begin a fry. . .
My dead father
starts to navigate.
In no time now
we will be home.

BREVIARY

The Pool (Courbet)

This is the pool
without the Sunday crowds:
no one stands
between the water
and its clouds.

This is the pool
as the hill-bristling trees
and the boulders see it,
when even the painter has left.

This is the pool
as it laps itself up.

*

Shadows

> Before there was no death,
> then her shadow grew with mine . . .
>
> — KAZIMIERA ILLAKOWICZOWNA

At first, no shadow;
only light.

It turned less bright
but I grew faster
than my shade.

Evening already:
light fades;
day ends.

My shadow extends
larger than life.

*

Café

He orders puddings, sausages, bacon, chips.
He orders his childhood to be set before him.
This is his mother's cook-up that he eats.
He chews and for a while is young again,
under the protection of her love.
He looks around him with lost eyes
when the plate is emptied of all but one hard rind.
Next, he will eat his way through one of her desserts.

*

The Young

They are the young.
They are taking the last bus to a party.
They are having a fantastic time.
They are fancying one another.
They are drunk out of their minds.
They couldn't give a shit about the future.
They are moving to a new beat.
They have no hang-ups.
They are doing their own thing.
They have every confidence in themselves.
They are the young.
They have no intention of becoming old.

*

Lingo

when my tongue explores
my twenty-six surviving teeth
it worries at the gaps
like sores or like someone
struggling for a word
fumbling for that
twenty-seventh letter
that would free her speech

     *

Hedgehog

He scoops himself into a huff
as our car-lights interrupt his journey.
I try in vain to lure him
from his bed of nails.
He strikes out with his spikes
the way that Aborigines fired spears
to deflect the test bomb's course.

     *

Periodical

When I told you I'd seen
a Robert Hass poem called 'Happiness',
you said 'Let's move to wherever
Robert Hass lives.'

Instead, I went back for the magazine
and brought it home to you
as if I believed in happiness
as something money could buy.

The Bottom Line

(1994)

THE BOTTOM LINE

[1]

Official standards, building regulations,
fair procedures for dismissing errant staff:
my brain is crammed with transient knowledge
– patent numbers, EC directives, laws.
I pause at traffic lights on the way back
to headquarters; windscreen wipers skim off
visions of this seeping stone-faced town:
a warehouse frontage littered with crates,
lovers locked in an umbrella-domed embrace,
consumers at a bank dispenser drawing cash.
I race the engine, inch the car towards green.

[2]

The kind of suit a man of this age
must wear: single or double-breasted,
turn-ups – or not – on the trousers,
usual lapels; the prescribed space between
the blue stripes of monogrammed shirts . . .
Problems which preoccupy me now, struggling
with pre-meeting notes, will pass away
like fashions: funny collars, ties
my grandchildren can scoff at, looking down
on forebears when, marking some anniversary,
the blanched album does the rounds.

[3]

Quality time at weekends, domestic bliss:
early pathways cordoned off by webs,
I slip out to the shops, return
to bring you tea and newspapers in bed.
On Sundays, every Sunday, I submit to the calm

of supplements, CDs, cooking smells.
All of the mornings of all the weekdays
I leave for work; my office bin fills
with the shredded waste of hours.
A pattern regular as wallpaper or rugs
and no more permanent than their flowers.

[4]

Anxieties you could elevate
to the level of a mid–life crisis
are mere reactions to your dreary days,
the boss's ire, tiresome assignments.
You scan the pink financial pages
on the way home, nodding off and on,
jaded, blinking at suburban nameplates
with each juddering halt the train makes.
Wives are parked by railings; silhouettes
of baby seats; a mumbled greeting, then
you unwind to family anecdotes, TV.

[5]

I am a trustworthy, well–adjusted citizen
at this stage, capable of a commanding
pungency in business talk, good grasp
of office jargon, the skill to rest
phones on my shoulders as I keep tabs,
the ability to clinch a deal convincingly...
I recognise a counterpart when our paths
cross in sandwich bar or jazz shop and we nod
to each other with a telling smile, maybe
recall negotiations where we held opposing lines,
all discreet charm now, agendas agreed.

[6]

A life of small disappointments, hardly meriting
asperity or rage, an e-mail cc-ed
to the wrong address, an engagement
missed, a client presentation failing
to persuade: nothing you can't sweat off
at gym or squash. But, in the dark filling
of the night, doubts gather with the rain
which, spreading as predicted from the west,
now leaves its mark on fuscous window panes;
and you wait for apprehensions to dissolve
in the first glimmer of curtain light.

[7]

Pressing tanned flesh, reaching consensus
over some outstanding fact, our well-
scrubbed, nail-filed hands feel soft.
Enough contact with the soil is made
weeding invasive seedlings from the lawn . . .
Best of all, undo the crested tie,
change into fawn slacks and turtle-neck,
white-fringed golfing shoes, commune
with nature between fairway and rough,
taking the air on a bracing Saturday
or sharing honours for the captain's prize.

[8]

When you unclasp your slimline briefcase,
the apple, deep green, high gloss
with waxen sheen, a tea-break snack,
glows among the acetate reports,
symbolising something you can't name
but crave for when your sales, morale
are low – peace, a meaningful existence . . .

You settle for a rental in the west,
family away-days, the company car,
and, who can tell, later you may rise
to a weekend cottage, hens, a bright-red door.

[9]

How did I get this far, become
this worldly-wise, letting off steam
to suppliers, sure of my own ground?
What did my dribbling, toddling stage
prepare me for? What was picked up from
rag books, sticks of coloured chalk, cute
bears, during those guileless, gap-toothed years?
So embarrassing the idiocies of my past,
seen from the vantage of tooled-leather
and buffed teak, hands-on management
techniques, line logistics, voice mail.

[10]

At the visitors' car park, the belts
of our trench coats flap with the wind;
we huddle in a confidential group
hoping to have pressed home the point,
a hollow Coke can tinkling on the street.
Then, despite this meeting of minds,
for one long second we run out of things
to say, permit thoughts chill as downturns
to stray into our heads until we contrive
the next move, check watch or schedule,
arrange matters arising, part on a jocose note.

[11]

Photos of my family – wife and sons –
framed in silver near my conference phone

inspire me to seize every chance I get,
make life better for the children
as my parents – sweat of the brow
and all that – did for me; my spouse
is most supportive, clued into the dog-
eat-dog mentality success requires.
Ferrying the kids to school in style
imbues them in the long-term with
some gainful aspirations of their own.

[12]

Pay day, the carefree junior staff
stroll back from the bank, flush with
spending power, indulging in the luxury
of ice-cream, crisps; a PA on maternity,
due to resume soon, parades her baby
like a trophy, weighs with friends
the pros and cons of a career break . . .
It is the wider picture I rake over in my mind:
how gearing can improve; whether to draw
the blind on loss-making subsidiaries
and let the liquidator worry about debts.

[13]

The hidden pain of offices: a mission
statement admonishing me from walls,
the volatility of top brass if sales volume
for a single line falls one per cent.
And customers' righteousness, their touching
faith in the perfectibility of man.
Yet even without the big compensations
– personalised number plates, offshore
tax breaks – I enjoy the hectic pace;
and when, stressed-out, I have an off-day,
I spend my way back to normality.

[14]

All this stuff here I've drudged hard
to own, installed alarms to keep,
could disappear tomorrow at the hands
of some dumb creep in shiny track-suit,
a suede-headed galoot out on bail . . .
Such negative conclusions deprive me
of the full potential of my things,
sailing my boat as often as I should,
shuttering the place for a spontaneous trip –
we give more dinner parties now, invite
boring, trusted friends to look around.

[15]

On the mobile to a client, or passing word
across a dealing room's array of desks,
the way you speak does not brook
disagreement – a patois of mutters and twangs.
Adjusting to home, tense still from
breasting the dense atmosphere of work,
it takes so little to set off a row.
One misplaced phrase and the avalanche
begins: a hail shower of rocks, ropes
failing to grip, your wife as an
ice-maiden throwing glacial looks.

[16]

Reversing into the designated slot
outside your duplex, leaping from
the leather seat of a four-wheel drive,
you feel your life has turned
up trumps; and there are always
further heights to strive for:
set up a consultancy, join the board,

be head-hunted by the rival firm . . .
You are groomed for better things,
well-positioned in promotion stakes,
dogged, uncompromising and still young.

[17]

The peace of Friday evenings after
staff have left the open-plan deserted,
before cleaners key-in for their shift.
Sun flakes out on the carpet, rays
highlight staplers, calculators, pens;
phones flop in cradles: Monday will
inaugurate another week, small talk
over instant coffee; new debenture stock . . .
Meanwhile, suspended between worlds,
I drum the plastic in-tray, stare down
at the frenzied city, disinclined to budge.

[18]

Women who matter in our lives
– secretaries, wives, one taking on
the other's features in the dark –
adapt their habits to our needs,
shrewd about what should be packed
for the tour of brand distributors,
which calls to allow, how to treat
our moods, our swears: we like our
secretaries efficient, young, breaths
of fresh air, able to laugh off risqué
jokes, remain tight-lipped as wives.

[19]

How much longer will this crystal water
flow, this snow come decked in white,

I wonder, as I pour out bottled spring,
brace myself for questions from the floor
about our new cost-cutting scheme . . .
Even when I mouth defences of our safety
record – latest filters, monitors in place –
I see my children's scornful faces, rivers
shimmering like metal, aluminium-clear,
quivering with farmed fish, squirming with algae,
grey snow lodging on eroded banks . . .

[20]

Before the car ascends the parking ramp
at nine, I drop my working wife off
with a ritual, perfunctory peck.
Tuna salad shared for lunch, a quick
check on appointments – we touch base
if schedules permit, save news of
office manoeuvres for our pillow talk . . .
I glimpse from here the nesting pigeon,
awkward, restless, treading on shells,
then load the spreadsheet's spurt
of ballpark figures, analysing trends.

[21]

In this downward phase of the economic
cycle, I despair of pre-tax growth,
the yield from R & D, lose heart.
Our boardroom's abstract art infuriates me:
dashed-off blobs and squiggles. Trash.
I resent the easy fortunes some make,
smarmy copywriters in white suits,
that painter flogging half-baked wares
for my likes to feel foolish near.
Time again to clear my desk; nothing achieved,
another bitty, gruelling, inconclusive day.

[22]

A torrential morning; drenched to
the cufflinks, I take calls from staff
complaining of sham ailments, voices
straining to sound hoarse or weak . . .
I think back like a parent to their
early promise: none of the we-have-
something-on-you vibes I get now
whenever I insist on strictness. Surely
they wouldn't go so far as to expose me,
trawl files to sniff out iffy deals?
All the things, with hindsight, I regret.

[23]

The nightmare prospect of retirement:
those pathetic cretins condemned to wring
every last comma from the morning paper –
Deaths column to For Sale – sparing
the crossword until later, keeping out
of their wives' hair, put to grass,
to mow lawns, lives devoid of contrast,
an onset of golf-fatigue and gloom,
eager to resume dictating vital memos
to that secretary, the one confidante
they trusted, the one sympathetic ear.

[24]

When the air crackles with threats
– disaffected personnel, final
notices, debts, legal proceedings –
I am lucky to be ex-directory
at home; and I lie low at work,
go aground, invariably *in a meeting*
if I'm pursued – other times, however,

need a high profile approach:
smiling as a football sponsor,
lashing the Budget in a trade mag,
lobbying a Minister for grants.

[25]

Valentine's Day attracts delivery men
cupping rosebud flames that will radiate
on desks through cellophane – no black
spots, no thorns: model of a world
where wars are misunderstandings, hate
is due to childhood traumas and will pass . . .
That people are basically good is agreed
at the canteen tea-break, life as plump
with expectation as the satin card
the postman brings; and love will conquer all
in its glass slipper, right to the final stroke.

[26]

Can a year really have passed since our
last Christmas shindig? Here I am
in the same rut, not a single resolution
carried through, deluding myself that
I'm still in my prime. Yes, it's that
time again: a factitious peace, a ceasefire
between camps, an ambience as sweet
as fake rot on marzipan fruits doled out
from desk to desk; tomorrow's gossip will
concern the boss who'll traipse in late,
suit crumpled, manner untypically mute.

[27]

The unoriginal sins we perpetrate, our guilt
shared like a Christmas bonus: mileage rigged,

spare parts purloined, an office laptop
commandeered for sports club use,
things troubling when the internal audit
section dreams up dodgy questions;
taxmen, too, the nightmare of close scrutiny
– receipts, excuses, bank statements
to prepare – and the attendant dread
of lay-offs, sackings, three-day weeks,
gaunt, haunting figures begging change.

[28]

Then the time comes when you know
none of your promise will be fulfilled;
the saving roles luck, fame, deliverance
from your job were meant to play . . .
You will slave on till pension day,
eluded by advancement, satisfaction, wealth.
In your head, some plangent melody repeats;
in your mind's eye, a preview of your part
as walk-on stoic, accepting failure in good
heart, battling home against the wind
this night the same as the last.

[29]

Stepping from a lunchtime bistro,
hitting the wet pedestrian-only streets,
I raise the logoed golf umbrella
for a noncommittal client, before we split.
Through the bad reception of rain
come memories of the kissogram French maid
disoriented in a downpour near the admin tower:
satins, bows so much at odds with
our stressed concrete, steel; her dainty
hesitations in the storm, a creature dazed
by headlights who starts turning heel.

[30]

A quite ordinary man, but go–ahead,
the sort you wouldn't throw a second glance
at in the street, let alone comment on.
If you happen to meet him, nothing will
cross your mind unless his smirk
dimly recalls someone you once knew . . .
Though his name won't mean a thing
at present, he is nudging forward, destined
for the top – watch the newsboy hold his
evening paper as he dashes down the steps,
gripping folders, lugging research home.

[31]

The white–cuffed sales rep, guarding
territory, does not add up in the age
of central warehousing; the few we still
keep on are doomed: jaunty, over-groomed men,
sharing jokes and samples at the check-outs,
waiting for a brisk assistant manager
to deign to acknowledge their existence,
counting pallets in a draughty store-room,
raising special offers to eye-level shelves.
Commission in decline, their smiles grow
thin; redundancy will come as no surprise.

[32]

Death, once brushed against,
does not seem in the least
like a stubbly ghost with scythe
reaping dry grass in the graveyard,
but shows up as a brash executive
cutting recklessly across your lane,
lights making eye-contact with yours,

ready to meet head-on as though
by previous appointment; ram home
your car horn like a panic button:
his cellphone's bell will toll for you.

[33]

Phase Two of our unit, I inspect the site
in hard hat and suit, furled plans
like parchment in my hand: a digger's teeth
grind pebble-crunchy, graveyard-yellow clay,
mud choking my oak-coloured semi-brogues.
Faced with such an earth-shattering foray
– the groundwork where progress is rooted –
I sense the desiccated souls of DIY types,
clawing their way through hardware bargains,
prodding at sprockets, widgets, screws,
figuring out some new useless device.

[34]

Guarding against mistakes at any cost,
I steer clear of the PA – lace
blouse and leather skirt – who seemed
ready to reciprocate my interest;
and I try not to fall for lavish gifts
from pushy, new-to-market IT folk
(tokens of appreciation, normal perks
– hampers, country house weekends –
from regulars are perfectly OK): no
rival jerk will do the dirt on me
in first-round interviews for Chief.

[35]

Out on the open road – sun visor, shades,
a satnav's guiding hand, the reassuring buoyancy

of tyres; blues and big-band discs plug gaps
between troubleshooting client operations.
Everywhere seems miles from everywhere,
conflated landscapes scale the heights,
as I check with my secretary by phone
that no shit has hit the HQ fan.
The man at the factory entrance-hut
directs me to the guest zone; I lean
back, grab my linen jacket from its hook.

[36]

Good to hold a stable job in these
recessionary times, friends receiving
letters of regret from the foreign parent,
no golden parachute on offer; yet
tempting just the same to make the break,
venture on a lucrative new challenge.
I scan the vacancies (*self-starter,*
forward-thinking, profit-responsible,
independent but committed to group culture),
conjuring my fate in black and white here,
in terms I can relate to, a dynamic role.

[37]

Scarcely to be acknowledged, even to myself,
days when the very sight of my wall planner
makes me sick, when – instead of tough,
decisive judgements delivered with a quick
peremptory scrawl – I sculpt a paper clip,
chew a ballpoint, gaze at the Alpine calendar.
Suit-coat removed, I scroll through e-mail;
there are press releases to issue, markets
to nail . . . I must switch back to fast track,
delegate; late again tonight, home to my
sleeping child, a wife's taciturn rebuke.

[38]

Over decades, I have said goodbye
to my retiring colleagues, signed
the sentimental cards slyly passed
around, tossed notes into collection
envelopes, stared at grey down fringing
a hand that squeezes mine, conveying
as much emotion as it dares betray . . .
We promise to stay in touch but, of
course, we never do after the hearty
speeches end (tributes, in-jokes from
friends) and they drop out of our cast.

[39]

Walking through the automatic exit,
talking heatedly about the downside
of a greenfield site, I am captivated
by a busker's tune: untainted, pure,
drawn from the rainswept mountainy mind
of an old man counting yearlings in the wind,
the log-shifting silence of his hearth . . .
That music keeps its nerve, unfazed
by the pressing business of the streets;
you continue – 'Right?', 'OK?' – but I,
thread lost, can only mumble and concur.

[40]

First day at the new firm, you treat
warily the insiders you've beaten;
too soon yet to know whose blitheness
camouflages venom. Left to yourself,
taking stock of your plush room, shocked
at the capacious desk-space you must fill,
you speed-read through the introductory

pack (staff pyramids, pie charts, stats)
and worry that – pressures of moving,
children's distress, apart – you may
have misjudged; money isn't everything.

[41]

Like some class of transsexual,
inhabiting the wrong body, you are
trapped in an ungratifying job,
losing self-esteem, but anxious
nonetheless to come plausibly across
as a motivated member of the team;
or is it an out-of-body experience,
so this isn't really you, a goal-
driven executive, setting fresh
parameters, laying down ground rules,
projections tripping off your tongue?

[42]

Creased with the pain of a piercing
duodenal, my thoughts drift to dead
comrades: I pick up from where they
left off, collapsing at a bus stop,
succumbing to a heart attack in bed,
and cut one free of his supportive rope . . .
Each funeral, my resolution was to listen
to staff problems but the real world
does not, alas, allow for much indulgence:
death-in-service pensions are the extent
of my role, lump sums for next-of-kin.

[43]

The flimsiness of steep buildings,
scintillant ice palaces of glass;

sun-spots, structures opposite are
mirrored, warped; filing cabinets,
work stations, rubber plants in tubs
prove amenable to public scrutiny.
It is like walking on air, the sheer
vertiginous layers of stacked light;
lifts surge through molten floors
or plunge to solidities of sculpted bronze,
revolving doors, terrazzo, guards.

[44]

A monumentally awful day, shopfloor staff
baying for your blood; sighs, grumbles,
union officials clamouring for redress . . .
Then the recriminations taking you aback:
like a drowning life, your past is
brandished on the far side of the desk,
your certainty about the fairness
of the way you run the branch is challenged,
old feuds reopen and, with tension high,
you still maintain control, adopt a mild,
sincere tone, just as the books advise.

[45]

A Sunday walk: bees nuzzling perennials,
something stirring under roadside furze.
I seldom find time to take in the view
that cost a hefty premium when I invested
in my prime-location home. I know what
umpteen fishing flies, horse trainers,
software packages – you name it – are called,
but not what this wilderness contains
before planning applications sweep it
all away – motor mowers blazing trails
to a culture of microwaves, antiques.

[46]

Not afraid of risks, not listening to
cagey advice; striking out from time
to time, irrespective of whose toes
you're forced to tread on – whatever's
needed to bring your plans on-stream.
However tight the ship, there will always
be some weak links in line management:
bypass them, oblige the shirkers
to shape up or go – any fallout from your
hardline approach may be made good in
due course; meanwhile, stand your ground.

[47]

All the profitless minutes I expend
on matters not recorded in my timesheet.
The clients' fees (so much per hour
plus VAT) should be reduced to take
account of idle daydreams: hotel trysts
with that ravishing sophisticate
from payroll, sneaking off towards
the border in twin bucket seats . . .
Jolted back from perfumes, limbs
– or thoughts of league scores, injured
props – I continue with put options, liens.

[48]

You could do it in your sleep, the dawn
trek through another empty terminal,
vinyl undergoing a mechanical shine,
gift shops shut – cigars, frilled silk
behind steel grilles – bales of early
papers bursting to blurt out their news . . .
Fanning stale air with your boarding pass,

if you look up from your business-class recliner
during the safety drill, it will be only
to eyeball the stewardess; you itch
to switch your laptop on, rejig the unit price.

[49]

Some networking is necessary to get
to the right people, turning on the charm,
having them eat out of your palm, but never
put entirely on the spot, everything off
the record, a once-only concession you
won't mention to your friends, strictly
between yourselves, without prejudice . . .
Futile dealing with less senior staff,
sticklers for detail, holding progress back.
At clubs, committees, conferences, make a point
of banging heads together, picking brains.

[50]

Sensor lights tested, alarm code set,
I burrow into the high-tog, duckdown duvet;
the number-crunching radio-clock squanders
digital minutes like there was no tomorrow.
Who will remember my achievements when
age censors me from headed notepaper?
Sometimes, if I try to pray, it is with
dead colleagues that I find myself communing . . .
At the end of the day, for my successors too,
what will cost sleep are market forces, vagaries
of share price, p/e ratio, the bottom line.

From
Quality Time
(1997)

YOU

Be yourself: show your flyblown eyes
to the world, give no cause for concern,
wash the paunchy body whose means
you live within, suffer the illnesses
that are your prerogative alone –

the prognosis relates to nobody but you;
you it is who gets up every morning
in your skin, you who chews your dinner
with your mercury-filled teeth, accumulating
garlic breath or weight, you dreading,

you hoping, you regretting, you interloping.
The earth has squeezed you in, found you space;
any loss of face you feel is solely yours –
you with the same old daily moods, debts,
intuitions, food fads, pet hates, Achilles' heels.

You carry on as best you can the task of being,
whole-time, you; you in wake and you in dream,
at all hours, weekly, monthly, yearly, life,
full of yourself as a tallow candle is of fat,
wallowing in self-denial, self-esteem.

THE NIGHT WATCH

I answer the door
to wasps.
A dawn chorus,
vibrato humming,
sheer wings
quivering in the dark.
A Biblical swarm.
Landing, flying,
increasing, multiplying.
Primed cluster bombs.
A sizzling pan.
A holiday traffic jam.
A battle dance:
taunting, sizing up
the enemy, ready
to bayonet-charge
with stings.
A Mumbai slum,
car horns, scooters,
cries of limbless beggars.
Stalactites of venom.
Gossips. Looters.
Refugees massed
on a platform
wailfully resisting
their fate.
A nervous spasm.
A panic fit.
The engine goes on
revving up for action,
a blistering
multi-pronged attack.
The star-coated sky
is blacked out
by the throng.

LAST FLIGHT

I

Winter frosts
kill off the wasps
who had escaped
the sticky end
of the jam-jar trap,
its sweet watery grave.

The hive in the roof
is too big now
for those few still alive,
old crippled nuns
in the cold cells
of a redundant convent.

II

A lone survivor protrudes from the grout.
No vigour left in limb or wing.
To spare it pain, I stub it out.
O wasp, where is thy sting?

SELLING OUT

I

We contracted to sell the lot.
The angle of attack of heavy rain.
The bedroom with the rising damp spot.
The dawn shunt of a gypsum train.
The night creak of boards, metallic pings.
The tree fungi like heaped-up plates.
The valedictory spider tying strings.
Swivel press. Clothesline. Blackbirds in spate.

II

When the sparrow tilted the balance of the pear tree.
When the apples were setting out their stalls.
When the scaly sea sparkled like a fizzy drink.
When the yew thirsted for the juices of the moon.
When your lavender deck chair sprawled
near the gangly hollyhocks.
When the palm tree – so alienated all winter –
fanned itself against premeditated heat.
When the robin came within two feet of your wellingtons.
When the neighbours were away.
When stamens bowed with gold dust.
When rust had yet to blight the lilacs.
When the white of the indecisive butterfly
was like the surface on a bowl of double cream.
When you returned upstairs
and stole a last glance at the view.
When you found the sky had misted over.
When the deed was done.

LIGHTING UP TIME

for Patrick Taylor

Rites of spring: roll out
your hibernating lawnmower,
dead grass wedged to blades;
line up the cans of paint,
sandpaper, brushes, rags.

*

The cottage garden in
the mauve light of delphiniums.
Lilies with honeyed tongues.
Bird notes in blossom.
A fern stretching its wings.

*

Vulcanised rubber snails,
plump as a colony of seals,
undertake the viscous journey
to make a meal of hosta leaves.

*

Those daffodils,
you'd know it was
their first time:

so open, so eager to please,
so bright, so upright,
so unaware.

*

The raw nerve of yearning
roused by hawthorn,
by the green of far-off hills
seen from your top-floor office
when sun pays out its light.

      *

That it might always
be spring, a held note.
That we might look forward
to long days of growth:

haze lifting like a screen,
waves peeling
off the Gulf Stream
one by one.

CUSTOMS

A small airport. A plane
lost in a fog of thought
      like a train nettle-deep
      in a siding. It has seen
mountain tops streaked with zebra
skins of snow, fields like cracks
      on an Old Master landscape,
      flickering cities – buried
treasure – through snagged clouds.

Early arrivals delayed,
the girl at the Hertz desk
      jokes with the passport clerk.
      A cleaner leans on his mop.
And the control tower
rising from the mist
      like a border look-out
      sets the Customs official
on a reverie of his own,

when the weight of January snow
buckled the roof on his
      solitary outpost; kicking stones
      along the byroad in July
– a tractor armed to cut hay
would bring a moment of diversion:
      as that engine dwindled, the stream
      could be heard more clearly,
the grass growing under his feet.

PARTING

I

the abandoned look of tracks
under a twinkling frost

criss-crossing at a junction
then going their separate ways

parallel rails
converging in infinity

which once bore trains
that ran on time

II

the ghetto diary lurches
to a sudden halt

a mystery train's brakes
screeching at a destination

of smokestacks and raked hair:
turn next to blank endpapers

where the narrative continues
on parchment skin, thin air

READING THE SIGNS

The ebbing tints of a winter evening
fall on walls, tower blocks, cobblestones,
tall statues of The Leader in his metal
greatcoat, tombs of soldiers known, unknown.

For a while the grandeur of old sooty buildings
is restored, architraves glow like coals,
and a doleful queue for rumoured pork
is transfixed by amethyst and gold.

The man at the apartment window stands
for a moment in the encroaching gloom
before he checks for electricity and finds
margarine light coveting his stark room.

A flat at the peak of a serpentine staircase:
young Literary Circle writers take the floor
under dusty plaster mouldings and peeled paint
to risk new poems, a typed Nineteen Eighty-Four.

Now, in brighter Nineties days, they can relax
at the outdoor restaurant near the tramline,
sun-dappled tables under apple blossom.
Their tripe soup and stuffed cabbage bides its time.

And they are free to wait; an editor –
still furtive from long habit – starts to pass
his latest issue round, reading the future
when blossoms float into his Coca-Cola glass.

UNDYING

from birth our countdown begins
muffled with heartbeats

*

at what stage does the dying start
at what point do you decide
it is not worth renewing the subscription
that it will be up to your successors
to repair the bathroom lock

*

what a waste
to create such radiance
then pitch it – body and soul – away
heat so unlike death
breath so sweet

*

marble is not the proper way
to enshrine her memory
whose name looks cold in stone
whose flesh creased with the least pressure

*

sans everything but mind
a mind alert to its collapsing shell

as if a child had intimations
of mortality and could foretell

the circumstances of his death
wise to the world he would be weaned from

    *

let's suppose we die
let's suppose they bury us like bulbs
let's suppose we rot rather than flower
let's suppose we are not punished or saved
let's suppose time and space are infinite
let's suppose life happens only once
let's suppose we die

    *

for as long as blood–oxygen
sprinkles your brain
and your mouth waters with life

    *

the unborn grow restive with delays
they need our space, our produce
they have destinies to fulfil
their passion fuels our desires

    *

we wanted to hold
on to our dead
to mourn them
when we felt the need

like pets caged
inside coffins
to be released
for exercise, fresh air

*

inconceivable they
could be forgotten

then our lives were
rearranged like chairs

their set places
at our dining tables

in our minds
were lost

we had let
them die

WATER

The miracle of water
is that it tastes of nothing,
neither of chlorine nor peat,
not of old tap fittings or dead sheep.

Water was the first mirror,
drinking images of beauty,
showing their wrinkled future
in the mildest breeze.

Water clings to its neutrality,
changes state at boiling point,
finds the level at which
tensions cool, limbs relax.

It is the splinter of ice in the heart,
the white blood of the snowman,
the burst main flooding
from Christ's frozen side.

HALLOWEEN

(on my mother's 70th birthday)

Summer is saved,
rolled up in carpets
of straw and hay,
         folded away
         like picnic chairs.
Autumn dusks
compose in mauve, rose,
magenta brushstrokes
         like celestial light
         poking through
the clouds in holy pictures
or rays squirting
from the thorn-pierced
         sacred heart
         above our parents' bed
(six of us sentenced to life
there in that room).
At rest under a marble
         headboard, does she
         watch out for a sign?
I tug at a dandelion
whose milky root
unravels underground;
         I smooth the coverlet
         of gravel that might be
a rash of goosebumps;
shuddering suddenly, she'd say:
Someone's walking on my grave.

THE ONE TWENTY PUB

after Wisława Szymborska

The bomb is primed to go off at one twenty.
A time–check: one sixteen.
There's still a chance for some to join
the pub's ranks, for others to drop out.

The terrorist watches from across the street.
Distance will shield him
from the impact of what he sees:

A woman, turquoise jacket on her shoulder,
enters; a man with sunglasses departs.
Youths in tee shirts loiter without intent.
One seventeen and four seconds.
The scrawny motorcyclist, revving up
to leave, won't believe his luck;
but the tall man steps straight in.

One seventeen and forty seconds.
That girl, over there with the iPhone
– now the bus has cut her off.
One eighteen exactly.
Was she stupid enough to head inside?
Or wasn't she? We'll know before long,
when the dead are carried out.

It's one nineteen.
Nothing much to report
until a muddled barfly hesitates,
fumbles with his pockets and, like
a blasted fool, stumbles back
at one nineteen and fifty seconds
to retrieve his goddamned cap.

One twenty.
How time drags when . . .

Any moment now.
Not yet.
Yes.
    Yes,
      there
        it
          goes.

SUN SPOTS

A hazy dawning.
The jogger's trainers
stained by dewy grass.

Insects mix and mingle.
Morning clears its throat
through a cock's crow.

A horse grows from sleep
to full height,
kick–starts into life.

I shut out the news,
gag the car stereo's mouth
with a Purcell ode.

And sun triumphs in the end
– resplendent, brassy, baroque –
trumpeting the day.

*

Autumn falters to a cube
of tawny light, a stage
where Chekhov is performed.

By now, the lavish
evenings of midsummer
have been squandered.

Isobars tighten like layers of clothes.
The year is an off-season dacha,
ready for boarding-up,

a play in which a band
is made out in the distance,
marching away. Wafting. Fading.

*And time will pass
and we shall be forgotten:
our faces, our voices, our pain.*

*

The momentary glint of tin,
the flash in the pan,
has remained precious this long,

long enough for the still life
painter's name to be unknown,
wiped out like flesh and bone,

like the bruised fruits
(liver plums, skull pears)
the viewers stalk

with hungry eyes,
ripe for the simple truths
the sun bares,

making light of water,
pinpointing
the pitcher's soul.

PIONEERS

for Olga Kelly and Tom Sheedy

How did we stand it?
Our squat bungalows plonked down
in the middle of a muddy field,
unfinished and unadorned.

Everything was unprecedented, strange,
edged with an expectant silence.
Pick and spade to hand, I manfully
staked my pride on an undulating lawn . . .

The house was ours; ours the pressured
water snarling from its taps; ours
the otherworldly quiet of its attic ribcage,
neat and insulated as a chaffinch nest.

Light fell gently on us sometimes,
gasping at the beauty of a morning glass
of orange juice, scooping a chute of sun
that dusted our sparse furniture with warmth

finding its way to dew-sprayed lettuce
left by our good neighbours on the sill.
Next to discarded bags of rubbish at the roundabout,
the precast concrete of the industrial estate:

forklifts, containers, CCTVs, plywood crates,
slavering guard dogs; wildflowers swept
clay ramparts under lumpy yellow carpets.
Environs so Iron Curtain, so consigned

to squalor, shoddiness and grot,
that when our poet-friend had finally
identified our nameless street,
Hello there, Comrades was his opening shot.

THE NEXT POEM

My next poem is quite short and it's about something most of you will recognise. It came out of an experience I had on holidays a couple of years ago. In fact, I'm pretty sure I'm correct in saying that it's the only poem I've ever managed to write during my holidays, if you could have called this a holiday – it bore all the hallmarks of an endurance test.

There's a reference in the poem to roller canaries, which become more or less mythical birds in the last line. I hope the context will make that clear. Incidentally, this poem has gone down extremely well in Swedish translation – which maybe reveals a bit about *me*! A word I'd better gloss is 'schizont'; if I can locate the slip of paper, I'll give you the dictionary definition. Yes, here we are: 'a cell formed from a trophozoite during the asexual stage of the life cycle of protozoans of the class *Sporozoa*'.

OK then, I'll read this and just two or three further sequences before I finish. By the way, I should perhaps explain that the title is in quotations. It's something I discovered in a book on early mosaics; I wanted to get across the idea of diversity and yet unity at the same time, especially with an oriental, as it were, orientation. And I need hardly tell this audience which of my fellow-poets is alluded to in the phrase 'dainty mountaineer' in the second section. Anyway, here it is. Oh, I nearly forgot to mention that the repetition of the word 'nowy' is deliberate. As I said, it's quite short. And you have to picture it set out on the page as five sonnet-length trapezoids. Here's the poem.

THERE AND THEN

and there they are
leaning over the bridge
figures from childhood
as if waiting all their lives
for my return

     *

evenings damp and vacant
                    as underground caves
the smoky boredom
                    permeating winter Sundays
the litter-swirling emptiness
                    after a hurling game
teachers and bank clerks adjourning
                    to the club-house bar

     *

I am out on the isthmus of school holidays
nesting in a bolstered tea-chest
feeding on two Lone Pine books a day

     *

granted one cloudless afternoon
crowds walked from town with towels
and tractor tubes to swim this river
as you memorised *Bello Gallico* passages
from a heat-curled textbook
for the imminent exam

     *

there is no end to this lane
in sight: look at the light
off in the distance

you would need to be young
to negotiate this gate
to run the gauntlet

of reminiscent greenness
saturating all sides
a corridor between two lives

*

blackcurrant bushes that ripened
in your youth bear fruit still

you could check them out this minute
remind yourself how memory tastes

look back through sleek black pupils
at summers picking them for jam

*

a childhood illness
the starched stillness of the bedroom
an anxious mother tapping out pills

*

the road I draw
is the one outside our door
it leads to mass, infants' class
Kilroy's toy shop, my cousins' farm

I am putting everything I have
into this picture

biting my tongue with concentration
clock hands join above the church
square-wheeled trucks haul sugar beet
a polka-dotted friesian strays
out of my farm set

for no reason at all
I add a big round steamroller:
now maybe I will win the prize

    *

that orchard was the last green fastness
glossy cooking apples, dock leaves, moss

cows, horses, goats, fleecy cauliflowers of sheep
two by two they grazed the flood-prone fields

wood smoke, gas lamps, willow pattern, deal
bellows, wholemeal bread, fuchsia sprigs

    *

and so much has disappeared
digging up your roots
bulldozing fields
where you knew every clover tassel
every thistle spike

    *

not just the way the dead fade
but also how the living
vanish into the living

dust off that face which greets
you in the street to find
beneath the carapace of age

the image unretouched
which scorched itself
into your very bones

place your fingers in the names
chiselled on your parents' tombstones
to believe that they once lived

and cared enough to part hair
floss teeth
choose your first communion suit

*

a few of us were making for home
finished our Legion of Mary visits

walking or taking our time on bicycles
wobbling along at the speed of speech:

as the church clock counted twelve
streetlights switched off

like a lapse of memory
darkness was declared

FAITH, HOPE, LOSS

1. I stumble on you, prostrate by the door, flat out in a frenzied search for a dropped ear-ring or stone, as if vowing to reform your life in exchange for the recovery of the trinket.

2. With mounting helplessness and rage, my route is retraced in my mind, until I suspect it was in the airport phone booth that I left the missing bag.

3. Losing a loved one. Seeing a daughter eviscerated by cancer, her kindly discoloured face beneath the numbered hairs.

4. To be one of the world's X billion people: reaching climax, anaesthetised with blockbusters and booze, delving in bins for found art, discarded food. Or one of the three unique species annihilated every hour as grasslands, open-cast mines, week-end shacks impinge.

5. The ditch of lisping water laced with greens, awash with sway-ing tendrils, dunked leaves, is cemented over; spring light of primroses extinguished; slashed briars where a robin summed up April dusks.

6. Bliss consists of the smallest things. The bus already there to meet the all-night train. Unhappiness lies in what we miss.

7. You are on your knees, convinced that what seems irredeem-ably lost continues to exist, keeping faith that – given time and patience – it will be restored.

NON ISSUE

Our new car, stopping at
the lollipop lady's command,
is bought with money saved
from the expense of children.
And this restaurant meal
is feasible because
there are no other
mouths to feed.

This brass bedstead was acquired
through denying ransom
to the unborn children
who demand our money
and our life.
That antique tallboy came
from their pocket money,
wall-hangings from college fees.

These pre-concert snorters
are equivalent in cost
to babysitter or au pair;
and this free love
we can make is safe
from bawling children,
smalls littered on the floor
as in an adolescent's room.

SONG

At Creevykeel

The sun climbs,
A cuckoo spreads its charms,
Limpid blobs of dew
Bind newly-minted grass
On the early-morning farms.

We follow a plot of death
But not to keen or whine
At this ancient 'giant's grave'
Where a cuckoo warms up
While the sun shines.

Death is an obsolete rite,
A shard of carbon-dated bone,
As remote to us who stray here –
Fresh from bed and breakfast –
As this cairn of skeletal stone.

The cuckoo chants.
Lambs bounce on springy feet.
The first fly of the year
Sweeps through a cottage window.
The day is gathering heat

At Creevykeel.

VARIATIONS FOR WIND

When a wind like this is blowing, it somehow comes home
to you that man has been flung into the world.

— ANDREI SINYAVSKY

I

Forget the gentle zephyr of legend,
the washday breeze dislodging suds

like cherry blossom from the line,
the therapeutic music of wind

at a bellows-driven, pine-crackling fire . . .
Whipped up by a cloud-furrowed

brooding sky, gusts lick the eaves
like flame, swig from window glass:

a hurricane crescendo drowning
naked cries, a day of judgement

as you rise from sleep to Gods
whom neither winds nor seas obey.

II

Think in terms of hiding
as storms hit their winter stride.

Raw wind gnaws your bones;
turn the other cheek,

turn from the foam-streaked sea
to the haven of the pub.

Knock back a hot whiskey,
discard the sopping anorak.

Keep your eyes peeled
for anyone in the room you know.

Through a headstrong plume
of cigarettes, begin counting days.

III

Sang-froid. The way the bird
would tune up every dawn.

Something set it going
like a car alarm; all through

atonal January, the strident
woodwind of the gales,

it tried to stave off harm
as though by scaling high notes

it could stop the flexing
cypress limbs it perched on

from toppling down upon us
in the next aggressive gust.

IV

You must leave – today, not tomorrow –
the face behind the ticket kiosk

seems to say. It's an ill wind
that blows: if not a Venetian sirocco,

the plutonium breeze ripping
through bilge-thickened seas,

a *force majeure* throwing spores
of incaution to the winds.

The sewage boat discharges
filmy cargo, like crude oil,

off beaches where Tadzios paddled
in gold stoneground sand.

V

That we will come,
ultimately, to nothing

– this the wind ensures,
threatening to break and enter,

belching black fumes of cloud
around the rheum-eyed moon;

and you start to understand,
looking out at where umbrellas

struggle like the bony wings
of prehistoric birds,

this planet is not habitable;
streets are paved with silver rain.

VI

Yes, we do have homes to go to
when the nights are cold and drab,

places we can be ourselves in,
universal potholed streets

along which someone scurries
through the shadows always,

the inlaid gem of a cigarette
above his leather jacket, jeans.

You sink into the fireside chair
that has assumed your very contours,

outstare the flames of coal a wind
is taunting, buff your muddy shoes.

VII

A churning, stomach-turning,
seasick sea: a gothic scene

as, once again, rain clouds –
ragged curtains – lacerate the moon.

Waves gasp ashore, collapse,
unload their concave burdens

and, sieved through shingle,
pour off surplus water on dry land,

rub salt into the wounded air.
Seas somewhere harbour

warmer colours, weathered copper
melding into verdigris. Azure.

VIII

After winter, like a chronic illness,
has kept up its tired routine,

the analeptic light which you
aspire to will strike soon

out of the blue: creepers stir
from purdah, decked with

festive blooms, butterflies
rise like the jubilant flags

of a liberated archipelago,
yellow flowers baste tall grass.

You recall how wild the roses smell
when doused by summer showers . . .

ALL

all journeying together
the living and the dead
all that are alive
all that will be dead
all that will be born
all that ever lived
remains accompany us
like meteorites
husks of dead bees
tusks of dead elephants
mandibles of termites
snouts of seahorses
spouts of whales
necks of giraffes
not a speck of moth's
dust is mislaid
wings of bluebottles
stings of scorpions
suction pads of leeches
gill chambers of fish
species certified
extinct on shale
still dwell among us
as alive once
as the neighbours
of our own future graves
who pass us daily
on the teeming streets

SIN

grant us sin, O Lord
we need to believe in sin
in the halo of pain

yielded by wealed buttocks
the body and blood savoured
in the beads of sudden jism

we need to believe it is wrong
to anoint each other with our chrism
as if lives depended on this

we need to believe it is wicked
to eavesdrop at the peak-hour rate
on cheap recordings of bored wives

do not forgive us, O Lord
our sense of emptiness after the event
our hollow cries of pleasure, woe

spice with a heightened shame
the slow ritual of removing vestments
the awe with which hands tremble

in the presence of transient flesh
that even to the naked eye
is Your own image and likeness

teach us to treat sweet secret passages
as dens of iniquity and filth
when, guilty and abashed,

we turn back to Your clasp

DECEMBER

That evening at the far end of the year, I was drafting a staff guide to the new EU Regulation. Gerry, stirring his tankard of tea, was responding to some Transit query on the telephone. Maurice's fountain pen, as usual, was in full flow, goaded by the demon of deadlines. All of us vaguely aware of the sun setting feverishly at our shoulders. One minute, its extravagance resembled the Caribbean postcard taped to the filing cabinet; the next, it was a lurid plate from an illustrated Dante.

Our Christmas party would take place later. The air was taut with anticipation. Gerry split a packet of Rich Tea biscuits and sighed for his dancing days. Showbands striking a chord with 'O Darling!'. Dimmed lights, distempered halls . . . The last plash of sunset, an abstract colour-field canvas, sharpened the outlines of buildings, the vertebrae of cranes stooped over the tax-incentive area nearby.

We lapsed back into another pen-scratched silence then. It would be a great night. A tree twitched off and on. Someone keyed-out on the corridor. The church steeples looked pathetic from our level – so small and helpless, stabbing at the dark.

TIME CHECK

To tell the hour, you need
an old-style wind-up wall-clock
swinging the lead of its pendulum,
marching in time with the seconds,
a child keeping step with a parade;

the sound of time when – too engrossed
to notice – we let it pass us by
or when it punctuates the silence
a lovers' tiff fomented, each moment
a drip of Chinese water-torture.

In the aftermath of a death,
the pendulum is stilled: a heart
snatched in a coroner's gloved hand;
released later, a pulsating fish,
the flicked blades of its fins

slicing through shaded streams.
Time must be heard no less than seen
as it goes around in circles.
A girl anticipates her first menses,
her harassed mother her last;

a dog barks from a distant farm
all through the vigil of a sleepless night . . .
The clock rations out your seconds,
checks them off, tots them up aloud.
Then its trance-inducing pendulum asks

for your childhood back, your life.

TALKING SHOP

What does it profit a man to own the poky
grocery shop he sleeps above, unlocking at eight,
not stopping until some staggeringly late hour?

Even before opening, he has driven his van
to the market, replenished supplies of bananas,
apples – nothing too exotic for local demand.

Seven days, he takes his place behind formica,
the delights of his mother's age preserved
in shelves of jelly, custard, sago pudding.

Peaches on his waterlogged display outside
will still be smarting from the previous day's
rain as though steeped in their own juice,

cabbage-leaves prismatic with drops.
A propped radio brings up-to-the-minute news
or, in slack periods, he reviews things

at first-hand, standing sentry in the doorway,
watching nobody come or go from the plain-
faced cottages opposite: once they unleashed

mid-morning shoppers; now wives work,
supermarkets supply all but a few spontaneous
needs: shoelaces, low-fat milk, shampoo.

Finally, having wound the shutter down again,
the life he leads is his business exclusively.
Perpetual light shines on the manual cash box.

You will see for yourself, through the slats,
the rows of cans like tin hats, suits of armour,
maybe hoarded as a foretaste of impending war.

SUCCESS STORY

Your name is made.
You have turned the company around,
downsized franchise operations,
increased market penetration
on the leisure side,
returned the focus to core business.
Man of the Month in the export journal,
ruffler of feathers, raiser of dust,
at the height of your abilities.

You don't suspect it yet, but things
are destined to go gradually downhill.
This year or the next you will
barely notice any change – your tan offsets
the thinning of your blow–dried hair,
you recharge your batteries
with longer weekend snooze-ins,
treat back trouble with heat pad and massage,
install an ergonomic chair for daytime comfort.

Behind closed boardroom doors
there will be talk: not quite
the man you were, losing your grip,
ideas a bit blah, in danger
of becoming a spent force.
The prospect of an early
severance package will be tested
delicately over coffee, low-key as
'Can you pass the sugar, please?'

The flamboyant young blood you trained
will start talking down, interrupting
half-way through your report
on grasping brassplate opportunities.
You will hear yourself say *In my day*

more often than you should.
Bite your tongue.
Brighten your tie.
Show your old readiness to fight.

HOME

when all is said and done
what counts is having someone
you can phone at five to ask

for the thermostat
to be switched to 'bath'
and the pizza taken from the freezer

THEM AND YOU

They wait for the bus.
You spray them with puddles.

They queue for curry and chips.
You phone an order for delivery.

They place themselves under the protection
of the Marian Grotto at the front of their estate.

You put your trust in gilts, managed funds,
income continuation plans.

They look weathered.
You look tanned.

They knock back pints.
You cultivate a taste for vintage wines.

They get drunk.
You get pleasantly inebriated.

Their wives have straw hair.
Yours is blonde.

They are missing one football card
to complete the full set.

You keep an eye out for a matching
Louis XV-style walnut hall table.

They are hoping for a start with a builder.
You play your part in the family firm.

They use loose change, welfare coupons.
You tap your credit card impatiently on the counter.

They lean over the breeze-block wall to gossip.
You put down motions for the Residents' AGM.

They have a hot tip for Newmarket.
You have the inside track on a rights issue.

They go over the top.
You reach it.

They preach better pay.
You practise it.

VOYAGER

I

He will live a little longer: sadness taints
the air like gas, a vapour of doleful music
escaping the radio's capsule; death signs
clarify like stars that filled his vision one night
on a river as eyes adapted to the dark,
heat lightning launched distress flares.

II

The boating holiday we'd planned to treat
him to: sedge and reed-beds; willows trailing
slender arms in water, as if from a skiff;
calm evenings with reading light till ten
when mayflies tantalise the slurping lake,
sun comes filtered through a sieve of leaves.

III

Rocks, lock gates, whirlpools, tidal flows:
his fingers trace the mapped obstacles faced
between the river's origin and the cold,
salt-preserved finality of sea; cut water
healing in his wake, he rows, as though
for dear life, towards the beating sun.

BRIDGE

after Mak Dizdar

I once
had
a plan

I would build
a million-span bridge
to the sun

Alone
out of that dream
survives

the foundation stone

lodged
in
my heart

BREVIARY

The Cow

after K. Schippers

The cow
is a funny artiste:
whatever the beast
has in mind
it always comes out
as a moo.

*

Winter Haiku

men in women's shops
　　women sizing up men's clothes
portents of Christmas

*

Oven Ready

a headless corpse
in a plastic bag
neck driven like a rivet
up its behind

remove transplanted organs
from the ribbed crypt
rinse the body
naked pink newborn

*

Off-duty

reclining in the garden overnight
your deck chair soaking up the moonlight

*

Trunk Road

I
hug
you like
a tree which
stands in the way
of a planned new road.
I throw my arms around you
like a protestor who will not
let the tree be felled, whose vigil
is silhouetted against dusk, while night
outlines bulldozers, trucks, blunt instruments
of
death.

From
Weather Permitting
(1999)

EITHER

They are somewhere in the world, pouring soya milk
on porridge during the dream-time before work,
        or sprouting thick fungal whiskers
        in a graveyard's penetrating damp –
the ones I used to know, with whom I lost
touch, who were once the mainstay of my
        gossip: squash partners, office colleagues,
        obnoxious neighbours, friends of friends.

As I speak, they scrutinise the milk carton's text
or subside more comfortably into the sleep
        that resurrection's long-haul wait entails.
        Our paths crossed, then grassed over again.
They are either alive and well or decomposing
slowly in a shroud; I could either call them up
        and chat, or confirm that they are ex-directory now.
        It is a matter of life or death.

FOUR DESTINATIONS

You travel under
cover of darkness

that lifts for the length
of a one-street village,

a hill farm scoured by
sour-milk yard light.

Then night comes
down again in sheets.

Tired and cold, you are
a fire inhaling its own ash.

      *

Regret is the hamlet across the bay
against which waves beat their brains
in winter, having lost all hope of change.

A door bangs. A cigarette sign swings
from rusty hinges. A slow piano theme
is rehearsed like an excuse.

      *

Why, as soon as the unaccompanied
cello suite begins, am I conveyed back
to the brittle wintry airport road,
your newly-widowed mother driving,
my arrival coinciding with a glacial
dusk, with the one customer left
to moderate the plate glass expanse
of an Arby's Sandwich franchise?

*

As the Friday-evening bus speeds from the city,
moonlight restores wildness to the fields.
We place our fate in the driver's hands,
having offered up our fares, hearts,
spinal cords, endocrinal glands.

BACKGROUND MUSIC

It is not music you are listening to, it is not
your song they are playing, but the time outdoors
those same chords struck: Mahler's hammer blows fell
as dusk crashed down like cymbals on the perspex
shell where the orchestra was pitted against
birdsong, the sky's membrane raised like a roof.

It is not the melody but the warm air it drifts on,
through a window open to let paint dry, a daughter
prying the piano keys for notes in the dull acoustics
of an immaculate white room; or a string quartet silhouetted
before a curving bay: you have travelled east into a second
spring, rays cascading through an ice-melt of blue glass.

And that pop-song: ignore the ear-rotting, saccharine words;
let it transport you back to school holidays, cycling
torpid afternoons away, circling the oblong square.
Stuccoed houses in a Mitteleuropa city, a Sunday heavy
with dust of ribboned war wreaths, history; dark-eyed surveillance
from backstreet bars, a gypsy guitar wafting like nicotine.

A bugler's reveille from his campsite, dissipating river mist.
An organ fugue through incense after a cathedral Mass
at which the host clung to the cupola of your mouth.
Scratchy childhood tunes, loudhailed by a carnival, croon
through bloated heat; you try to sleep amid the corncrake-hoarse
excitement – cross-hatched sounds that fuse in memory now,

a Charles Ives symphony improvised on the spot.

THE CELTIC TIGER

Ireland's boom is in full swing.
Rows of numbers, set in a cloudless blue
computer background, prove the point.

Executives lop miles off journeys
since the ring-roads opened, one hand
free to dial a client on the mobile.

Outside new antique pubs, young consultants
– well-toned women, gel-slick men –
drain long-necked bottles of imported beer.

Lip-glossed cigarettes are poised
at coy angles, a black bra strap
slides strategically from a Rocha top.

Talk of tax-exempted town-house lettings
is muffled by rap music blasted
from a passing four-wheel drive.

The old live on, wait out their stay
of execution in small granny flats,
thrifty thin-lipped men, grim pious wives . . .

Sudden as an impulse holiday, the wind
has changed direction, strewing a whiff
of barbecue fuel across summer lawns.

Tonight, the babe on short-term
contract from the German parent
will partner you at the sponsors' concert.

Time now, however, for the lunch-break
orders to be texted. Make yours hummus
on black olive bread. An Evian.

JET AGE

Years, centuries, millennia will pass. Highways and airports
will be reclaimed by twitch grass or covered with sand.

— IVAN KLÍMA

The stories we will regale our grandchildren with,
titanium whales plunging to within inches of our lives,
diving down on cities, capsules stacked above the tarmac
before wheezing to a breathless halt (where swaying grass
will replace windsocks, fuel-trucks rust on apron cracks).

Spread-eagled tonnage taking off, a magic carpet rising
on its dust, vapour trails like silver rails to glide along,
live cargo strapped to padded seats commanding sight of land
stranded in sea-water; clouds like rose-tipped corries,
exhausted quarries, frozen canyons, unconquered peaks . . .

So inured to mystery were our people, we will say,
they took for granted sprayed glitter of night cities,
towns riveted to the ground, but stirred from newspaper
or snooze to adjust their watches and their headrests,
choose capriciously among the complimentary liqueurs.

NOR

'There didn't have to be 2,000 diseases
of the skin', I remember someone commenting.
Nor 17,293 painfully slow routes through the vomitory
before being thrown to the lions of death.
Nor 11,416 ways of feeling wounded.
Nor 89,010 gradations of loneliness
calibrated on traffic islands, country lanes.
Nor 29,109,352 reasons to toss and turn at night.
Nor stage fright, nor honeymoon cystitis.
Nor *esprit de l'escalier*, nor so many calories in cheese.
Nor sexually transmitted fatalities, nor smoker's cough.
Nor 400,000,000 tons (live weight) of humanity
to experience these things, nor however many
newborn pounds were dragged screaming, added
to the tally, since my opening line.

IN MEMORY OF ALOIS ALZHEIMER

(1864–1915)

I

Before this page fades from memory,
spare a thought for Alois Alzheimer,
called to mind each time

someone becomes forgetful,
disintegration vindicating
his good name.

II

His is the last image assigned
to the ex-President who has slipped
from public view; soiled sheets
give credence to his thesis;

his territory is marked out
by the track of urine
dribbled along the corridor
of the day-care centre.

III

Lie closer to me in the dry sheets
while I can still tell who you are.

Let me declare how much I love you
before our bed is sorely tested.

Love me with drooling toxins, with carbon monoxide,
with rope, with arrows through my heart.

THE VICTIM

I

The victim is male.
In his early thirties.
That's all the police will reveal for now.
Relatives have yet to be informed.
A post-mortem has yet to be scheduled.
The coroner's beeper is sounding its alarm.
What faith, tribe, gang he subscribed to.
Whether he had been involved or not.
Whether it was a random killing.
Whether it was a revenge attack, a tit-for-tat.
Speculation can await tomorrow's papers.

II

Until he is given a life.
Until he is given an address, wife, children, job.
Until he is a man with a history, a past.
Until the mystery of his death is cleared up.
Until the blood is swabbed from his chin.
Until the mud is laundered from his clothes.
Until someone claims his body
for family or nation or God.
Until guilt, forgiveness, innocence,
blame have been apportioned.
Until he is given a name.

END OF THE PEACH SEASON

The peaches are no longer in their prime:
Although their cheeks keep up a summer show,
They are living now on borrowed time.

To score with knives such beauty seems a crime;
But, underneath the skin, dark bruises show
The peaches are no longer in their prime.

Like dying wasps in grass who cannot climb,
The sun is losing altitude and shows
It is living now on borrowed time:

Pinched skins, with which streaked sunsets chime,
And wasp-bored wells of syrup go to show
The peaches are no longer in their prime.

Bud and blossom (*still life*) first; then slime
(*Memento mori*) ends their rose-hued show.
They are living now on borrowed time.

Scrape out the mould, the pockmarked heart of grime,
Expose the sallow tissue that will show
The peaches are no longer in their prime,
They are living now on borrowed time.

COMING OF AGE

What age would my parents have been on our excited day-trip to
the city when, during a bone-china lunch in the convent parlour –
served under the oily portrait of the haloed founder – my wimpled
aunt remarked that they would pass for twenty?

> What I do know
> is how young
> my dying mother was.
>
> How difficult it became
> to recognise her
> in her final weeks.
>
> How – down to her black
> cancer-painted nails –
> she looked as though
>
> she had lived
> to be the oldest
> woman on earth,
>
> as if it would take
> an archaeologist
> to excavate her grave.
>
> How my aunt, despairing
> of the limitations
> of a walled-in life,
>
> would revoke her order.
> How my father's darkest
> chapter would abruptly shut.

How my sister, below
the age for admittance
to the wards,

was plied with goodies
in the hospital shop:
all the chocolate

she could cope with,
all the fizzy orange
she could drink.

TO LOVE

the dead woman
in the living girl.
The child in the woman.
The tree planed
against its grain
into a coffee table.
The blossom in
the inner chamber
of the crab apple's heart.
To love the squawking
baby bird underpinning
the full-spanned hawk
and the silk purse
of piglet skin
stashed in the jute
sack of the sow.
The meadow grass
taking root
in the tarred car park.
The wolf howling
through the chimney
of the mongrel's throat.
The race memory
of unfenced space
agitating the battery hen.
The ancestral ape
in the chauffeur-driven
man with diplomatic plates.
Even the flu virus
which lays you low
but has its own
agenda to pursue,
like moss in paving slabs,
cracks in frescoes,
hearthrug sparks.

SNAIL'S PACE

I look down on the snail as on a container ship
seen from a plane, its slow pace an illusion
caused by distance, filigree silver wash a ruff
of sea spray. It is on its way, no doubt, to feed
off my garden, cold mucous mouth watering at the thought
of a sweet-and-sour meal of compost, leaves.

I raise a foot, needing to hear a shell's crunch,
a squelch against cement. Or I might nip inside
for salt to liquidate it, watch the textured stretch-
fabric flesh fizz into extinction; no one is sentimental
towards snails, oozing as though squeezed from rusty tubes.
Yet I let this specimen pursue its sluggish routines in the end.

The horns scout like a ship's antennae, ready
to warn but pointless when faced with aerial attacks.
I even know the damp ivy-clad segment of the back wall
where it skulks on dry days, lurking in its chestnut shell,
sticky with phlegmatic glue; and though sometimes I reach over,
prise it off to teach it who is boss, I can never quite rise

to the callousness required to play God with its life.

VOTIVE CANDLES

Burning candles toast
a corner of the church:

To your good health,
happiness, success . . .

One lighting the next
like a nervous

chain smoker's cigarette:
little rockets, boosters,

launched to heaven,
knuckle-white with pleading.

When they gutter,
stutter, dwindle, taper off,

what is left
of inflamed hopes

is a hard waxen mass,
a host;

the shard of soap
with which

God washes
His spotless hands.

A STATION

after Jenó Dsida

An official announcement crackling like deep-fried fat
that our branch-line train would be three hours delayed.
A garbled explanation, some reference to points failure.

And so this Thursday night, I stamp feet on the platform's pier,
venturing to the edge of choppy dark, like a man walking a plank.
Back in the yellow, dank, retch-smelling station building,

I read maps cracked on walls, see pierced hearts squeezed
in felt-tip between names; a revving engine raises,
dashes hopes, abandoning me to loneliness again, a pattern

repeating like the taste of supper in my mouth, thoughts
of betrayal in my mind. The blood is faltering in my veins.
A pale man, slumped near the blinded ticket kiosk, eyes

the clock; a young woman, tightening her veil of silence,
looks aside – it would be good to hear companionable sounds.
No chance. I listen as my inner demons prophecy what cruxes

lie in wait. Telegraph scaffolds line embankments.
Peter could snooze until cock-crow. James drools into
the neat pillow he has made of his scarf. John,

sleeping rough on concrete, keeps watch on his bad dreams.
Restless, I resume my platform vigil, fear streaming down
my forehead in the signal light's unyielding red.

Then, like switching tracks, I start to pray that my train
might never arrive, that my journey be indefinitely delayed,
forward connections missed, that my cup might pass from me.

TOMORROW

I

Tomorrow I will start to be happy.
The morning will light up like a celebratory cigar.
Sunbeams sprawling on the lawn will set
dew sparkling like a cut-glass tumbler of champagne.
Today will end the worst phase of my life.

I will put my shapeless days behind me,
fencing off the past, as a golden rind
of sand parts slipshod sea from solid land.
It is tomorrow I want to look back on, not today.
Tomorrow I start to be happy; today is almost yesterday.

II

Australia, how wise you are to get the day
over and done with first, out of the way.
You have eaten the fruit of knowledge, while
we are dithering about which main course to choose.
How liberated you must feel, how free from doubt:

the rise and fall of stocks, today's closing prices
are revealed to you before our speculating has begun.
Australia, you can gather in your accident statistics
like a harvest while our roads still have hours to kill.
When we are in the dark, you have sagely seen the light.

III

Cagily, presumptuously, I dare to write 2038.
A date without character or tone. 2038.
A year without interest rates or mean daily temperature.
Its hit songs have yet to be written, its new-year
babies yet to be induced, its truces to be signed.

Much too far off for prophecy, though one hazards
a tentative guess – a so-so year most likely,
vague in retrospect, fizzling out with the usual
end-of-season sales; everything slashed:
your last chance to salvage something of its style.

HAY BARN

Riches of hay, hoarded
away in the barn, a cache
stuffed under a mattress,

were withdrawn over
winter, wads forked out
from a frosty cart.

Loose clumps
poked from smoking
mouths of cattle

who itched long
alligator chins
on wattle posts.

Though ransacked,
whittled down,
the hay smelt yet

of dusty summer,
of the beehive domes
swept dreamily home

on a horse-drawn float,
listing, hem brushing
against the uneven field,

sides ripping on thorns,
losing wisps to
a hedge-congested lane;

then unclasped, uncorseted
from twine bindings,
added to the stockpile

with sweaty, shirtless heaves
of men relieved
to have crammed each cavity

before the rodent-patter
of rain, creating a sanctuary
again, love nest,

escape hatch
for brooding hens
with dung-speckled eggs.

Ruminate on abundance
there some Sunday
after church,

still in your suit,
rooted to the ground
with awe.

NEWGRANGE

in memory of Miroslav Holub

> *They waited.*
> *They waited in vain.*
> – HOLUB, 'The Earliest Angels'

I

Light scans the megalith, on the winter solstice,
nosing forward, sniffing its way into the chambers,
twitching its rays like the whiskers of a laboratory rat.

It confronts the dark like white armies of lymphocytes.
It coats the walls like cholesterol on a middle-aged aortic arch.
Its glow is a 4 a.m. hospital corridor, a barium x-ray picture.

II

When you visited Newgrange – an off-colour autumn day –
you were seven minutes late: five thousand years
and seven minutes too late for admission;

so, you were refused access to the tomb, which loomed
before you like a time-operated safe; the tour guide,
a centurion, stood guard at the carved entrance stone.

III

Though no lab apparatus could have predicted this,
you were four years, nine months too early for the tomb,
where now you chart the frequency of light

at the tunnel's end and formulate a chaos theory
based on the flap of an angel's wing,
the velocity required for taking death by storm.

INTERIM REPORTS

for Teri Garvey

That precious time in bed
just before you rise for work.
Every second counts.
You live each minute
as though it were your last.

*

The formica tables
    and plastic chairs
of station cafés,
    roadside diners,
staff canteens;
    of hospitals where
relatives nurse
    styrofoam cups
and wait for word.

*

A long illness bravely borne.
Words that crop up in obituaries.

The stress on every syllable
in its euphonious phrase.

*

How are things?
How are you keeping?

How's the world
treating you?

Are you having
a nice day?

Have I caught you
at a bad moment?

How soon do you expect
to know for sure?

Should I ring back when
you're more composed?

     *

Thank God for morphine
where pain management is concerned –

though, granted, it can have some side effects
(vertigo, facial flushing, bradycardia, palpitations,
vomiting, constipation, confusion, drowsiness, nausea,
sweating, orthostatic hypotension, hypothermia, restlessness,
mood swings, dry mouth, miosis, micturition difficulties,
ureteric or biliary spasm, raised intracranial pressure).

     *

When someone first asks of you
'Is he/she still alive?'
you will be well
into injury time.

     *

And where does the suffering go?
Down the hatch of the dialysis machine?
Ejected with a colostomy bag's waste?

Does it leave a flesh wound on raw innards,
notch the heart like a furrowed face?

Does it seep down, sweat and blood,
to the lower water table, or bubble up
like methane from a smothered mass grave
where an underground stream surfaces
through porous rock, a running sore?

                    *

The whisper of the word 'hospice'.
The hush at its heart.
The sedated body laid out on starched sheets.
The soul billowing on puffed pillows.

                    *

The sisters in the children's unit
            couldn't have been kinder.

The bereavement support group
            helped us come to terms.

                    *

He had a comfortable night,
            the nurse assured me.

Her body was no longer contorted;
            she looked like her old self.

I felt I could detect a smile,
            as if he recognised me.

Her breathing became laboured,
            I pressed the emergency bell.

It was impossible to believe
    this was the end.

We had some good times together
    in spite of everything.

DEADLINES

The suspense of hanging
      around for an arbitrary call,
passing the years until

you're summoned, pacing
      between walls without
a firm appointment:

Read a glossy magazine.
      Break the crossword code.
Sit it out in your office,

driven to distraction
      by the workload;
at home, restore the paint

a malicious nail has
      scarred your car with;
threaten lawyers' letters

on your noisy neighbours;
      study the small print
in the share prospectus.

Your time will come
      when it gets a minute,
refusing to be pinned down,

despatching you at whim
      with a mercifully sudden
heart attack, snapping your back

in a car accident, setting
        your nightwear alight
in a hotel inferno,

taking your memory away
        so that you can't quite
put a name on its blank face.

TOWARDS A CESARE PAVESE TITLE

(Verrà la morte e avrà i tuoi occhi)

Death will come and it will wear your eyes.

Death demands the handover of your eyes.

Death eyes you, stares you in the face.

Then death assumes the running of your eyes.

Death powders cheeks, shadows eyes.

Death would take the eyes out of your head.

Death will seize your assets, cut off your eye supply.

Death lashes out at your defenceless eyes.

You are up to your eyes in death.

Death takes after you, eyes the image of yours.

You would recognise death with your eyes shut.

Death will give you dagger glances, evil eyes.

Death makes eye contact at last.

Death will come and it will steal your looks.

9 A.M.

A metal clatter of shutters.
A shattering of the street's silence.
A turning of keys, an unbolting of doors.
A reversing of 'CLOSED' verdicts.
A striped sun-awning is goaded
from its lair by a long pole.
Mobile signs are placed strategically
on the pavement, the direction of arrows checked.
Blue security men, not yet on their guard,
step out for a smoke or breathe the light.
The gift boutique smells of buffed wax polish,
the cosmetics section atomises into perfumes.
Brasso revamps an estate agent's image.
Two beer-reeking tramps, disturbed
in doorways, fold up blankets blearily.
Jewellers unlock their strongroom stock of gold rings
and bracelets, slip them back into plush velvet displays.
Name-tagged managers drip bagged coins into tills.
Flowers, bleary-eyed from all-night truck journeys,
revive in cool vases, open wide.
Dust is taken in by vacuum cleaners
or brushed aside, swept towards gutters.
A hairdresser assesses a fringe
of tepid water with her hand.
'The usual' for a bakery customer means
a roll and butter, a tea-break muffin.
Bacon, egg, sausage in a coffee shop.
A newspaper, a slice of toast.
9 o'clock and all goes well.
Everyone is present and correct.

FRIDAY

We are driving home.
Work is over, the weekend ours
       like a gift voucher
to spend as we feel inclined.

       We pass the armed guard
of whitethorn, the guard
       of honour of poplars,
until our favourite

       half–mile stretch
where a canopy of branches
       spans the road
like a triumphal arch.

       Our car tunnels into
this leafy underpass,
       entering its funnel,
its decompression chamber.

       Sheep are shearing fields;
lambs bound like woolly dogs
       just released from the leash.
We have squeezed through

       the filter of trees
and now, renewed, detoxified,
       we are on the downward
slope towards home.

ONLY

It is only skin.
It can be artificially cultured these days.

It is only breath.
As often sour as sweet.

It is only nerve tips.
Invariably sensational in response.

It is only lips, one on top of the other.
Shedding their unsavoury scales.

It is only warmth.
Everyone hovers around the 37° mark.

It is only hormones, emitting primitive signals.
Easily reproduced under laboratory conditions.

It is only blood.
The dilation can be clinically explained.

It is only desire.
An impulse inspired electrochemically.

It is only a fluttering heart.
It has a finite number of strikes.

It is only one organism among many.
A million clones could be arranged.

It is only that your moment has arrived.
It is only for now.

TO A LOVE POET

I

Fortysomething did you say? Or more?
By now, no one could care less either way.
When you swoop into a room, no heads turn,
no cheeks burn, no knowing glances are exchanged,

no eye contact is made. You are no longer
a meaningful contender in the passion stakes.
But a love poet must somehow make love,
if only to language, fondling its contours,

dressing it in slinky tropes, caressing
its letters with the tongue, glimpsing it darkly
as though through a crackling black stocking
or diaphanous blouse, arousing its interest,

varying the rhythm, playing speech against
stanza like leather against skin, stroking words
wistfully, chatting them up, curling fingers
around the long flowing tresses of sentences.

II

Never again, though, will a living Muse
choose you from the crowd in some romantic city –
Paris, Prague – singling you out, her pouting lips
a fountain where you resuscitate your art.

Not with you in view will she hold court to her mirror,
matching this halter-neck with that skirt, changing her mind,
testing other options, hovering between a cashmere
and velvet combination or plain tee-shirt and jeans,

watching the clock, listening for the intercom or phone.
Not for your eyes her foam bath, hot wax, hook-snapped lace,
her face creams, moisturisers, streaks and highlights.
Not for your ears the excited shriek of her zip.

Look to the dictionary as a sex manual.
Tease beauty's features into words that will assuage
the pain, converting you – in this hour of need –
to someone slim and lithe and young and eligible for love again.

LIFE CYCLE

in memory of George Mackay Brown

January. Wind bellows. Stars hiss like smithy sparks.
The moon a snowball frozen in mid-flight.
George is rocking on his fireside chair.

February. The sea loud at the end of the street.
Ferries cancelled. Snowdrops seep through dampness.
George is sitting down to mutton broth.

March. Oystercatcher piping. Early tattie planting.
Gull-protected fishing boats wary of the equinoctial gales.
George is tired by now of his captivity.

April. Cloud boulders roll back from the Easter sun.
The tinker horse, a cuckoo, in the farmer's field.
George is taking the spring air on Brinkie's Brae.

May. Scissors-tailed swallows cut the tape, declare summer open.
A stray daddy-long-legs, unsteady on its feet as a new foal.
George is sampling home-brew from his vat.

June. Butterfly wings like ornamental shutters. Day scorches
down to diamonds, rubies before being lost at sea.
George is picnicking with friends on Rackwick beach.

July. Another wide-eyed sun. Its gold slick pours like oil
on the untroubled waves. Shoppers dab brows as they gossip.
George is drafting poems in a bottle-green shade.

August. Pudgy bees in romper suits suckled by flowers.
Well water rationed. Trout gills barely splashed.
George is hiding from the tourists' knock.

September. A brace of wrapped haddocks on the doorstep.
Mushrooms, snapped off under grass tufts, melt in the pan.
George is stocking up his shed with coal and peat.

October. Porridge and clapshot weather. Swan arrivals, divers.
Sun hangs, a smoking ham, suspended in the misty air.
George is ordering a hot dram at the pub.

November. Rain shaken out slantwise like salt. Hail pebbles
flung against the window to announce winter's return.
George is adding a wool layer to his clothes.

December. Three strangers, bearing gifts, enquire the way
to byre and bairn. A brightness absent from the map of stars.
George's craft is grounded among kirkyard rocks.

DELEGATES

Today, we have no responsibility for the world.
We are in transit between airport lounges.
It is Tuesday in one jurisdiction, Monday in another.
We cannot be tied down, we are on the run like fugitives,
sheltered by date lines and time zones, escaping tax
regulations, weather alerts, dodging the present tense.

*

Container boats – ferrying
imports, exports – can be
seen from our mezzanine.

A backdrop to negotiations
like a painted seascape
framed on an office wall,

turned to when minds wander
or memories are rifled
for near-precedents.

*

A strategic break. Mass migration towards the wash room.
A lemon squirt from your shrivelled member, then out again
to drum up support for your proposal: hands, perfumed
with liquid soap, gesture as you outline your rationale.

*

Always a harried official,
plastic ballpoint in mouth
like a thermometer, checking
the viability of a draft
the viability of a draft

beginning with the words,
'Notwithstanding the provisions of . . . '

*

An end-of-term mood
in the July conference rooms:
microphones switched off,
booth lights dimmed,
the open spaces
of the corridors
thinned of population,
attachés pressing 'o1'
in the mirrored lifts,
interpreters returning
to their mother tongues.

*

Friday night delays
of flights to capitals
by national carriers,
the wait for take-off clearance.

Jackets folded, stowed with duty-free,
balding heads lie back,
soak up news distributed
by smiling cabin crews.

*

Rushing the glass
                arrivals door,
you pick your
                expectant daughter
from the throng,
                playschool painting
elevated at the barrier
                like a name-board.

BUYING A LETTERBOX

Another mouth to feed.
Our best face
turned to the world,
catching the brass
eye of the sun.

Should we buy the type
that snaps shut,
a trap scattering
bills and final reminders
like feathers, fur?

Or the limper kind
that yields easily,
tongue slobbering around
the postman's hand,
yet still eats anything,

digesting the bad news
as casually as the good?

WEATHER PERMITTING

I

The August day you wake to takes you by surprise.
Its bitterness. Black sullen clouds. Brackish downpour.
A drift-net of wetness enmeshes the rented cottage,
towels and children's swimwear sodden on the line.

Dry-gulleted drains gulp down neat rain.
Drops bounce from a leaking gutter with hard,
uncompromising slaps: and, like resignation
in the face of death, you contemplate winter

with something close to tenderness, the sprint
from fuel shed to back door, the leisurely
ascent of peat smoke, even the suburban haze
of boiler flues when thermostats are set.

You warm to those thoughts as you sit there,
brainstorming ways to keep the family amused,
plans abandoned for barefoot games on dry sand.
Handcraft shops? Slot-machine arcades? Hotel grills?

In truth – manipulating toast crumbs backwards,
forwards at the unsteady table's edge – you'd prefer
to return to your bed as if with some mild
ailment, pampered by duvet, whiskey, cloves.

II

Let it rain.
Let the clouds discharge their contents like reserve tanks.
Let the worms burrow their way to the topsoil
from whatever dank Sargasso they were spawned in.
Let dampness rot the coffin-boards of the summer house.
Let the shrubs lose their foothold in the wind,
the nettles lose their edge, the drenched rat
with slicked-back hair scuttle to its sewage pipe.
Let the tropical expanses of the rhubarb leaves
serve as an artificial pond, a reservoir.
Let the downpour's impact on the toolshed be akin
to the dull applause on an archive recording of a love duet.
Let the bricklayers at the building site wrap
pathetic sheets of polythene around doomed foundations.
Let the limb ripped from the tree's socket
hover fleetingly in the air, an olive branch.
Let a rainbow's fantail unfurl like a bird of paradise.
Let a covenant be sealed, its wording watertight.
Let the floods recede.
Let there be light.

III *After Giacomo Leopardi*

The storm runs out of wind; nature, which
abhors a silence, fills the vacancy with birdsong.
Deserting the airless, low-ceilinged coop,
the hen repeats herself ad infinitum. Replenished
like the rain-barrels, hearts grow sanguine.

Hammering resumes. Humming. Gossip. Croons.
Sun strides down lanes that grass has repossessed,
takes a shine to the brasses at the hotel where,
by the window she thrust open, the chambermaid
is marvelling at the cleansed freshness, calm.

Balm of mind and body. Will we ever feel
more reconciled to life than now, ever
know a moment more conducive to new hopes,
eager beginnings, auspicious starts?
How easily pleased we are. Rescind

the threat of torment for the briefest
second and we blot out dark nights of the soul
when lightning flashes fanned by wind
ignited fire and brimstone visions.
Sorrow is perennial; happiness, a rare

bloom, perfumes the air – so that we breathe
with the ease of a camphor-scented chest
from which congestion has just lifted.
Lack of woe equates with rapture then,
though not till death will pain take full leave

of our senses, grant us permanent relief.

CHURCHYARD VIEW: THE NEW ESTATE

On their side, inviolable silence.
On ours, hammering, pounding,
sawing, clawing out foundations
with the frenzy of someone buried alive.

*

We like our dead well-seasoned.
Newly-ground soil disturbs.

*

She could wind him round her little finger
that is now solid bone.

*

My halogen light with sensor
alert for resurrections.

*

Every crow suspected as a raven,
every pigeon inspected for vulturehood.

*

They mark their death-days among themselves,
bake a mud cake, make candles of wax fingers.

*

Young since they were born.
Young since they were teenagers.
Young since they staged a coming-of-age

bash in the tennis club hall.
Young since they played non-stop
basketball for charity sponsorship.
This being young could only go on for so long.

*

Crab-apple windfalls
at the cemetery wall
no one collects for jelly.

*

The churchyard in shadow
like a north-facing garden.

*

Our freehold title
when the mortgage is redeemed.
Their graves to be maintained
perpetually by bequests.

*

Call my wrong number
in the small hours of the night.
Remind me how bad
things might – will – be.

*

A lip-puffed, ear-blocked, glow-nosed
head cold is what they feel nostalgia for.

*

How much it took to sustain their lives:
heaps of gravel, travel coupons, steel pads,
roll–on deodorants, bran flakes, tampons.

*

The dead seem more at ease in autumn
as the time to hibernate comes near.

*

Written before they were born,
these books foretold
anxiety and strife and war.
And yet they were born.

*

In our pine bed, we hear them stir
when floorboards creak, pipes cheep.

*

The prehensile clasp of the dead
grasping at prayer books
with straw–yellow claws.

*

Most die over a lifetime.
Others die all at once,
missing in action.

*

The child's coffin
like a violin case.

A pitch which parents' ears
can hear through clay.

*

Buried talents lie.
Hoards unexcavated by posterity.

*

Scan the obit columns, uniform as war graves.
Check the maiden names, the regretting children.
Whole cities and towns wiped out.
A plague on all your houses.

*

A hearse in rush-hour traffic:
a ghost at the feast.

*

Two sisters
who wished each other dead
languish side by side.

*

All behind them now.
The blushed fumblings of sex.
Interventional radiology.
Expense account lunches.
Games of bridge.

*

Death is the aftertaste of life.

*

Those who fester better than others.
Those who manage it more neatly.
Those fussy about the order
in which their organs decompose.
Those who discover an aptitude for death
they never had for life.

*

The blackness of
the cemetery blackbird,
its song an octave lower.

*

Above prison–high walls,
the trees – up to their knees
in slaughter – protest their innocence
to the outside world.

*

Who had a crush on the girl
six headstones away.
Who couldn't muster
the courage.
Who wouldn't make
the first move.

*

Paupers' anonymous plots.
Families in layers like bunk beds.

Crypts where coffins rest
on shelves, left luggage.

The rusted, railed-off holdings
of those whose souls

appropriate a private
heaven for themselves.

      *

Add the total suffering of these bodies.
Deduct their combined pleasure.
What doth it profit a man?

      *

As you were built on bone,
your house was built on sand.
Not a stone will stand upon stone.

A painted wall is a white lie.
You will crumble to the ground.
Your house will sicken, die.

      *

I stare at the graves
like a sailor gazing out to sea.

      *

A skull smashed,
    the crust of concrete
is sledged open –
    dust to dust –
welcoming an addition
    to the family.

      *

For whom growing pains, walking frames,
crash diets, price rises, self-esteem
were live issues once upon a time.

*

Days when death comes so close,
you say No to life.
Days when you could show death
how to live.

*

Should this end in spring
when death is overwhelmed
by winding sheets of green?
Or Halloween when
I overnight with friends?

FAMILY ALBUM

A rose window, rescued
from the Reformation axe,
was unearthed in the henhouse
of a children's adventure story.
I read about it, waiting in the car
for my father, as a shivery evening
descended on the village like an Asian flu.

                *

The empty Atrixo jar is what survives
of our mother's hands: hands that plumped pillows,
milked drinking water from the pump, spread suds
and beeswax polish through her children's lives.

                *

Rained-out day-trips.
Vain buckets, spades.
        The beach like
        newly-laid concrete
where, growing boys,
we ached to build
        our castles
        in the healthy air.

                *

July. My mother and I are in the kitchen.
Sun, outlined behind mist, swaggers into view.
Radio tuned to Athlone for the requests show,
she soaks the charred saucepan to which
a crust of porridge sticks, scrapes laval
streaks from a blue-rimmed egg-cup, squeezes
a plastic bottle for the last dregs of detergent.

I dry the dishes, leave her then, stuffing the gullet
of a circular washing machine with clothes,
adjusting the crank on the manual wringer.
Russian vine invades the outdoor toilet,
where newspaper tearings substitute for tissue.
In my spongy sandals, I walk the cinder paths
between sweet and sharp competing fragrances.

Morning glories tighten their grip. Spurred nasturtiums.
Lettuce hearts harden. Beyond the hedge, bordered by silk
poppies – red slept-in party dresses – the dip and rise
of headscarved women cycling on High Nellies to the town.
Sound waves of conversation ripple through the heat.
Insects hum like chainsaws in a rain forest. Larks
about their business. A moist rubber-mouthed frog.

And snuff of dog roses. And wasps on house calls.
And a sudden outburst of church bells. And great
surges of silence. And my sister's skipping rhymes.
And berries roasting on their stalks, like fish grilled
on the bone. And a grasshopper's rhythms, a bamboo
thwacked by a bored child along park railings.
And permed dahlias. And days and days and days of this.

                    *

No work. No school.
          Sunday, January 20th 1963.
Wary cars are testing
          fresh clots of snow.
Crinkled seals of ice
          unbroken on the puddles,
rain–barrel frozen tight,
          what might our outlook hold
when the icicle sword
          guarding the bay window
corrodes and we gradually
          drift apart?

*

The front door ajar: a black hole
through which a hurling commentary
curls, like smoke shavings off tar.
I play with cousins in a trailer
lined with grain shot, locks of hay.

Free till milking, uncles in oaten socks
lean towards the radio from timber forms.
Later, hair brilliantined, Old Spice
and soap outflanking vapours of hot cow,
they will make a dash for the Sunday dance.

Calf mash bubbles in a cauldron
on the range. A hen, flapping with
hurt pride, is evicted from the kitchen.
The sun locates an opening in the clouds
to slip through, rendering things precious

for a second: our chubby, toad–like
Volkswagen; straw roof thatch; chunks
of turnip that spill, gold winnings,
from the pulper when my brother
shoulders the iron handle's strain.

*

The crane, throwing its weight around,
jib pointed towards the future,

distracts me with a shade not seen
since primary school: gobstopper blue.

I suck the paintwork white
with greedy eyes.

Now the gobstopper becomes
a demolition ball:

hurled against the wailing
walls of childhood,

it starts to taste
of love and aniseed and fear.

*

No exams this year.
The summer break is under way.
Days are brimful of potential.
My father takes me on his sales drive
to small towns near the county border.

Broad face cleared of thistle–spiky
bristle by a safety blade
– worked up to a lather
with shaving stick and brush –
he is glowing with good health,

glad of the company, the chat.
We overtake a bakery van, almost
able to catch the doughy draught of soft
white bread, cracked terracotta crusts
we'd love to pick holes in.

A milk churn on a donkey cart;
the farmer – legs dangled next
to an outsize orange wheel – salutes.
Hay-scented air streams through
our side-windows like thyme.

Crops reach out with a flourish
or are raked and baled and bound.

We laugh at the clapboard church
we pass but cross ourselves nonetheless.
Guess how many dogs we'll see

between here and Clogheen?
We each make a stab.
Dogs asleep in dung-scabbed farmyards.
Dogs lunging from boreens at our tyres.
Dogs hobbled to inhibit straying.

Down one steep, narrow-waisted road.
Up another.
Tracing the stout-walled perimeters
of a demesne; the disused railway line
an abandoned, meandering, flower-hemmed lane.

Council men with drippy cans of bitumen
stand in the shade between potholes.
He is so alive, my father, he can talk, drive,
become animated about a gymnastic stoat,
lacy patterns sun stencils through the trees.

He smiles at some remark of mine.
Tonight, he will repeat it to my mother
as she fills the ringing tea pot
with hot water; and, dinner eaten, will
record it proudly in his diary like a sale.

                    *

Oranges were my exotic fruit
when young: gaudy leatherette
of skin, profuse sachets of juice.

Then peaches. I must have reached
eleven by the time of my first-hand
encounter with an uncanned peach,

pronouncing the ripe word to the grocer
who drew one from its nesting place,
laying it to rest in my disbelieving palm.

*

Grey. The dishwater disgorged in anger against the kitchen wall.

Grey. Cotton vests worn under home-knit sweaters, to shield
against chest colds, damp rooms, harm.

Grey. A fog of affection and alarm dense enough to isolate you
from the world.

Grey. The pipe smoke signalling peace when your father lit up.

Grey. The dust multiplying neatly on the venetian blinds after she
had died.

Grey. Still the colour in which your dreams preserve that house.

Grey that could bud suddenly into dayglo picture books, American
comics, love displays.

*

A lashing wet February night. Cold jabs of wind.
I park my bike. Stark unholy rainwater rushes
down the gutters of my exposed nose.

What a miracle it would take to step back
into my leaky shoes and enter the bleak,
unheatable cathedral (mosaics of angels,

wings gold-tipped like nibs; statuesque Marys
sheltering beneath the cross's beams) with faith
as firm as mine was then; ending a retreat,

we elevated rosary beads and scapulars for blessing,
roused to 'Hail Queen of Heaven' at the organist's
first hint; incense like a whiff of paradise.

Then trailing the May procession on its petal-strewn route
through the seminary grounds, apple trees in blossom,
high schoolboy voices breaking into hymns.

Women wearing veils and Child of Mary gowns.
The canopied archbishop attended by seminarians.
Sodality banners. Bunting. Papal flags. Divine pageantry.

       *

No, maybe I won't opt for a liquorice whip
or a powdery flying saucer after all; I swap
my 6d coin, sporting a silver greyhound,
for a cream pie (enough pennies yet to buy
ten candy cigarettes at lunch-hour).

The upper crust of chocolate is flecked
with little coloured dots that give my tongue
a sandpapery feel, exactly like our cat's,
the goo underneath like chewy ice-cream
wedged into the sugary inlet of a cone.

Though I'm tempted to start from the flat
wafery bottom, squared out like graph paper,
I work down conscientiously from the top,
gapped teeth meeting no resistance.
I drag the pleasure out all the way to school.

       *

Saturday morning, our father ferries us to town.
A pound of this, a scoop of that, from fragrant sacks
of seeds, pellets, phosphates, feeds in Sutton's yard.
A pair of brass hinges at Molloy's hardware.

The library's squeaky-clean linoleum for Enid Blyton's
Secret Seven, a doctor-and-nurse story for our mother,
our father wavering between two gory wars.

Salmon-coloured stamps licked into savings books.
The sweet, addictive smell of pulped sugar beet
wafting our way on a raft of factory steam.
Bills to pay for clothes we'd tried on appro.
Then back to the car, pulling faces at passers-by,
while our father eyes a rival's cabbage plants,
doused and counted into hundreds at the market.

A busker plays a tarnished trumpet. Hawkers gesture.
Capped men off country buses check used suits for thickness.
Half-heads, teaty bellies, hard-salt flanks, smoked streaky
grace Molony's bacon window. My brothers and I caffle,
tire, then face out racing clouds until the world begins
to spin – like when our father swings us to dizziness,
sets us down on the kitchen's unstable ground.

NOCTURNE

Time for sleep. Time for a nightcap of grave music,
a dark nocturne, a late quartet, a parting song,
bequeathed by the great dead in perpetuity.

I catch a glance sometimes of my own dead at the window,
those whose traits I share: thin as moths, as matchsticks,
they stare into the haven of the warm room, eyes ablaze.

It is Sunday a lifetime ago. A woman in a now-demolished house
sings *Michael, Row the Boat Ashore* as she sets down the bucket
with its smooth folds of drinking water . . .

The steadfast harvest moon out there, entangled in the willow's
stringy hair, directs me home like T'ao Ch'ien: *A caged bird
pines for its first forest, a salmon thirsts for its stream.*

BREVIARY

Departures

He has made up his mind.
He is on his way,
in mud-stained trench-coat,
five-day stubble.

To judge by his bag,
he is determined to stay.
His knock on your door
will mean trouble.

Real trouble.

*

Web Site

Silk stretched out
like a retractable tape,
taking the measure
of the leafy site.
Planet's guyropes.
Latitude. Longitude.
The world dangling
by a thread.

*

Jack

The longer he is dead
the less our memories are eclipsed
by that bald-moon look his friends
could not identify him with.

His hair begins to grow,
his beard will need a trim.
We are nearly back
on speaking terms with him.

*

Edward Hopper

Everything in Silbers Pharmacy has become redundant:
gravid flasks of watercolour fluid cracked,
doors softened into rot, dispensing drawers
and hardwood counters sold to dealers as a job lot.

Patent cures were superseded like that archaic lettering
on the fascia, mutant diseases succeeding one another
as a new century outmanoeuvres an old. The image alone
stays immune, conserved in varnish like formaldehyde.

From
Exemplary Damages
(2002)

OUT OF CONTROL

Worry on, mothers: you have
good reason to lose sleep,
to let imaginations run riot
as you lie in bed, not counting sheep
but seeing sons and daughters
like lambs led to slaughter
in the road kill of Friday nights.

Remain on standby, mothers –
you never know your luck –
for the knock that would break
the silence like the shock
of a metallic impact against brick.
Keep imagining a police beacon,
a blue moon shattering the darkness.

Lie warily, mothers, where,
eighteen years before, conception
took place in the black of night,
a secret plot; wait restlessly,
as if for a doctor's test,
to find out whether
you are still with child.

HEART TO HEART

Heart, how well we've come
to know one another,
though we've never met.

We are like blood brothers,
pen friends communicating
through bright ink.

'We must arrange a rendezvous',
we say; but the red–letter day
is continually postponed.

Heart, we grew up together –
until, by now, your
walls are plush with fat,

a mud–spattered car after
a long journey – but have
yet to meet in the flesh.

What, I wonder, do you look like?
Those turnip–shaped
ox hearts in butcher shops,

aesthetically aligned
on metal plates, cuddling up
like litters of new pups?

Heart, you stood by me
always, adjusting your beat
as the occasion required,

slowing to a funeral march
or hastening to match the pace
of love's provocations.

We were inseparable when
you took your first sip of blood.
You shared my rapture when,

one magic morning,
plovers rose from fields
like doves from a conjurer's hat.

Heart – pump, sump, soak-pit,
purification station –
keep up the pressure:

fight to the last white
corpuscle, squeeze
the last drop from my life.

BLOOD RELATIONS

I

Who descended from whom.
Who has whose eyes.
Whose nose.
Whose bone marrow matches whose.
Whose blood group.
Viscous as crude oil.
Sticky situations.
Four times thicker than water.
Brought to boiling point
at the least slip of the tongue.

II

Blood is what earns you
a sponsor's place
at the baptismal font
cradling your newest niece;

or, sporting a paper crown,
the right to dish out breast of turkey
at the Christmas get-together,
test the firmness of pink ham;

the privilege to share
in triumph or disgrace,
put up bail, act as guarantor,
face the midnight call.

III

Cells dunked in plasma,
fruit in syrup.
Clots, blockages, oxygen loss.

Such scope for bad blood.
The potency to pump 8,000 litres in a day.
100,000 beats worth.

More than your hardening
arteries may find
the capacity to forgive.

HIGH SPIRITS

Knowing time is not on their side, the old make no bones
about enjoying a night life, catching up, scraping the best
from the years that are left; sneaking out while households sleep –
2 a.m. or 3 – under a moon draped with loose-fitting clouds
like a pale grandmother dwarfed by her dressing gown.

There is safety in numbers for the old; but the young,
returning home in disco fashions or long satin debs gowns
are repulsed, disgusted by the withered skin-flaps
shamelessly exposed through low-cut nightdresses,
pyjama stripes clashing with tartan bedroom slippers.

A man stops suddenly, starts, laughs hysterically, whispers
confidentially in a wispy voice; a shrieking woman beats
on the laundrette window, demanding a pennyworth of sweets.
Another seeks directions to the teacher's house from no one:
she must hand in homework before her birthday party begins.

The high spirits of the old provoke pandemonium.
Boosting the decibel levels, their sons and daughters
cause a traffic snarl-up by cruising the dawn streets
for straying parents whom they will find blissfully happy
though suspicious of the strangers offering them a lift:

a parent who has no reason to miss his spouse, since she
is not dead – just temporarily mislaid like house keys;
a parent without a worry in the world, unless you count
an anxiety to check that her shoes are still snug in the fridge,
her infant son with chicken pox still sleeping soundly in the box room.

CLINICAL ELATION

I

In the out-patients' cubicle,
    you shed the paper gown
and dive, head-first, for cover –
shirt and sweater – relieved
your sentence is deferred.
Reprieved, you melt back
        into the city crowd, the rush-hour
        cortege of cars unmoved for miles.

How fresh this stale world seems:
        like the aniseed smell of wildflowers;
sweet globes of pineapple-weed squeezed
between fingers on a riverbank
from which supple trout are spotted
fluttering in pools, then glossing
        over moss and stone, a pianist's
        hands angling for glissando notes.

II

You are in your stride now,
        in denial, walking away from trouble,
elated as a child catching a first dramatic
glance of the flickering wide-screen sea
behind guest houses with No Vacancies,
rest homes for retirees, souvenir shops
        gritted with sand – spades and windmills,
        tubes and water-wings displayed outside.

Then the huge expanse of unimpeded
        ocean leached through hazy light;
one right turn more grants barefoot access.
The family car brakes – like a beached

wave – to a halt: the scene compressed
into perspective from a dune top
      but stopping at nothing, hinting
     at the infinity you race towards.

SATURDAY NIGHT FEVER

Playing tonight at the X-Ray-Ted Club,
The Chemotherapies, drugged to the gills,
the lead singer's pate modishly bald.

And who will your partner be?
Alzheimer, the absent-minded type,
with the retro gear, everything a perfect mismatch?

Huntington, grooving his hippy-hippy-shake routine?
Thrombosis, the silly clot, trying to pull a stroke?
Angina, who can be such a pain, and yet is all heart?

Raynaud, decked in ice-blue, coolest kid around?
Dear sweet Emphysema, so exercised she hardly
has a chance to catch her second wind?

Cancer, the rogue, ever-gregarious, spreading himself
around, groping his way niftily to a breast?
Parkinson who is already restless for the next number?

They sweat it out all night under the lightning strikes
of strobe lights flashing like an ambulance – such fun
that nobody, as they groan with pleasure, dreams of sleep.

YEARS AFTER

And yet we managed fine.

We missed your baking for a time.
And yet were we not better off
without cream-hearted sponge cakes,
flaky, rhubarb-oozing pies?

Linoleum-tiled rooms could no longer
presume on your thoroughgoing scrub;
and yet we made up for our neglect,
laid hardwood timber floors.

Windows shimmered less often.
And yet we got around to
elbow-greasing them eventually.
Your daily sheet-and-blanket

rituals of bedmaking were more
than we could hope to emulate.
And yet the duvets we bought
brought us gradually to sleep.

Declan and Eithne (eleven
and nine respectively at the time)
had to survive without your packed
banana sandwiches, wooden spoon

deterrent, hugs, multivitamins.
And yet they both grew strong:
you have unmet grandchildren,
in-laws you never knew.

Yes, we managed fine, made
breakfasts and made love,

took on jobs and mortgages,
set ourselves up for life.

And yet. And yet. And yet.

CAVE DWELLER

The baby, at the end of its
umbilical tether, awaits delivery
bubble-wrapped in an amniotic sac.

The doctor is alert
to every knock the foetal heartbeat makes
at the womb's front door.

The father has bought
a cellophane-sheathed
baby seat for the family car.

The mother is ready
to stifle cries of distress
at the wellhead of her breast.

Wool blankets to hand,
they are all on standby
like a search and rescue party

keeping vigil near a cave.

EXEMPLARY DAMAGES

Our one true God has died, vanished under
a rainbow's arch, banished like a devil
scalded by holy water; but our lives remain
eternally precious in the eyes of man.

We love one another so much the slightest
hurt cries out for compensation: sprain your
ankle in a pothole and City Hall will pay
exemplary damages for your pains.

We are equal under law as we once were
in His sight – just as He kept tabs
on the hairs of our heads, the sparrows
surfing the air, we are all accounted for,

enshrined in police department databases,
our good names maintained by the recording
angels of mailshot sales campaigns,
rewarded with chainstore loyalty points.

      *

How will there ever be goods enough, white goods,
dry goods, grave goods, munitions, comestibles,
to do justice to all the peoples of the world?

Enough parma ham, however thinly curled,
to serve with cottage cheese and chives
in the cavernous canteens of high-rise buildings?

Enough rubs and creams, suppositories and smears,
mesh tops and halter necks, opaques and sheers?
How will there ever be enough flax steeped for smart

linen suits, enough sheep shorn for lambswool coats,
enough goats for cashmere stoles to wear on opening nights,
enough cotton yarn to spin into couture tops, flak jackets?

And can we go on satisfying orders for baseball caps, chicken nuggets,
body toning pads, camomile salve for chapped lips? And what quantity
of dolphin-friendly skipjack tuna meets a sushi bar's demands?

And how much serviced land remains for leisure-centre building,
how much hardwood forest has been cleared for grazing, how many
quarries can still serve as landfill sites for agribusiness waste?

And will there be sufficient creatures left to brighten up
our morning drives with road kill? Will the fox's brush-fire
be extinguished, the hedgehog's yard-brush swept aside?

What hope of raw ingredients for peroxide bleach, wheelie bins,
beach thongs, gluten-free bread, protective welding masks,
trucks transporting cars like reptiles ferrying their young?

*

Let's call it a day, abandon
the entire perverted experiment,
refuse to collude any longer with
the crude manipulations of sex,
the need for extra housing stock,
the record pressure on hospital beds.

Scrap the misbegotten concept
altogether, let the noxious rivers
wind their serpentine way towards
the caesium-fished, oil-slicked sea,
the stores of pesticides evaporate
through the widening ozone hole.

Burn the lot, the speculative rot propagated
about extra-terrestrial intelligence,
the self-help books to combat fear and stress,
the rules for ethical genetic engineering,
the blunt facts about cloning, the Bible tracts,
the glib self-deceptive upbeat texts.

Take it away, the latest theory on
bowel cancer and stem cell research.
Tear from limb to limb the handbook
on palliative care with its matter-of-fact
chapters on genitourinary disorders,
charts for accurate measurement of pain.

Let's not bestir ourselves to purge
the unholy mess, our daily urge to dispose
of rosy tampons, soiled baby Pampers,
home-delivery pizza styrofoam,
the hardening mustard crust of sewage,
thirst-quenching diet Pepsi cans.

It was all destined to end badly, near
the reactor core; or at the city dump
where fridges pour out their gaseous souls
and black plastic sacks spill synthetic
viscera for pillaging shanty dwellers
to scavenge, reap what we have sown.

MISSING GOD

His grace is no longer called for
before meals: farmed fish multiply
without His intercession.
Bread production rises through
disease-resistant grains devised
scientifically to mitigate His faults.

Yet, though we rebelled against Him
like adolescents, uplifted to see
an oppressive father banished –
a bearded hermit – to the desert,
we confess to missing Him at times.

Miss Him during the civil wedding
when, at the blossomy altar
of the registrar's desk, we wait in vain
to be fed a line containing words
like 'everlasting' and 'divine'.

Miss Him when the TV scientist
explains the cosmos through equations,
leaving our planet to revolve on its axis
aimlessly, a wheel skidding in snow.

Miss Him when the radio catches a snatch
of plainchant from some echoey priory;
when the gospel choir raises its collective voice
to ask *Shall We Gather at the River?*
or the forces of the oratorio converge
on *I Know That My Redeemer Liveth*
and our contracted hearts lose a beat.

Miss Him when a choked voice at
the crematorium recites the poem
about fearing no more the heat of the sun.

Miss Him when we stand in judgement
on a lank Crucifixion in an art museum,
its stripe-like ribs testifying to rank.

Miss Him when the gamma-rays
recorded on the satellite graph
seem arranged into a celestial score,
the music of the spheres,
the *Ave Verum Corpus* of the observatory lab.

Miss Him when we stumble on the breast lump
for the first time and an involuntary prayer
escapes our lips; when a shadow crosses
our bodies on an x-ray screen; when we receive
a transfusion of foaming blood
sacrificed anonymously to save life.

Miss Him when we exclaim His name
spontaneously in awe or anger
as a woman in a birth ward
cries out to her long-dead mother.

Miss Him when the linen-covered
dining table holds warm bread rolls,
shiny glasses of red wine.

Miss Him when a dove swoops
from the orange grove in a tourist village
just as the monastery bell begins to take its toll.

Miss Him when our journey leads us
under leaves of Gothic tracery, an arch
of overlapping branches that meet
like hands in Michelangelo's *Creation*.

Miss Him when, trudging past a church,
we catch a residual blast of incense,

a perfume on par with the fresh-baked loaf
which Miłosz compared to happiness.

Miss Him when our newly-fitted kitchen
comes in Shaker-style and we order
a matching set of Mother Ann Lee chairs.

Miss Him when we listen to the prophecy
of astronomers that the visible galaxies
will recede as the universe expands.

Miss Him when the sunset makes
its presence felt in the stained glass
window of the fake antique lounge bar.

Miss Him the way an uncoupled glider
riding the evening thermals misses its tug.

Miss Him, as the lovers shrugging
shoulders outside the cheap hotel
ponder what their next move should be.

Even feel nostalgic, odd days,
for His Second Coming,
like standing in the brick
dome of a dovecote
after the birds have flown.

CALLING THE KETTLE

No matter what news breaks,
it's impossible to think straight
until the kettle has been boiled.

The kettle with its metal back
strong enough to take the strain,
shoulders broad enough to cry on;

plump as the old grandmother
in her woollen layers of skirts
who is beyond surprise or shock,

who knows the value of allowing
tears to flow, of letting off steam,
of wetting the tea and, her hand

patting your cheek, insisting – as she
prevails on you to sit and drink – that
things could have been much worse.

HEAT WAVE

Heat brought the day to its senses.
We are not used to such direct
expressions of feeling here
with our wishy-washy weather,
our dry intervals and showers,

our clearance spreading from the west;
rain and shine – ham actors –
mixing up their lines.
But there it was, the real thing,
an unstinting summer day,

not rationing its latitude for heat,
not squeezing out its precious metal
meanly between cracks in cloud.
Sunflower dishes tracked a solar path
across the radar screen of sky.

Apples swelled but still fell
short of breaking point.
The taut skin of black currants
would spurt open at a touch.
Ripening grain was hoarded

in the aprons of corn stalks.
A bee paused as if to dab its brow
before lapping up more gold reserves.
Tar splashed the ankles of cars
as they negotiated honey-sticky routes.

Foxglove, ox-eyed daisy, vetch
jostled for attention on the verges.
Spiders hung flies out to dry.
A coiled snake – puff adder
or reticulated python – would

have thrived in that environment,
mangoes supplanting gooseberries.
Were the river not reduced
to the faintest trickle of juice
it might have furnished

cover for a Nile crocodile
with sloped back patterned
like heat-soaked patio bricks.
A sudden low-lying cat dashed
between houses like a cheetah.

Had that sun made itself heard
it would have sounded like the inner
ferment of a cask of vintage wine,
the static on a trunk-call line
when someone phones out of the blue . . .

Birds retreated into silence, perched
deep inside leaf-camouflaged trees,
having nothing meaningful to add,
no dry-throated chalk-screeching
jungle note that would fit the bill.

A day that will spell summer always
for the child, too young to speak,
who romped outside among flower beds,
his mother's voice pressed thin and flat
as she summoned him languidly back

to the cool, flagstoned kitchen,
ice-cream blotches daubed
like sun block on his pudgy face.

A BOWL OF CHERRIES

for Pat Morrison

I

While, granted, life may not be
a bowl of cherries on the whole,
Osias Beert gave literal expression
to the more upbeat view in his
sixteen hundred and something
painting, *Still Life with Cherries*.
Its glow – a wood–burning stove –
caught my eye in Stockholm
one harbour-stiffening winter.
Long–spired churches sniffed
the icy air; berries were served
on branches like arctic cherries.
Silhouetted pine trees shivered;
their saw–toothed outlines
chattered in raw snow.

II

Although the season of cherries
is brief, the painter set aside
his griefs to let joy have its way,
each puff-cheeked fruit in its first
flush of youth, a trumpet-blowing
cherub; the roe of some exotic
species plucked from juice, not brine;
the rods and cones of the sun's eye.
The painter's plate is full now
and he is satisfied with his lot
even if the rot will set in soon
and the freshness is pure deception
lasting no longer than cherry blossoms

tossed on snow when north winds
enjoy their final fling.

III

There are times, his painting
seems to say – and this is one
of them – when, despite all
evidence to the contrary, life is
(and no denying it) a bowl of cherries.
Just look at this picture: so rich a crop
that some have dropped off the edge
like coins spilt from a collection plate.
And, though Osias may be far off
the mark where truth (whatever
about beauty) is concerned,
the cherries – bite-size apples –
tempt with their own improbable
knowledge and the cold viewer's
eyes helplessly assent.

TULIPOMANIA

And who on earth would blame them,
those Dutch merchants prepared
to give up everything they owned
for the pearl of great price
that is a tulip bulb?

What house wallowing in canal mud,
like a rigged-out ship marooned
in harbour, could hold its own,

however secure its moorings,
against the ground-breaking tulip egg
that incubates in spring, sprouting shoots
of incandescent plumage: tangerine feathers
rippled with pink, streaked with aquamarine?
And who, with his priorities in place,
would hesitate to exchange
his very home for the tulip that leaves
no blood-red trail of perfume
but proceeds to make its bed
in the tactile gloss of satin sheets?

What crinoline gown, what silk
chemise, slithering to the boards
of a lead-windowed bedroom,
could compare with this stranger
bearing arcane knowledge from
a stream-splashed crag in Tien Shan
or the snow-melts of Tashkent?

Who wouldn't want to fade out
in a blaze of glory? Who wouldn't
sacrifice himself on an altar
of urn-shaped tulips, a pyre
of flaming crimsons, smoky maroons?

Who wouldn't be the better
for the lesson of those petals,
dropping off like share values,
precious metal rates,
leaving time to meditate on fortune,
speculate on loss?

LOVE LIFE

You really have to hand it to them.
They let nothing stand between them
and love's work; even in the face
of inequality and AIDS, admit
no impediment that would detract
from glossy theories of attraction
(*Put your seduction skills to the test*
with this month's questionnaire . . .),
'love' and 'forever' sharing the one
sentence like a king-size bed.

You really have to marvel at men
chivalrous enough to let themselves
be mesmerised by model bodies
conjured up on websites,
at women brushing up techniques
to keep their men on side,
despite courtroom reports
of barring orders, statistics
for divorce, incompatibility
on housework rotas, sport.

You have to recognise
the nobility in this busy,
cost–effective era of devoting
tranches of scarce time resources
to nail-painting, e–mail vigils,
rose bouquets, singles dinners,
basement bars, lace uplift bras,
discounting the mounting evidence
of chins, thinning crowns, downward
projections for the future.

You have to concede the idealism
it takes to get dressed up
to impress, then divest each other
of glad rags, down to the last
sad tufts of private hair; in an age
of hygiene hyper-awareness
to allow tongues explore where they will
as the muscular grip of the heart
tightens with excitement, a breaking
bag of waters ready to let rip.

Miraculous how the old ways survive:
gazing into another's eyes like precious
stones – spurning scientific findings
about hormones, seminal vesicles,
gametogenesis, selfish genes.
Voices dim, discreet as recessed
lights, over a bistro meal;
aired confidences, bared souls;
fingertips meet on the wine-stained
gingham cloth, feet entwine.

And so a new generation comes round
to the problem pages of teen magazines,
mastering the body-language needed
for hanging out at shopping mall
McDonald's or music megastore,
navels pierced, tiny skirts and shiny
cropped tops sneaked to weekend clubs,
unknown to parents offered curt
assurances about who'll be where
tonight, who with, till when . . .

And so your grandparents' names
are back in fashion, your twinkly
grandparents by whom the word 'sex'
was never expressed in your hearing,

whom you could never remotely imagine
making what we now call love.
'Still going on', as the great,
supposedly fouled-up Philip Larkin
(in an entirely different context)
wrote, 'all of it, still going on!'

THE LADS

Technicians, overseers, assistant
depot managers, stock controllers.
Old fashioned nine-to-five men
who rose moderately up the line.
You can pick them out in tea break
identity parades at the Quick Snack
café, bellies extending under
diamond-patterned sweaters.

They tuck into a fry – it's pay day,
after all, a day of their lives,
and their wives, a bit too fond
of calorie counting, restrict
fry-ups now to Christmas,
the odd holiday B & B.

The lads still flirt, as readily
as the next man, with the waitress
and break into synchronised grins
at her snappy repartee.
But it's mainly sport the talk
embraces these times, though
their playing days are over,

apart from the veterans' league,
a pre-pub Sunday game
of pitch-and-putt.

That there are worse fates
they know well enough;
and who'd want to be
among those bosses
monotonously talking shop?
Not for all the BMWs
in the world would they swap.

One of the lads takes to the idea
of early retirement with a convert's zeal.
Not that he feels old or anything –
never felt better, in fact, give or take
the back complaint, his smoker's hack . . .
It's just that the kids have gone
their own strong-willed ways
and the wife works part-time
in the plastics factory crèche.

Before the lads pocket
their hands, stand up to go,
they check their lotto numbers,
bantering about the jet they'll charter
to Thailand when their syndicate wins.

Nibble on a bacon rind
discarded on the mopped-up plate.
Life tastes great some days.

THE CLERICALS

How slowly, in those pre-flexi days, the cautious hands
of standard-issue civil service clocks moved, leaving you
impatient to change into flowered polyester frocks,
cheesecloth skirts, bellbottoms, platform shoes,
finding the sequinned night still young at 2 a.m.,
held in its velvet embrace under the gaze
of a ballroom's crystal moon, a disco's excitable lights.

Marys, Madges, Kathleens, it seems an age
since you guarded public hatches or sat in cream
and mildew-green gloss-painted offices, updating
records, typing carbon-copy letters on demand
for bosses, serving them leaf tea, checking the tot-ups
for payment warrants on slim adding-machine rolls,
date-stamping in-tray correspondence, numbering files.

The years have not been at all kind to you.
Your lives have not withstood the test of time:
not a spare cardigan draped on a chair-back,
not a card-index, not a hard-copy file remains
from the glory days of 1970-whatever when
your generation held the monopoly on being young:
twenty-firsts, all-night parties in a friend's friend's flat . . .

Your youth was snatched from your manicured grasp,
lasting no longer than the push-button hall lights in red-brick
houses where you returned by taxi in a pay-day's early hours,
barely allowed time to step inside and locate your bedsit key
before the darkness resumed: you unlocked the warped
plywood door in the eerie silence of a sleeping corridor,
set the fluorescent alarm clock on the prowl for morning,

undressed, flopped on the foam mattress, dreamt.

FULL FLIGHT

Vapour trails:
worm casts left
by burrowing planes;

a wake of surf
on the shipping lanes
of an inverted sea;

pink streaks squirted
at dawn from an aerosol can;
straight lines drawn

by an unsteady hand;
wing tracks rutting
flight paths.

*

All eyes on the check-in screens, families
locate their airline's zone, before passing
through the x-ray vetting and the plexiglas walkway
to lounge around Departures, dressed in loud
anticipation of another climate, the blow-dry hot-air
blast that will greet them on arrival like a tour guide.

Boarding, in row-order, is called for raucously
at last; carry-on bags are manoeuvred into
narrow bins or stored discreetly under seats,
duty-free vodka bottles jangling like foreign coins.
Belts snap shut, cameras are flashed, blockbusters
deposited on laps, children plied with puzzle books.

The airline magazine is yanked from its
elasticated pocket; newspaper readers settle
on sports; business-class curtains close ranks;

a mix-up in a seat allotment is resolved.
Film themes and jazzed-up classics serve
as ambient music, the plane swerving into action.

Mist lifts from runway grass; a wedge
of leftover moon nestles on a shelf of cloud.
Engines gather the reckless speed
needed to raise wings to a higher plane,
to take off from the long flight path
of the tarmac, a dead-end country lane.

Below the dimmed cabin, a miniature
world – every detail faithfully reproduced –
can now be spied: rivers slop out into the tide;
lakes are potholes gouged in buckled mountains.
Then the land draws a borderline in sand.
Out on a limb, dangling over water,

nothing is seen except waves shuffling
their packs, the metallic dazzle of sea
like the video screens – as yet blank –
on which in-flight movies will be viewed.
The cabin crew, patrolling their beat, smile.
Passengers relax, take the weight off their feet.

                    *

Arms outstretched,
sunbather on an inflated bed,

the overhead jet
is just that interval

from take-off at which
the stewardess announces

We shall shortly be commencing
our in-flight cabin service.

It might equally be
a speeded-up version

of Bede's fable:
a mechanical sparrow

hightailing it above
that transient banquet hall.

       *

From there, the world is recreated as collage:
waves like a cancelled air mail letter
the artist includes for its ethereal blues.

Then inland over glued-on fields:
wheat a yellowing newspaper page,
furrows the strings of a Picasso guitar.

       *

Casting cloud aside
      like passive smoke,
the descending plane
      dips to an elevation
where the Atlantic's
      chop-and-change
is witnessed from
      the safe distance
of a window seat's
      reviewing stand,
a gold coast of sand
      outlined by yellow
highlighter pen:
      stepped waves,
boats towing
      trails of foam.

Then tufted fields
        crop up; wheels
put out feelers,
        anxious to
touch down
        on solid ground.

                    *

Having retrieved their sliding cases from the carousel,
they leave the steel-clad baggage hall, declaring nothing,
follow trolleys to where tanned holiday rep,
regional HQ driver or exiled daughter waits;

then proceed beyond car rental stands,
tourist reservation booths, bureaux de change,
out into the shock of open air, the stink
of kerosene, the racket of taxis echoing

through the underpass, of courtesy coaches,
terminal shuttles . . . They have arrived.
Ears still popping, they make small talk,
unzip a purse or money-belt for local bills.

Now they are part of the ring-road traffic
they had pitied from the air, barely moving,
cogs in concrete wheels, passing vast hangars,
double-glazed houses devalued by flight-path noise.

Sheraton registers its name repeatedly in neon:
inside, uniformed crews are allocated rooms;
a bleary wayfarer, all the day's connections missed,
checks in for sleep. Travellers go on being routed,

defying laws of gravity, the risks of law-defying
hijackers, of pilot error, radar failure, lightning storms,
metal fatigue, having texted their ETA
to grounded office colleague, lover, spouse.

VARIATIONS ON YELLOW

[Yellow Device, by Patrick Scott, Ulster Museum]

Sun brushes the mountain
before landing on a field
      so lush with buttercups
      they might yield
a painter's yellow pigment
or be cultivated as a cash crop.

    *

What does it say of nature's taste
that its décor of choice for waste ground
is invariably the common or garden dandelion,
its over-egged yellow such a flashy colour
to splash out on, compared, say, to the subtle
primrose with its beeswax glow of light?

    *

      The swelling yellow sun of early May lures you
westwards again: a country bolt-hole, weekend hideout,
lakeside shack, some perch you can escape to,
      draw back creaking shutters, air out dusty rooms.

    *

The relief when a cloud,
      eclipsing the sun, steps out of the light
and fishermen in yellow oilskins
      glisten like the yolk of a guillemot's egg.
A kittiwake takes the plunge, snatches
      a slapstick fish clear of the waves.
It's anyone's guess what may happen next.

    *

You want to hang on for as long as this
yellow painting radiates illumination,
the way someone in a lunch-break
music shop hesitates to walk out
on a mezzo in full flow: you'd like
that light to shadow you down
the street, pursue you to your desk.

IN TOWN

The wizened country woman
with smoke-tanned skin
is foraging for provisions
among supermarket shelves.

Her floral headscarf is
as broad as it is long,
her fur-trimmed coat
a hand-me-down,

brown bootees patched,
the bag with her
pension money
darned at the strap.

When she pays
at the checkout
for oat flakes, stock
cubes, baking soda,

a cake jammed
inside pink icing,
she is ready for home,
all set for her cottage

along a back-road
that hedges its bets
between the clapped-out
sandpit and the handball alley.

A crocked Ford car,
abandoned by her son,
waits faithfully on
its pedestal of blocks.

Her sheepdog noses weeds
like an ant-eater
or snaps at a passing tractor
to speed it on its way.

Lean cows graze nearby:
udder bells – wind
chimes – brush against
rushes, wildflowers.

Thistles burst open
like worn sofas,
their downy stuffing
puffs and blows.

She keeps a holy water
font topped up, a gleaming
set of willow pattern,
a leatherette car seat

to put visitors at ease,
enough dry peat to see
her comfortably through
an average winter.

She is on her bike now,
the talon of the carrier
safeguarding her groceries
in an iron grip.

REMAINDERS

The street seller of newspapers
is growing old.

One glance and you can tell
that a lifetime of violence
has taken its toll.

War and murder have been
meat and drink to him.
Think of all the catastrophic news

of which he has been the bearer,
all the sensational headlines
he has put through his hands,

all the scandal he has spread,
all the famous dead of whom
his tabloids have spoken badly.

At day's end, when he checks
how many papers are left,
he counts them pensively,

as if preparing a defence,
as if each were a year for which
he simply cannot account.

THRUSH AND ANTI-THRUSH

Definitely not, in the thrush's case,
a matter of fine feathers making
fine birds; yet its speckles lure the eye.
Jumpy also, a tad insecure,
walking with a sack-race hop,
legs propped at an awkward angle
like a dodgy bracket on a home-built shelf.

The brown wings and crown
are its least attractive features
by a fairly long shot,
bringing to mind musty smells
and past their sell-by-date
mushrooms, festering brain-dead
in the vegetable drawer.

Marks should be deducted too
(purely on lapse-of-taste grounds)
for its liposuction diet of flabby snails;
insects picked like scabs from walls;
rubber-band worms coiled round its snout,
gormandised the way the Dutch toss
pickled herrings down the hatch.

Enough rubbish you'd assume to choke
the drains of any gullet, until you catch
the rapturous return journey of song:
rococo notes that cry out for transcribing
on calf parchment with a calligraphy quill –
the opposite of magpies which, for all
their preening, can't rustle up a note

between them, scraping the barrels
of their rapid-fire throats;
pointedly attired in well-pressed

morning suits, though lacking in finesse,
rattling on about nothing,
jarring like a car struggling
to start, the ignition failing to engage.

But it's the thrush's tune
the light expires to, day slipping
through the gnarly fingers of old trees;
a music inducing the absurd spectacle
of a man (myself, say) looking to a bird,
of all things, in a digital epoch,
for entertainment, maybe even truth.

WHILE STOCKS LAST

As long as a blackbird
still mounts the podium
of the aspen tree, making
an impassioned plea for song.

As long as blue tits, painted
like endangered tribesmen,
survive in their rain-forest
of soaking larch.

As long as the trilling lasts
above the office car park
and hands tingle to inscribe
in the margins of buff files,

'The skywriting of a bird
is more permanent than ink'
or 'The robin's eagle eye
questions these projections.'

ENGLAND

Without nostalgia who could love England?
— ANNE STEVENSON

Somewhere out there, England lingers
under the bushy brow of thatch that juts
above half-timbered houses in Home Counties.
A mill village survives where a raft
of flag irises rises near the grain loft
and the vicarage garden party is tastefully
announced on a hand-painted sign.
A family pile in Queen Anne style,
available at a knock-down price,
catches the needle-sharp eye
of a Lloyd's 'name' in the auction pages
of *The Field* or *Country Life*.
The hand-crafted. The home-made. The family-run.
Pink briar roses sink their claws
– like painted nails – into the gable walls
of listed cottages at Winchelsea and Rye.
Jersey cream dissolves in steaming scones
at the Salvation Army cake sale.
A smell of new-mown hay, of boiling jam,
of hops vented through an oast-house cowl.

England is still out there somewhere,
an owl roosting in a cobwebbed barn.
You can overhear a pub argument about
the best brew of beer, best-ever shepherd's pie.
Alistair Cooke is delivering his four millionth
'Letter from America'; so many record-breaking
West End performances of 'The Mousetrap' or 'Cats';
the ten thousandth revival of 'An Inspector Calls'.
Tin-plate, ration-coupon laughter from the audience
of a radio panel show; Lilliburlero marching
on the BBC World Service, Big Ben chiming
to the second with the tea-time news,

the sig tune for 'Coronation Street' a national anthem.
Johnners greets listeners from Lords
as sunlight is rolled out along striped grass.
The tabloids have murder in their hearts.
That and exclusive photos of the latest
female tennis sensation at wet Wimbledon.
Scoreless draws in the Premier League.
Soft going at Newbury and Kempton Park.
Rain stopping play at a county cricket fixture.

Pastel-painted timber seaside chalets.
Miles of white clifftop caravans like dumped fridges.
A day-trip across ridged Channel waves:
cheap pints of bitter in the car ferry bar,
chips with everything in the cafeteria.
English Breakfast Served All Day in Calais.
Vera Lynn. VE celebrations. Our finest hour.
Poppy wreaths, brittle as old majors'
bones, wilt beneath the stony-faced
gaze of the Great War memorial.
Shakespeare settings by Roger Quilter
and Gerald Finzi in aid of the church tower
restoration fund, the vicar's wife doing
the page-turning needful for the accompanist.
A few tremble-lipped parishioners, feeling
their age, clear throats as the harmonium
is tuned and lend their bronchial best
to 'The Day Thou Gavest, Lord, is Ended'
while watery light through leaded glass
lands, like a housefly, on the brass plate
commemorating the valiant dead of Ladysmith.
Elgar's 'Pomp and Circumstance' arranged
for the Queen's visit by the colliery band.
Ralph Vaughan Williams's 'The Lark Ascending'
in rehearsal at the Free Trade Hall.
Gurney's Severn mists, Housman's blue
remembered hills, Hardy's wind and rain.
A Wilfred Owen troop train falling silent

at an unscheduled stop; or Edward Thomas's
halting express at Adlestrop taking on board
a consignment of pre-war blackbird song.
A brawny chestnut shields the clover-fattened
cattle in a hedgerowed field from searing noon.
Water-colour enthusiasts choose the ideal
viewing point to capture the flamboyant sunset.

The quiet courtesies. The moderation.
The pained smiles. Things left unsaid;
passed over in silence, an unwritten constitution.
Miles of graffitied tower blocks, near treeless
motorways wide as triumphal boulevards.
Race riots in Brixton and the North.
The peal of street-pleasing steel bands at Notting Hill.
Allotment cabbages with gaping caterpillar wounds.
Words like *tavern* and *shires* and *lea*.
Blazered Henley. Top-hatted Ascot.
Black herringbone for the Royal enclosure.
The wine-jacketed coach driver pointing
his blue-rinse passengers to the loos.
A single-room supplement for Christmas
at a refurbished Grand Hotel in some down-at-heel,
sea-eroded, once-genteel Edwardian town.

Romantic England is neither dead nor gone,
nor with Olivier in the grave.
It is out there somewhere still; plain-speaking
Stanley Baldwin's 'corncrake on a dewy morning,
the sound of the scythe against the whetstone . . .
a plough team coming over the brow of a hill'.
Homely John Major's England still holds its own
somewhere: 'long shadows on county grounds,
warm beer, invincible green suburbs, dog lovers'.
Goodly, portly Sir John Betjeman envisions his England:
'oil-lit churches, Women's Institutes, modest
village inns . . . mowing machines on Saturday afternoons'.

It is somewhere at the back of the mind,
like the back of a newsagent's where plug
tobacco is sold; shining like the polished
skin of a Ribston Pippin or Worcester Pearmain.
It preys on imagination, like pleated ladies
sporting on bowling lawns; like jowled men
of substance nursing claret in oak-panelled
smoking rooms of jovial private clubs.
See it all for yourself – the quadrangled choir school,
the parterred garden with the honesty box,
the fox-hunting colonel on his high horse,
the Gothic Revival haunt leading through
a topiary arch to gazebo, yew maze,
pet cemetery – on your jaunts about
cobbled market towns, treks down lanes
rutted with what surely must be haywain wheels.

Listen to England as it thunders from Pennine becks
like a loud speech heckled by a Hyde Park crowd.
Listen to its screaming day traders, its bingo callers,
its Speaker demanding 'Order!' in the lower chamber.
Listen to the big band music to which couples
relax at the Conservative Club dinner dance.
Listen to the wax of silence harden
round the red leatherette upholstery
after closing time at the Crown and Rose;
steel shutters come down hard on the Punjab Balti;
grease congeals on the mobile kebab stall.
Listen to the tick of its Town Hall clocks,
like a Marks and Spencer shirt
drip-drying above a chipped enamel bath.
Listen to the silence in which England finds its voice.
It declaims this sceptered isle, this earth of majesty.
It claims some corner of a foreign field.
It chants while the chaffinch sings on the orchard bough.
It chants history is now and England.
It pleads green and pleasant land.
It pleads for all its many faults.

LAST WORDS

What an absolute creep
Philip Larkin
seems to have been.

Have you read
the letters yet?
The biography?

Did you watch
the tele-prof
cut him down to size?

And, true to form,
he proved a sleazy
bastard to the last:

as he was dying,
he squeezed his
nurse's hand

(she should,
strictly speaking,
have ordered

him to keep
his filthy paws
to himself),

while he croaked
as best the
throat cancer

(which he'd brought
on himself with
smokes and booze)

allowed: I am going
to the inevitable.
So negative always.

So obsessed with death.
1.24 a.m., the time.
Except for the nurse,

he was alone – no
visitors, of course,
at that unearthly hour;

no wife or kids
to line up tearfully
around the single bed.

A selfish swine
without doubt;
and, by all accounts,

no great loss.

WAR POET

There is talk of a ceasefire but the poet will hear none of it. If a lasting peace in that distant, barbaric land is really on the cards, he's damned if it will happen until his poem is complete. Only this morning, he felt another surge of inspiration. Images inundate his mind: a bomber plane budding with engines; a wounded man whose guts jut out like the service shafts of the Pompidou Centre ...

His will be the war poem to end all war poems. A sure-fire competition winner. Now suddenly this premature bullshit about peace: intermediaries, UN envoys, neutral venues, exploratory talks. How can they do this to his poem, before it's had a chance to speak its lines, to influence the outcome of the war? Can the TV bulletins of scorched gables, camps of toothless refugees, famished children – the very scenes that triggered off his poem's wrath – not hold out for a short while more?

But there's hope yet. Negotiations may collapse. Hardline factions may refuse to sign up to the deal. Splinter groups may form. He feels a little steadier. Yes, he'll knock that poem into final shape if it kills him. He will live to see it carved, an eternal flame of words, in the marble columns of a solemn war memorial. The opening stanza – perhaps misquoted slightly – will be publicly trumpeted on commemoration days.

He fumbles for a cigarette, paces his balcony at the sylvan writers' retreat. His morale is on the rise. He knows in his bones the war will – *must* – go on.

NO, THANKS

No, I don't want to drop over for a meal
    on my way home from work.
No, I'd much prefer you didn't feel obliged
    to honour me by crashing overnight.
No, I haven't the slightest curiosity about seeing
    how your attic conversion finally turned out.
No, I'm not the least bit interested to hear
    the low-down on your Florida holiday.
No way am I going to blow a Friday night's freedom
    just to round out numbers at your dinner table.
No, I'm simply not able for the excitement
    of your school-term coffee mornings.
No, strange though it may seem, your dream kitchen
    holds no fascination whatsoever for me.
No, there's nothing I'd like less than to get
    together at your product launch reception.
No, I regret I can't squeeze your brunch into my schedule
    – you'll be notified should an opening occur.
No, I don't appear to have received an invitation
    to your barbecue – it must have gone astray.
No, my cellphone was out of range, my e-mail caught a virus,
    I had run out of notepads, parchment, discs, papyrus.
No, you can take No for an answer, without bothering
    your head to pop the question.
No, even Yes means No in my tongue, under my breath:
    No, absolutely not, not a snowball's chance, not a hope.

NOT YOURSELF

Monday, you take the accordion out of its case in rain,
                          begin to busk.
Tuesday, you complain that the raïto sauce with your hake
                          is far too garlicky.
Wednesday, you temp as a PA in a software solutions firm,
                          filing your cherry-red nails.
Thursday, you will be the youth arranging for his sailboard
                          to be tattooed with a nude.
Friday, you gain consciousness after your last-chance operation
                          to beat prostate cancer.

Monday, you will be a gate-leaning farmer, watching tall wheat
                          ripen like bamboo.
Tuesday, you are on duty at the beauty salon, adding volumising
                          shampoo to crestfallen hair.
Wednesday, you will be fitted with a spinal stimulator, if metabolic
                          complications are resolved.
Thursday, you are a salesman picking your teeth as you leave
                          a small-town hotel.
Friday, with your fellow-envoy, you try your damnedest to revive
                          stalled peace negotiations.

Monday, you joke with other widows about the bloke who calls
                          the bingo numbers.
Tuesday, you are a parcel-lumbered motorcycle courier,
                          jousting with gridlock.
Wednesday, you will block the undertaker's lane, unloading
                          a consignment of veneer.
Thursday, you stack up cushions for a clearer view from the seat
                          of your adapted car.
Friday, you will attack defence computer systems worldwide
                          with your virus.

Monday, you bring the best case you can to the attention of
                                    the sentencing review board.
Tuesday, you lock yourself inside an orthopaedic corset to save
                                    your back from strain.
Wednesday, your slow fast-lane driving is greeted with the accolade
                                    of a two-finger salute.
Thursday, you know the acute pain of seeing your new purchase
                                    at half the price you paid.
Friday, you administer morphine to a doubly incontinent patient
                                    in a dank public ward.

Monday, you will iron white shirts like a carpenter
                                    planing a plank of deal.
Tuesday, you feel a cold coming on as you banter to your passengers
                                    on the tour coach.
Wednesday, you will broach the subject of a barring order
                                    with your younger kids.
Thursday, you will change into uniform before collaring
                                    your guard dog for patrol.
Friday, you will wake up stark naked, wearing only
                                    your lover's arm.

Monday, you are a leotard-clad ballet dancer rehearsing
                                    for Coppélia at the barre.
Tuesday, you are a car mechanic in a pit: dirt infiltrating skin,
                                    grit irritating a graze.
Wednesday, you are the mindless old man whose happy release
                                    his family prays for.
Thursday, you will give birth to a child, smuggled like a refugee
                                    under your tarpaulin.
Friday, you will struggle across the fairway, humping your golf bag
                                    like an oxygen tank.

Monday, either as a bank's investment analyst or flipping burgers
                                    in a fast-food chain.
Tuesday, the unsame . . .

AT THE SEMINAR

I

An electronic blip from house-martins as they pass
an open window at the conference centre; frantic birds,
on errands of mercy, transporting relief supplies to tricorn beaks.
We sneak a glance at mobiles for text messages.

Crawling across the hotel lawn, sun puts mist in the shade:
a transparent morning now, our vision unhindered for miles.
A golfing party, armed with a quiver of clubs, aims
for the bull's-eye of the first hole; others, near a pool
blue as our EU flag with its water sparkle of stars, dry off:
shrink-wrapped in towels, they sink back into resort chairs.

II

For serious objective reasons, we are informed, our keynote
speaker is delayed; the Chairman's interpreted words
are relayed simultaneously through headphones:
In order to proceed to a profitable guidance for our work
which will be carried out with a feature of continuity and priority . . .

I see the lake basking in its own reflected glory, self-absorbed,
imagine turquoise dragonflies, wings wide as wedding hats,
fish with scarlet fins, water-walking insects.

I intervene. I associate myself with the previous speaker's views.
Discussions go on in all our languages as I unscrew
still mineral water, bottled at some local beauty spot.
Certain administrations suffered cuts as they weren't entrusted
with new attributions likely to fill in the logistical gap
resulting from the inference of the frontierless economic area . . .

In two hours (less, if – with luck – that stupid clock has stopped)
our final workshops will convene in the break-out rooms.
Then it will be time to draw conclusions at the plenary,
score evaluation forms, return to our respective floors
to dress down for the bus tour of the Old Town.

III

Now the rapporteurs start synopsising
the workshop findings on felt-tip flip-charts.
The Chairman is summing up: *New challenges*
overlook the world scenery in our global stance . . .

Lily pads strut across the lake like stepping stones;
fish risk an upward plunge; martins – plucking
sustenance from thick air – lunge at their mud nests.
Hold the world right there. Don't move a single thing.

GERM WARFARE

As saints kissed lepers' sores, caressed rank beggars' wounds,
    I ought to thank God for the way you
    Spray me with your germs, my fellow travellers.
I should take it like a seraph, or at least like a man,

Ingest your pestilence with relish, meditate indulgently
    On sprinklers dousing a striped lawn,
    Feel proud to hothouse your viruses in my lungs,
Pick up stray bugs like hitchhikers, pets needing a good home.

So by all means go on sneezing in that spunky style of yours:
    The convulsion, the eruption, the paroxysm, the pile-drive,
    The dog yelp, the orgasm, the gale force, the squelch,
The caught short, the sudden brake, the snort, the screech owl.

Let it all hang out, therefore, whatever it happens to be.
    You with the unprotected schnozz, as though a hanky's
    Prophylactic would sin against your principles, your faith,
You who pass your plague around like cough drops,

You can be relied upon to prop yourself beside me
    On the bus, telling your cellphone how much
    You suffer, as you present me with hard evidence,
Certain that a problem shared is a problem halved.

The morning before the long plane journey, the crucial interview,
    The special date, whenever hoarseness begins to tighten
    Round my throat like a noose, thoughts wander back to you,
Eyes water, touched by the largesse with which you showered me,

Smitten to the core by your infectious charms. Bless you!

SO MUCH DEPENDS

The red barn. The Vermont farm
you fled from to the city
or vowed you'd retire to some day.

The barn at your grandparents'
in Kansas where you stowed away
one preteen summer, happy

to be left alone, at sea on the prairie,
hay spilling before cutter blades,
waves breaking on an inland shore.

A battened-down barn, holly-berry red
against the first dusting of snow.
Chevron-patterned wagon doors.

The grocery store forty miles off,
an upstate Amish village planted
among neat-drilled horse-tilled fields.

There will always be room
in the scheme of things for a red barn.
You may depend your life on it.

Inhale cured fodder, grain, manure.
Admit winter cattle to the stalls.
This is your clapboard cathedral:

pillars, nave, aisles, weather vane.
Wheat is separated from
chaff here, sheep from goats.

Come back, Grandma Moses, lead us
from the desert of downtown
to the promised land of the red barn.

TIME PIECES

How long a day lasts.
It starts at dawn,
goes on all night,
right into the small
hours, makes time
for each minute
individually.

                    *

How long days take.
An evening when you wait
for the phone to ring
as if for a watched kettle
to come gasping
to the boil and sing.
A week in which your lover
broods the situation over.
A summer marking time
before exam results.
The breathing space
the lab requires
to prove your GP
right or wrong.

                    *

The grandfather clock keeps
time under lock and key,
counts the seconds like a miser
inside walnut-panelled vaults.

Its chimes disturb light sleepers,
hold them in suspense

until another hour's demise
is hammered home.

*

The word *forever* as used
in a pop song chorus.
The word *vintage* as it occurs
in the second-hand shop-talk
of the clothes store – say, in
this label: *Vintage Slip, 1980s.*

*

When we settled in
        to the new house,
distancing ourselves
        from our sour past,
secure at last in exultation,
        we knew we would
never again be as young
        as we were then;
nor had we been for years.

*

        My contributor's copy
of *The New Younger Irish Poets*
        already liver-spotted with age.

*

And to think
of her once-new
bijou town house –
sleek, chic, state-of-the-art,
latest in everything –
advertised for sale
'in need of modernisation'.

＊

Seems only yesterday
you woke in this same
bedroom and dressed
for the same steady job,
here where you will wake
again for work tomorrow,
your yesterdays adding up
to thirty years of waking
since you were waved off
by hands it now takes
memory to flesh out.

＊

Like the snow in Joyce's story
that falls all over Ireland,
on the living and the dead,
grey hair has lodged
on most heads of my generation
and the first flurries start
to take root in the next.

＊

December 31st: punch line to your diary.
The date when time runs out.
When you may take your case no farther.
When you must sign off, watching your
dead – in passé glasses, retro gaberdines –
lag farther behind, as you place your faith blindly
in a new year's resolution of your plot.

＊

It comes almost as a relief,
the long-anticipated voice
creeping down the line:
the phone call you had
coming for a long time,
for years of nights;
a dark secret, a rodent
gnawing at your sleep.

*

Travel as a backward step.
You journey until you find
a meadow where wildflowers
grow with pre-factory-farming
copiousness, a horse-drawn
landscape where hay is saved
in older ways, to revive
the life you lived once,
catch up with your past.

*

Whatever it was you feared
has not come to pass.
Not tonight at least.
Whatever it is afflicts you
will not last.

Your siege will lift.
You will take the risk
eventually to say,
'Things really were unbearable
way back then.'

*

How briefly a day
lasts, unravelling so fast
you can't keep pace.
You are at the morning
bus stop, wondering
if you definitely
locked the hall door
when, what seems
like seconds later,
sunset struts by
in all its sky-draped
finery, its evening
wear, and you are
unlocking the hall door.

*

Wiping clean the day's dark slate,
sleep sweeps you off your feet,
leaves you dead to the world
in your bedclothes, shrouded in sheets.

Foreseeable Futures
(2004)

SERMONS IN STONES

Mountain peaks
    aspire to wisdom.
Passing like molten
    glass through fire
and water, they thirst
    for knowledge
pure as driven snow.
    What mountains
know is gleaned
    from rifts and faults
and shifting plates,
    a faith moving
across millennia,
    sermons in stones
handed down
    in granite seams.
It is towards mountains
    that we lean
for answers,
    scanning their
weathered folds
    as if each
shimmering outcrop
    hinted at some
bedrock insight,
    gold reserves of truth,
looking to their
    carbon–dated strata
for the longer view.

SOFT FRUIT

The ephemeral life-cycle of a ripe raspberry,
its beady fruit an enlarged mayfly's eye,
everything about it tentative, dissolving
like an ice-cube in your palm, where you
toss one around absent-mindedly, content
to fritter away a sun-sated July day.

Filmy pink, styrofoam light, faintly obscene,
those atoms of fruit split between fingers,
smudge whatever surface they rub against.
Taste one and it makes a stab at bitterness
but proves too gentle for the role, a softie –
lush, slushy, surrendering to the condition of a jam:

a pulp, like treaded grapes, the seedy paste
bubbling in the hectic kitchen when steamy
windows must be sealed to keep out greedy,
sweet-toothed wasps ... Spice up your life
with madras, chased by a raspberry sorbet
or whip up a taste for raspberry crème brûlée.

Surrender. Feel hard-and-fast intentions melting
in the presence of a raspberry chocolate crunch sundae.
Drink to your own health with a brandy-based
raspberry liqueur that has come to fruition, matured
in heat, distilled near jam-jar traps on windowsills.
Hold back unblemished specimens for freezing,

for defrosting when icy winter bites: preserving
summer's patois, looking not the least
like clean-shaven apricot or pouting peach,
but (how appearances deceive!) as if each
were as burred as a cat's raspberry tongue –
the purring cat that scoffed the cream.

BROTHERS AT SEA

We inlanders don't have a sea leg
to stand on when we laze along the prom,
unable to establish much rapport
with the hazy waves, unable to identify
the spiky birds that bob ashore,
then flap nervously elsewhere;
unwilling, in the stiffish breeze
ruffling the strand, to chance our arms
lying back on damp sheets of sand
in a wager that the sun might overwhelm
the heavy odds of cloud; nor will we throw
discretion to the winds – shed an anorak
or doff a cap – merely for the sake
of a cool holiday appearance.

Without surfboard, rod or dinghy
as prop, we lack an adult alibi
to match childhood's spade and bucket.
Should we roll up our trousers,
wade ankle-deep, risk letting water
steep our boneheaded knees?
We enjoy at best a nodding
acquaintance with the sea,
strictly restricted to summer,
limited to day trips, involving
hefty excavations of fresh air,
all-you-can-breathe ozone
densely textured as candy floss
sold in a slot machine arcade.

While there is the clear option
of training the coin-op telescope
on cliffs, our preference is for
rushing a limp vinegar-dripping
bag of chips and battered fish

to the snug car for a steamy meal,
then – irrespective of the weather –
to fall into line with a whipped
ice-cream cone for atmosphere,
letting the fussing, fretting waves
in the foreground create a scene.
We might down a beer in the Mermaid Bar,
pit ourselves against the rifle range
until the small change of our luck runs out.

Though we're ready to make our excuses –
that raw breeze, the forecast rain –
and all set for reversal from the sandy
car park, for easing our journey
home by the picturesque route,
we steal one more quizzical look
at the way those fleet-footed waves
tiptoe across the shore before, losing
balance, they fall flat and withdraw.
Shrieks of five-a-side beachballers
reach our wind-pummelled ears.
A shivering family gets into the swim.
Grasping for some final payback,
we stare as if anticipating revelation.

As if waiting for some explanation to sink in.

NATURAL CAUSES

Summer smells to high heaven
     like this lavender garden
where chilled nectarine soup
     infused with mixed-fruit
syrup and fresh mint
     spiked with more than
a hint of anisette liqueur
     is served on the lawn
while every blade
     of grass is ratified
individually by the sun.

     *

Cézanne can bring himself to paint
only a corner of the summer farmyard.

This is as much as he can take in at once
such is the intensity of what he finds.

Wheat, ripening into Van Gogh yellow,
is lifted above the daily grind.

Monet, abroad at all hours with his easel,
traces the relationship of light and hay.

Stacks are shaped like sun-baked pies
packed for a crusty farm worker's lunch.

     *

The conveyor
belt of spring
and summer
moves so fast
it soon reduces
flowers to rubble
in its impatience
to press onwards
along its petal–
strewn route,
its primrose path.
A smattering of
snowdrops melts.
Daffodils, yellow
chicks, lie bruised
and limp–necked.
Lilac, laburnum,
whitethorn flick past
like fabric samples.
Mangled cherry
blossoms fall as
polka dots on cars.
Nature – no soft touch
for sure – changes
its mind about
which pastel colours
it should favour
and moves
capriciously on:
fresh–faced flowers
barely stalked
within its sights
when they are mown
down in their prime.

*

Then the warm spell runs out of steam.
We must settle for mean temperatures,
a nip of autumn at the tips of branches,

the whole show folding its tent before our eyes,
leaving us cold, putting a damper on our hopes.
Some chill sense lingers that we have crossed

a boundary, are entering a final phase:
the frosty reception of breath at morning
like the plumes on a funeral carriage,

depressions circling the weather map,
storms at sea, ice inching along roads,
the slippery slope towards winter.

SEPTEMBER

Late honeysuckle lushness.
Fields of barley bristle.
Oatmeal thrushes ransack berries.

Along a lane, cooking-apple green,
a mare – tail a sun-bleached
stook of corn – is reined in.

Mist has lifted from the river
which rides side-saddle across the weir.
The year has switched its engine off

to save fuel on the downward run,
revelling in every cloud-break,
in hailstones of grain,

lofty trailers of baled straw,
pyramids of peat storing
mummified winter heat.

Combine harvesters will soon
return to yards, like planes landing
at base after reconnaissance.

Bees devour nectar at a pace
scarcely concealing desperation.
Dipped in a stream, where willows bow,

deferring to their own reflections,
cows are herded from an Aelbert Cuyp
(one of those Dutch paintings that incite

art critics to cream off their richest
prose: *drowsy heat, dewy peace,*
golden calves, pleated water).

Gather blackberries while you may:
let loose their inky juices on blank vellum.
Illuminate your findings like a scribe.

FORESEEABLE FUTURES

I   *The New*

The distinctive
        Irish bungalow,
built by instinct,
        needing no plans,
just the heft
        of direct labour
and the odd day's
        back-up from
a local handyman.
        Look how quickly
        it takes shape,
breeze block showing
        through plaster
like visible panty line.

II   *Mid-Terrace*

With prices spiralling through the roof,
you could I suppose come round
to loving this lacklustre house
and such grounds as it stands on.
It's the best you can afford.

Maybe – if you decided to buy –
the wrought-iron staircase curlicues
would grow on you, the plywood veneer,
the tiled fireplace, the cemented-over garden
where you could almost squeeze the car.

III *Planning Permission*

Right at the corner of the lane
where the wren is feathering its nest

and the scent of hawthorn is a condiment
adding spice to spring, a planning notice

has been planted, staked down like a sapling.
You make the wary approach
of someone scrutinising a suspect
package, a booby-trapped device.

IV *Viewing Recommended*

Strutting about your house,
as though we already own it,
we find the place on best behaviour,
everything done and dusted.

We superimpose our lives
on your lives, paste our heads
on to your bodies, grind coffee
in your kitchen, hack back

your garden privet, make love
furtively in your bedroom
where the *en suite* tiles
leave much to be desired.

V *Testing*

The soil mechanics jeep makes a beeline
for the centre of the former wheat field.
Hard-hatted men are setting up equipment.
Wheat will have yielded to concrete
before the growing year is out.

LORD MAYO

You have come to a bad end, Lord Mayo,
to find yourself lodged in digs next to mine.
Yours is the grave my house looks down on.
Or would if your tomb could protrude
like a well-fed belly through your waist-band
of nettles and ground elder and brambles.

Fancy not having a lackey who can make
the railings stand to respectful attention,
keep you sealed off from mere mortals,
lend the rusted bars a bit of class with a dab
or two of paint, lop off that ridiculous
top hat of ragwort and silk poppies.

It's a strange reversal of the old order
that you should be mucked about
without frieze coat or gaiters, while we –
fast-forwarded a century and a bit later –
are double-glazed, centrally heated,
en suite'd, dry-lined, living it up.

What a state you are lying in,
for a man of your stature, having
shrunk to this rectangle smaller
than a billiard-room, your name the mud
of a poor Irish county, a bogged-down
empire on which the sun never rises.

Or – to be impertinent and frivolous at once –
it connotes the mayonnaise option at the sandwich
counter. And such chop-licking wraps,
such goat's cheese and aubergine melts,
such sushi specials and antipasto misto
are now served in our lunchtime delis.

You'll observe how uppity the peasants
have become: hurtling off-road 4 by 4s
(the new coach and four) from crèche
or ironing service, ordering carry-out
meals – Indian, Thai, Chinese – no less exotic
than florid shrubs uprooted from the colonies.

One thing, I'll say, Lord Mayo, in your favour:
song thrushes love to bits the berries
that sprout from your personal yew tree
(a yew that responds eerily to gales),
unbuttoning them lustily like a scullery maid
undone in some stately basement kitchen.

As for the elderberry bushes, clustered
at your feet like a pleated curtain
on a four-poster bed, how appropriate
in your lordly context is Heaney's image
elevating those ball-bearing berries to 'swart caviar'.
Use your silver coffin-plate for daintiness

when you scoop them up to taste: a dish fit for a king.

SEVEN AGES

Teens are wrapped round one another
like cars locked in the embrace of lampposts
after closing time in clubs and bars.

Twenties, having shacked up in a bedsit,
save for a house deposit and the outlay
for the full works on the Big Day.

Thirties – circumnavigating the neighbourhood –
are on the two-car shuttle between school gates,
face painting, violin lessons, junior sports displays.

Forties hope to prove themselves enlightened
when moping-and-tantrums syndrome strikes
their back-chatting, drumkit-bashing young.

Fifties, at leisure to relieve the child-minding
side of their children's pressures, wheel
squealing granddaughters to sleep in buggies.

Sixties try to ignore signs of decline but still
accept a sorely-needed lift from son or daughter
to the support-group meeting or out-patients' prefab.

Seventies blab on about deteriorating standards,
wish their children hadn't relocated at such distance,
live for Christmas reunions, bide their time.

BOY SINGING SCHUBERT

A late-night silence beds down
at that dreamy hour when house lights
dim to long-life bulbs on landings
and one day leads to another.

The silence of deepest cyberspace
to which unsaved data is consigned.
The flat summer silence of a midlands village –
canal barges tethered like donkeys,

tourists snug in pubs, swans at large
like spume trapped at a lock-gate.
The silence of a log-warmed farmhouse
overcome by fumes of snow.

*

The silence to which our class of raucous boys
was reduced when, pending our teacher's return,
one of our number started unexpectedly to sing.

Forehead pressed as firmly to the desk as an injured temple
to cool metal, he avoided eye-contact with our ridicule,
our scorn, concentrating solely on song:

peak notes ascending the halo-capped summit
of Mary's statue, flowers arranged as a May altar
at her clay feet – ruck-leafed primroses; bluebells

the sky-blue of tricky jigsaw pieces; dewy sprigs
of lilac plucked that morning. *Ave Mar-e-e-a, gratia plena,*
Dominus tecum, benedicta tu in mulieribus.

FREE RANGE

A fistful of gold
      – chickenfeed –
doled out from a sack
      is enough to mobilise
a brazen procession of hens,
      falling into line,
feeding against the grain,
      then breaking ranks again,
drifting absentmindedly away.
      One goes chugging
towards the orchard
      where apple trees stoop
under the weight of fruit
      roosting in branches.
Another – taking wide, determined
      police-like strides –
hits upon an indefinite
      line of enquiry
as it vaguely scrapes
      evidence together,
scratches around for clues,
      peruses every last speck,
keeps its pecker up
      leaving no stone unturned.
And this one bobs
      above the wavery aftergrass,
bottle-top crown
      and foam-rubber wattle
an extravagant opera costume:
      a full-dress rehearsal as
it sounds that languid note
      always so evocative of summer
and leaves it floating
      in the air, dangling
by the skin
      of its hen's teeth.

BOOK SALE

Seizing, as if in panic,
armfuls of reduced-price classics,
        bound in sombre, artful jackets,
he is determined at last to take
        a stand on *Crime and Punishment*,
come to terms with *The Rights of Man*,
        surrender to the power of *Leviathan*,
renew youth like a library book:
        remembered times past when –
cushioned from hardship, lying astride
        an easy-chair or in the wood-panelled
reading room of a summer garden lair,
        an aromatic tea chest marked *Ceylon*,
he plunged headlong into adventure,
        knowing contentment like the back
of his page-turning hand, oblivious
        to the rota of household chores,
the squeegee singing of a thrush,
        the tennis ball's monotonous crush
on a gable wall, the canter
        of an empty meat tin blowing
like perpetual motion near the bin,
        cows ripping out chapters of grass.
He expects more substance from
        his reading now, of course,
and these books he stacks up
        at the cash desk have a weighty feel:
You must change your life is what
        he wants to hear them say,
There is still time to begin.
        They will fill his shelves like resolutions,
tasks he must get round to some day soon:
        that leaking tap, that creaking door,
that bathroom fungus needing close attention.

NON-STOP CHRISTMAS

Christmas is always coming.
It steals sneakily up on you,
snapping at your heels, ready
to pounce like a pantomime wolf.
Or it looms ahead like a road block,
a juggernaut impossible to pass.

Christmas is always near at hand.
You find it lurking in the attic: hidden
with the Santa things you landed
at the right price in a summer sale;
lingering in the brittle fringes of the artificial
tree you store beside the water tank.

Christmas is always on the cards,
for the child addressing the North Pole,
for the emigrant booking tickets
on the no-frills airline website,
for siblings singing from different carol sheets,
raking over old coals at the hearth.

Christmas is always brandished above your head,
a carving knife; or it looks you sharply in the eye
like a tack with a rip of crepe paper attached
that brings garish paper-chains to mind in hazy July.
It tumbles from a cupboard in the shape of hoarded
decorations: folded golden tinsel concertinas.

It is always Christmas in the house
where a useless crewel-work gift can't
be disposed of tactfully, where broken
toys are tripped over, where the non-shed tree
needs to be stripped of glittering baubles
like a court-marshalled soldier's gongs.

Christmas is always showing its ugly face
like the switched-off neon Santa in the pub
left to drive his reindeers up the walls in summer.
A few unmelted flakes of fake snow hang on
for months to a corner of the butcher's window.
Extra tonic stocked in case of visitors goes flat.

The Christmas season is always declared open.
The word slips out with indecent haste in a TV
advertisement and when the hotel's securing deposit
for the office party must be rounded up by August.
Christmas is always striking like a seasonal virus.
There are only ever so many days still left.

EEL

after Eugenio Montale

Eel, wee sleeket
siren of icy seas,
lashing out
against the choppy
tide, slipping
from the iron fist
of Baltic waters,
unable to resist
the lure of distant
estuaries, streams
drenched in
freshwater perfumes,
not hindered
even by drought
when the trail
of current runs out
to a gravelly trickle,
muddy dregs of slime,
and the sunshine,
flooding a net
of chestnut trees,
throws light on
her inward advance:
eel, laser beam,
headstrong as a torch,
lean as a whip,
sharp as a love-
tipped arrow,
brooking no delay,
drilling to the core,
the pith, of rock,
flailing past
stagnant gullies,
sparking hopes

that counteract
the ashen heart
of darkness,
flashing like a
curled-up rainbow,
like the pools
of your green eyes,
and she mirrors
your every move,
proving you to be
– admit it –
her kinswoman,
her truest sister
under the skin.

LOW-FAT

I worry like mad about
        the pork sausages man
I see some mornings
        unloading his refrigerated truck
when I am stuck in a backlog
        of commuter traffic.
He just doesn't seem at all
        cut out for the job,
not strong enough to be
        lugging those backbreaking
cartons – low-fat though
        some are labelled –
of gold-medal sausages,
        laden boxes
of hickory-flavoured rashers,
        too bashful to ignore
the way the shop owner –
        meeting demands for
newspapers and milk –
        hasn't a civil word to spare,
not brash enough to fob off
        the prowling warden
by lobbing an evil eye.
        He'll never hack it,
though he gives it his best,
        mimicking the gait
of a bigger man,
        owlish schoolboy glasses
flashing like gold medals
        above the tottering boxes
as a taxi horn taunts him
        for blocking rights of passage,
a bus driver gestures
        with two uplifting fingers,

a mounted policeman pounces
        from his motorcycle
and the fat is definitely
        in the fire this time.

THE LIGHT OF OTHER DAYS

I freely admit to having always
detested John McCormack's voice:
the quivering tenor pitch,
the goody-good way he articulates
every in–dee–vid–you–al syllable,
prissily enunciating words
like an elocution-class nun.
And – though clearly not his fault –
the hiss on old 78s is oppressive
as if he had a fog (*sic*) lodged in his throat,
as if a coal fire in the parlour where
those songs supposedly belong
were leaking methane
through the gramophone horn.

Or perhaps that surface hiss
is the dust coating mahogany cabinets,
their Sunday-best hush
of wedding-gift china,
tarnished silver trophies,
inscribed retirement salvers,
cut-glass decanters
that have lost their shine;
the locked parlour gone musty
as the cover of Moore's *Melodies*

(shamrocks, harps and wolfhounds
wriggling their way out
from an undergrowth of Celtic squiggles).

McCormack's mawkish rendering
of *I Hear You Calling Me* nauseates
so much the gramophone could be
winding me up, deliberately needling me,
applying surface scratches to my body,
tattooing my skin with indelible images
from the Eucharistic Congress of 1932
when, for the mass congregation,
he sang *Panis Angelicus* in that
ingratiating way of his, sucking up to God.

Why do I bother my head tolerating
this travesty? Why don't I force him
to pipe down, snap out of my misery
like an 'Off' switch, send the record
spinning against the wall at 78 revolutions
per minute, rolling it like his
rebarbative 'r's before I throw?

Am I compelled to let it run its course,
an infection, wait until the stylus
lifts its leg to finish, because, well,
this sickly song calls back to mind
a father whose tolerance for such
maudlin warbling knew no bounds?
Could he, by some remote chance,
be the special guest expected indefinitely
in the stale, unaired parlour
laid with deep-pile carpets of grime?
Does McCormack's loathsome
voice succeed in restoring
that father figure, at least momentarily,
remastering him from dust?

THE HOME TOWN

Our town needed no attention from the fast-talking city, to boost
its self-esteem, shrugged off its lack of name-recognition status,
the absence of an entry in the standard tourist guidebooks.

Flash-flooded paddocks were the nearest we came to creating a splash.
The cathedral took tame inspiration from its Pisan counterpart.
Our hill quarried for silky lime would scarcely warrant a coach tour.

To while away spare time, there were Sales of Work in aid of foreign
missionaries, mixed doubles golf competitions, Lenten plays, clay
    pigeon
shooting tournaments, the New and Capitol cinemas to view permitted
    films.

Had your parents not exercised the hard choice on your behalf,
you might not – all things considered – have settled on it as the first
spot on earth you'd adopt as birthplace; but it more than sufficed.

And a bond deepened between you: you responded to its easygoing wit,
its readiness to lift a hand, took pride in its sizeable stadium, watched
the river flee beneath the bridge like a non-stop mainline train.

        *

Hardly a day passes that the town does not cross your mind,
and though, officially, you've left behind the confines of its square,
acquired what lawyers call new domicile, it still answers to home.

And when you cut through it now, on one of those impatient trains
making hasty tracks for elsewhere, its back is turned disdainfully,
its garden hedges prickly, its householders otherwise preoccupied.

As far as can be seen, your traitorous face – reflected in carriage
glass – doesn't ring the faintest of cathedral bells and only the family
headstone is still willing to claim you unbegrudgingly as its own.

You remember a town where lives seemed doomed to fail: factories
to pack up, able-bodied men to bail out for England and its building
    sites.
Now even a nail-bar thrives, the Chamber of Commerce outlook is
    upbeat.

Any sadness you feel when leaving is on your side alone, crocodile
    tears
as far as the place is concerned; yet you always quicken to its name
emblazoned on a container truck, its accent picked out in the city
    crowd.

VIGIL

Life is too short to sleep through.
Stay up late, wait until the sea of traffic ebbs,
until noise has drained from the world
like blood from the cheeks of the full moon.
Everyone else around you has succumbed:
they lie like tranquillised pets on a vet's table;
they languish on hospital trolleys and friends' couches,
on iron beds in hostels for the homeless,
under feather duvets at tourist B & Bs.
The radio, devoid of listeners to confide in,
turns repetitious. You are your own voice-over.
You are alone in the bone-weary tower
of your bleary-eyed, blinking lighthouse,
watching the spillage of tide on the shingle inlet.
You are the single-minded one who hears
time shaking from the clock's fingertips
like drops, who watches its hands
chop years into diced seconds,

who knows that when the church bell
tolls at 2 or 3 it tolls unmistakably for you.
You are the sole hand on deck when
temperatures plummet and the hull
of an iceberg is jostling for prominence.
Your confidential number is the life-line
where the sedated long-distance voices
of despair hold out muzzily for an answer.
You are the emergency services' driver
ready to dive into action at the first
warning signs of birth or death.
You spot the crack in night's façade
even before the red-eyed businessman
on look-out from his transatlantic seat.
You are the only reliable witness to when
the light is separated from the darkness,
who has learned to see the dark in its true
colours, who has not squandered your life.

BEFORE

A carpet-cushioned
hush as you arrive
at the marble check-in desk,
bringing your watch
up to speed on local time.
Registration forms.
Credit card impress.
The porter – cabin bags,
suitcase in tow – shows you
to your made-up room.
Elevator pings.
Linen trolleys.
Furniture polish spume.

*

Alone in your designated office,
you take in the back-of-buildings view,

trying to make vague sense of the procedures
set out in the manual you've been handed.

This first day grows longer by the minute.
A telephone keeps ringing in your predecessor's name.

*

When the morning presenter enters,
the studio door shuts behind her
with an emphatic thud, leaving her alone
with a flood of requests in that sealed
and leakproof capsule, an astronaut
awaiting the producer's countdown.
Bungalows where house lights come

on stream, as curtains fall on dreams,
will soon grow fully attuned.
Workers with radio–alarms will be roused
by her call to take up their arms and rise,
her voice getting carried away above farms,
bedsitters, office blocks, transmitter masts
like fir trees in which a dawn chorus sings.

*

Ahead of schedule,
the truck driver breaks for freedom
near the city's edge.

From car level, what you glimpse
is a pencil perched behind
an ear; a glint of steel

from a cigarette lighter,
a tabloid like a docket
in a swarthy hand.

*

The apprentice hairdresser
happy in blonde streaks of sun
could wait outdoors all morning
for her agitated boss to open late,
breathlessly confessing to a mislaid key.

*

A show apartment.
Unoccupied space like unpolluted air.
Fresco–fresh bright walls.
White couch, chintz drapes.
State-of-the-art prints.

Spotless ceramic splashbacks.
Unworked marble worktops.
The steely assurance
of the self-cleaning hob.

*

The day approaches.
You begin to fold some clothes
in readiness: the pink towelling
dressing gown, the sensible
nightdresses, still in cellophane.
You try to recall what kind
of bedroom slippers are the norm
and must make sure to jot down
health insurance numbers
and other facts you'll need
when you sit in Admissions
with your holiday holdall
pretending to read old horoscopes
in tatty cast-off magazines.

*

The full-fry pall envelops you
half-way down the fluffy
stairs-carpet to the hall.
In the breakfast room,
another couple, seated next
to sports trophies, wedding photos,
is swapping sibilants.
Crunch of corn flakes, toast.
Clash of cup and saucer.
Splenetic fat is heard
hissing in the pan
as the chatty landlady
appears from the kitchen
clutching hot plates

with a cotton dishcloth,
wishing you good morning,
hoping you both slept well.

*

In staid, straight-backed velvet chairs
around a gleaming convent dining table,
your school debating team has five minutes
to prepare its case against the motion.
Practised scales leak from upstairs.
Corridor giggles are inflamed by a nun's shushes.
You block-letter notes on prompt-cards.
There is no arguing with the clock.

*

Before the paint roller
makes its sweeping statements,
lisping gummily along,
the room is stripped down;
picture marks are like the traces
of discarded clothes.
The modesty of furniture
is safeguarded by sheets.

*

Check the plates are heating.
Flick the speck from a champagne glass.
Pick a loose thread off your sequinned dress.
Straighten your necklace.
Adjust your hair in the mirror one more time.
Steady the candles in their silver holders.
Start, as if taken by surprise,
when the doorbell rings.

*

Lights in the Community Centre
generate excitement.
What's up?
What's on tonight?
A Lions Club AGM?
A ballroom dancing class?
A drama group rehearsal?
A youth disco?
A whist drive?

*

As you climb the arts centre steps,
expectation mounting,
the organiser forewarns you
that the body count
is lower than anticipated.
You make your entrance,
nodding to the few acquaintances
who brave the austere seats.

*

Riffle through your notes.
Repeatedly clear your throat.
Skim a promotion brochure.
Try to look composed
when the bubbly
broadcast assistant arrives
to lead you to the studio.

*

Before proceeding
with my business,
I eat lunch in a small
malt-smelling pub
well off the beaten track

and, though my fate
lies with the main road,
I linger in this backwater,
storing for future use
the view I had
until now relegated
to a background detail,
a windscreen saver.
I will be glancing
over my shoulder
as I speed away.

Reality Check
(2007)

DIVERSIONS

Lean on the green recycle bin
    in the yard where roses run amok,
scent intensified by last night's rain.

Lift your eyes to the sunlit hills: hedge-
    perforated fields are first-day issues
tweezered askew in your childhood album.

Rest on the laurels of your elbows.
    Consent to mind and body going
their ways amicably, a trial separation.

       *

Even the distant glimpse of a dozen
    hormone-puffed cattle can sometimes
be enough to raise your spirits from their rut.

Or an uncouth stream – only slightly
    the worse for farm waste – topped up
from some unfathomable source.

You ache to touch the hem of its current
    as you drive by, reach out like a willow leaf,
contrive a way, in passing, to partake.

CASSANDRA

after Hans Magnus Enzensberger

For years, all we showed
    her for her pains
were two deaf ears,
    as she fumed over
global warming,
    emitting dire predictions
in her smoky voice:
    catastrophic floods etc.,
high-rise high-rent condos
    marinating in brine . . .
Though we'd buried
    our heads for ages
like spent fuel rods,
    her prophecies are
a hot topic suddenly
    on every chat show.
There's not a taxi driver
    who can't repeat
her words like racehorse
    tips, a dead cert.
Her rumours spread
    at hurricane speed.
Her hoarse phrases
    – 'before long', 'too late' –
sink in at last.

        *

Hang on a minute, though.
How many years does
'before long' add up to?

How late is 'too late'?
How up-to-date is she on
current scientific R and D?

We carry on as bravely as we can
in these uncertain times:
4 x 4s at every door.

Low-fare airlines for cheap access
to nest-egg second houses.
All-year strawberries in supermarkets.

Business as Usual signs
displayed on hoardings everywhere,
with so much construction underway.

BREAD AND BUTTER

The rich abundance of the still-life
        painter's palette: glistening
pitchers; pewter kitchenware
        battered like windfallen fruit;
fatted watermelons, grapes
        and apricots; bushy heads
of cauliflower in season.
        And sweetmeats. And bread.
Bread that no more has
        a season than the air;
keeping bakers awake all night,
        worrying over loaves.
A corner is nicked from this roll
        painted with eggshell delicacy;
maybe the artist, unable to desist,
        picked absent-mindedly at
the burnished crust, as when
        a restaurant diner – all eyes
on the menu – fumbles with
        the basket of plaited rolls.

                    *

Where to start? Remembered batch pans wrapped
like exquisite gifts in tissue paper when you were
despatched townward on your bike for a family loaf.
Mushy white sliced in waxed Coady's Bakery packaging.
Home-made brown soda, rough and ready, signed off
with a dividing cross, yet reconciling divergent elements –
salt, buttermilk, baking soda, wholemeal flour – devising
a viable compromise among them all. A harvest loaf with
ornamental bark to carve through and reveal its inner grain;
leaving a trail of crumbs, like sawdust, on the breadboard.
Char-marked nan, flat as blini pancakes, chewy as pizza
base, coriander-enhanced, ghee-brushed, Sri Lanka-shaped.

Unconsecrated hosts, surplus to the church's needs, doled out
by the school nun, savoured as a wafery ambrosian appetiser.
Brie-like wheels of flour-dusted sourdough – moist of crumb
and crisp of crust – cooling on the wire racks of a coffee shop
the time you stopped in pastel-painted clapboard Telluride.
The over-the-top iced raisin-and-walnut loaf your mother
loved to embellish further with a coating of lime marmalade.
Toast the moment of surrender when the fat hits the pan
and you yield to the full breakfast experience – bacon, sausage,
pudding, field mushrooms, potato cakes – mopping up
egg seepage with a dripping dodge of well-fried bread.
Exotic morning offerings, topped with poppy seeds, fortified
with sun-dried tomatoes, you first sampled with bureaucratic
caution at the Euroflat Hotel in the EU *quartier* of Bruxelles.
All the slices of life bread has treated you to . . .

    *

Fast-moving, computer clock-watching, speed-dating,
Ireland in its high-tech phase digests its daily bread as rapidly
as text messages or chews it over at a lunchtime desk
with an urgent request for a ballpark profits forecast.
Office juniors form a bread line for chilli pesto rosso,
baba ghanoush, baby spinach, yellow peppers on ciabatta.
Then the tough decisions: Chai latte? Mocha macchiato?
Best stick strictly to your health regimen: frosty fruits
smoothie, organic caesar salad wrap, plastic tub
of watercolour melon chunks, detox glass of wheatgrass.

    *

Irish taste buds configured in the bread and butter
era, the donkey cart to creamery age that no longer
dares to speak its shabby name, shamefully hunger
sometimes for the old values of the ham sandwich
in a scruffy lunch-hour pub: fat-framed meat in oval
slices, pink folds arrayed on greaseproof paper,
ready, at the half-twelve rush, to be sandwiched with

a wedge of processed cheddar, a slobbery tomato ring
lobbed in for good measure, a tattered lettuce leaf
revived under a cold water tap; white sliced pan
of pre-focaccia, pre-tortilla days, buttered up incautiously
by the wheezing, plum-faced, sleeve-rolled barman;
cracked plate slapped down – take or leave it –
on a sudsy Guinness beermat. The great mainstay.
Plain or toasted. Pressed into service too with thermos
flask of home-brewed tea for a quick roadside elevenses
between house calls: the salty ham boiled or roasted,
mustard boosted, pale or wood-smoked; rarest of all,
the joint reserved for special occasions – Christmas,
christenings – honey-glazed, clove-studded, carved thickly
from the bone, ridged with a kitchen knife's serrations.

*

The butter must be very good in Ireland.
When my American friend spread the word
'butter' on a hot Santa Fe day, her *butta*,
liberated from flat-earth Irish gutturals, roundly
pronounced its curvature, emphasised the 'butt'.
And, as a knob of solid sun was melted down
for heat above deserted New Mexico streets,
a cool grey Irish day flashed nostalgically
to mind: a lunchtime nip out to the bakery
for a crust-flaking demi-baguette,
an oven-warm sultana-implanted scone,
three foil-wrapped butter portions.
I see a Tipperary meadow, cows
flinching from insects, fly-whisk tails
patrolling dung-encrusted hindquarters . . .
Imagination, straying further, reaches
a misty autumn morning, hassocky grass,
spectral shadows, congealed cowpats:
right time and place for moulded cups
of mushrooms to reveal themselves
abruptly, as though parachuted to my feet.

Take some home for breakfast.
Stuff to the gills with chopped herbs.
Smear with garlic butter.
Sear to a tanned hide on the stove lid.
Toast some doughy muffins.
Fan the flames.

*

Could anyone not
live contentedly on bread
    and butter alone?

CROWD SCENE

It's like watching a film...

— WISŁAWA SZYMBORSKA, *'The Terrorist, He's Watching'*

Warm weather has brought out a good crowd.
They are everything I could have hoped for:
forming orderly queues, scooping up globes
of ice-cream, calmly streaming in and out of shops,
checking purses for what spending power is left.

Both sexes, all age groups are represented fairly
among these extras. A pedestrianised street is perfect
for my needs; and how controlled those people are,
all here voluntarily, not one betraying the least
hint of resentment at what is scheduled next.

Hard to grudge some pride that things
are panning out exactly as I'd plotted,
that the capacity gathering is faithful to my plan.
I could embrace them, they are so accommodating,
as if they know they serve a greater cause.

All that will remain, when I have slipped away,
is for the coded statement to be issued through
a trusted channel: screens will flash with breaking news,
shreds of ashen evidence be sifted; the rattled government,
caught offguard, will find holes blown in its defences.

Having rehearsed the details of this crowd scene
so often in my mind, it seems already starting
to vanish into the past. Now let the future arrive.
Today's turn-out could not remotely be improved on.
They are having the time of their lives.

AND ON WHAT

and on what
presumption
parents
may one ask
do you blithely
give life
act as catalyst
for future
generations
grant your
bodily urgings
precedence
over mind
blind impulse
sweeping
reason away
in a surge
of preconceptions
your creative juices
frustrating inhibition
obscuring
the margin
of error
between
your instinct
for survival
and your
perpetuation
of death's
lineage

INTERCESSION

God and humankind meet on uncommon ground.
They just don't speak the same language.

He plays hard to get.
They try to smoke Him from His lair with incense.

They flatter Him with glittering vestments, prayerful
patter, gilded portraits, po-faced processions.

Both sides operate to incompatible agendas.
Priestly mediation fails to close the widening rift.

Their loudest pleas, tempered by
musical settings, fall on His deaf ears.

No, they can't hear what He is saying either.
No, they can't see His side of the story.

The generation gap that separates them
reaches back to the pre-galactic universe.

He thinks in terms of infinity.
They urge research to prolong human life.

He casts His pearly gates before a chosen few.
Before the rest, He raises hell.

His commands are not their wish.
They yearn for riches, youth and beauty.

He bestows gifts of osteitis, earthquakes, infant deaths.
They shake their fists, proclaim their disbelief.

THE CALL

When we call on God, we always find him out,
away on business maybe, lost in a world of his own,
performing miracles for distant universes, volunteering
to undergo humiliation all over again on another planet's
equivalent of a cross to which his credulous disciples
nail their colours as a drowning man clings to a mast.

He is otherwise engaged perpetually – lines busy;
no menu of options offering access to the top –
his supplicants fobbed off with white-collar staff,
parochial-minded men handling his clients like constituents;
clerical workers undertaking to pass on petitions, insisting
the final decisions fall totally outside their sphere.

We are disillusioned by this failure to meet us face
to face, his abdication from fair play when all we ask
is mercy for patients sweltering feverishly through blue
surgical gowns, a softening of his line on chronic pain,
repeal of whatever law ordains that those dealt a poor
hand must suffer the consequences for life, a birth scar.

Is it conceivable that he still dotes on the very hairs
of our sceptical heads, eavesdrops on every arbitrary
phrase, like some benign celestial Nicolae Ceauşescu?
Or is he no longer on speaking terms with mankind,
dismissive of the species as a bad day's work, leading
his campaign trail to more docile outposts of his empire?

Has he ceased believing in his mission statement, lost faith
in his epoch-creating role? Can this universe have spun out
of his control, his conglomerate diversified so much that
a personal touch, a hands-on customer service, is unviable?
We want him to summon a mass gathering like an extraordinary
meeting of shareholders, feed facts to the multitudes this time.

If he has died, where are the oozing wounds to which our doubting
fingers can be applied? What are the chances he may rise again?
Once, his beatific smile graced all our houses like an ancestral
photograph or the graven image of a charismatic President or King.
Now the blanched patch left in its place must be brushed out,
the wall painted over, a hall mirror found to occupy that space.

AFTER HARVEST

Tanked up with grain,
the armoured high
and mighty combine
harvester discharged
its barley into trailers
and left the field
to tractors, balers.

Polished-off acres
of striped gold
could be a newly-laid
timber floor: more like
a pristine showhouse
now than a field as
old as the hills.

AN ULSTER LANDSCAPE

('*The Old Callan Bridge*', *1945, John Luke*)

Impossible to treat this
post-war idyll – hedged off
from the real world –
seriously at first glance.

The July day is baked
to perfection by the sun;
warm stones in twisty
cobbled–together roads

batched like bread rolls.
Every wish has met its
match. The bridge with
a river to cool its arches.

The horse with copious
oats. The cows with
grazing on demand.
The hatted man and

grandson who take
to country ways in
summer's marching season.
The dog chasing

children chasing friends.
Hard though it is,
realistically, to place much
faith in the painter's

vision of an Ulster
eternally untroubled,
he still submits his
testimony as credible.

This is the gospel truth
according to John Luke.

ALL OVER IRELAND

Snow was general all over Ireland . . .
    – JAMES JOYCE, 'The Dead'

What's general all over Ireland is definitely not snow. Sandbag-
bulky clouds, about to splurge on rain, close in sulkily on all
four provinces, allowing them no quarter, flushing them out.

Rain adds layers of flab to the river where anglers in oilskins
prospect for trout. A downpour drowns the banter of two neighbours.
A course inspection at Leopardstown leads to cancellation.

Rain climbs hills on which foot-rot sheep, dipped in precipitation,
graze with a lamb or two in tow. Rain, not snow, is what blurs
perspectives at furze-lined tourist beauty spots in Kerry and Mayo.

Rain meaning whatever was sent to torment the couple lugging
home a heavy bag of groceries, each grasping a plastic handle.
Rain not snow. On a ruined castle crumbling like a water biscuit.

On a heifer lying low with her drooling mouth full. On a mangy stray.
On a blinking lake. On roofs where zinc tanks corrode and starlings
practise courtship rites. On a night nurse in the sodium-lit car-park.

The man shouldering a wicker basket of racing pigeons to the station
takes a beating from the rain, as do the sleek racehorses making
a run for it in the beech-hedged grounds of sheik-owned studs.

Rain is general too in the village near the landfill quarry:
it's pensions day in the sub-post office; the creaking door
of a derelict thatched cottage plays second fiddle to a gale.

Rain joins isolated farms where border collies cap each
other's barks, like gossip passed from mouth to mouth. Rain
plinks on the glass dome shielding plastic roses on a grave.

It touches the raw nerves of gaudy window boxes, drums liquid
fingers on the corrugated transit warehouse where cattle destined
for live export to dry Libya or Egypt await their marching orders.

It tries the patience of a foreign film crew hoping the sun will wriggle
out from cloud, and the lodger for whom a limp window-envelope
marked *Don't Delay! – Save Money Now!* is the day's only mail.

Rain hammers the builders' hut as a bricklayer shuffles the deck.
Damp patches taint the Old School Restaurant and the Rectory
B & B. Drains back up in the side-street panel-beater's yard.

Rain, bombarding windows, pours out its feelings to a room where
a blue screen-saver flickers like a gas flame and a youth revises
for the Garda exam. It throws cold water on a bridal photo shoot.

The minimum-wage man expertly meshing empty supermarket
trolleys is well used to the rain. So too is whoever arranges
the optimistic beachball and bucket display at the seafront kiosk.

Tub-thumping rain, snubbing the prayers of grain farmers, finds
a welcome in the striped metal barrel at the downpipe and tops
the highest-ever levels measured at Belmullet since records began.

Commuters rush from the bus as if fleeing a catastrophe. Some wear
soaked newspapers as headgear. A woman, doggedly taking her
constitutional by the golflinks, pauses under the awning of an oak.

Rain pesters the baffled Latvian au pair, on the deserted platform,
who fumbles for her contact number. It droppeth on the church hall
that is now a lottery-aided heritage centre for a town down on its luck.

The breadman delivering catering pans to the electroplating unit's
canteen has never seen such rain. Not since yesterday at least
when it seeped through the felt on his flat-roof kitchen extension.

The pelt of the Atlantic Ocean receives the rain like a protective
spray on a pair of crocodile tassel loafers. A brightly-pegged
row of tracksuit bottoms sags on a housing estate clothesline.

Tomorrow, yet again, instead of snow, the forecast will hold out
the promise of *a dull day everywhere, with rain and drizzle,*
cloud formations like the tissue of a compulsive handwasher's brain.

Rain is general all over Ireland. It lashes the glass panels of the James
Joyce Bridge. Falls on the house where Bartell D'Arcy's song caused
grief one distant Christmas. And upon all the living and the dead.

THE CLOCK

With only one story to tell, the clock strikes
a monotonous note, irrespective of how
musical the bell, how gilded the chimes
its timely conclusions report through.
Time literally on hands, it informs you
to your face exactly where you stand
in relation to your aspirations, stacks up
the odds against your long-term prospects,
leaves your hopes and expectations checked.
Keeping track of time to the last second, it gives
the lie to all small talk about your reputedly
youthful looks, sees through the subterfuge
of dyed hair, exposes the stark truth beneath
the massaged evidence of smooth skin.

REALITY CHECK

I   *Death*

Death does not come cheap
and is paid for in lumpectomies.
In bone marrow skimmed from relatives.
In sterile hardware ransacking soft parts.

In the clamped aorta of the donor heart.
In students poking round a tube-occluded bed.
How precious death must be to make such
vast demands, exact such satisfaction.

II   *Consultation*

What you want to hear him say is
Nothing to worry about – it's perfectly normal.
What you hear him say is *I'm afraid . . .*
grounds for concern . . . high-risk age-group.

What you want to hear him say is
It's quite routine – it will soon clear up.
What you hear him say is *The biopsy results*
are back and I won't beat about the bush . . .

III   *Observation*

Every attempt at escape is thwarted here,
the waverings of the heart monitored by
the cardiograph: no hearsay evidence,
no incriminating script passes undetected.

All-night patrols keep you under surveillance,
permanent guard. Tomorrow, treated with
the deepest suspicion of malign behaviour,
you will be frisked for smuggled polyps, growths.

IV *Operation*

After the endoscopic tests and x-rays,
the guilty verdict is pronounced.
Handcuffed to a metal intravenous stand,
you are escorted to the central operations room.

Your defence team briefs you on the nature
of the charges, your complete lack of immunity.
The futility of appeals. The special precautions
to be taken. In the event of. Just in case.

V *Textbook*

The smaller the swelling the greater the danger.
80% are benign but surgery is always
advised, though removal poses a serious
risk of permanent damage to the facial nerve.

If not removed, there's a solid chance
the lump will prove eventually malignant.
If removed, it may grow back.
If malignant, it will almost certainly have spread.

VI *Broken Man*

Smashed cars, scraped together in the salvage
yard, are scarred for life, shattered into
atoms of chromium and glass, too crushed
ever to qualify for roadworthiness again.

Your mind had suffered some unspeakable
collision, its impact written all over your face,
as if your brain were panel-beaten crudely
back to some simulacrum of normality.

VII   *Bandaged Heart*

(cast stainless steel by Cecily Brennan)

The heart should be cast in steel
to spare it human feelings, wrapped
in a bow of bandages, a tourniquet to stem
the flow from blood–corroded arteries.

It is as if the heart had hardened
before its lava could yield up the molten
secrets of its chambers, congealing into
reflective metal, a love object of surgical steel.

VIII   *Analysis*

And who among the angelic orders will compensate
us for the gift of life? Who will make good our gains?
Who will be designated to help us come to terms
with the emotional strains of music we've endured?

How can we recover from the recurring attacks
of lovemaking we've known? What counselling
might reconcile us to our children's growing success,
allay the trauma of being spoilt for choice?

MEETING POINTS

You shake hands with fellow delegates
in the conference room, interpret the rakish
Italian's playful mime, swap business cards
and direct line numbers with the Dane –
shirt sleeves ironed sharp as hatchet
blades – twiddling his country nameplate.
Once your final position on derogations
is sketched out with a plastic hotel pen,
the draft directive highlighted in dayglo lime,
no Chairman's *tour de table* will faze you
when your time comes to answer for Ireland.

   *

  Boarding at Brussels,
the Minister for Rural Development,
  laptop strapped on shoulder,
is throatily feeding Gaelic
  to a cellphone, having
taken his case to Europe.
  Stooping below the awning
of the luggage rack,
  the Minister for Agriculture
loosens his tie, settles back
  for pre-dinner apéritifs
and off-duty piss-taking
  with his suited entourage.
Bliss. If only smoking
  were still permissible.

   *

Another EU Working Group session in some
hosting Member State; another boardroom-style
layout in a hotel ballroom, the regulation baize
covering a multitude of joined-up trestles.
Eager microphones lean to overhear our
multi-lingual debate; the Chairman – clinking
a tumbler to call the room to order – makes
a start by summarising the agenda items.
En marge babble abates; back-up staff
in the wings are busy with attendance sheets,
juggling departure details, airport taxi needs.
A revised draft directive is circulated, hot from
the photocopier like clothes folded from a drier.
An expert sub-group will surely be among
some delegation's proposals; for now,
the Chairman is kicking to touch, fielding
questions about the pie-charts and graphs
that lend colour to his PowerPoint presentation.
Beyond the drawn velvet curtains, the gull
scream of a car alarm, the glassy rumpus
of empties from a passing brewery truck.

                *

Such happy release when,
the meeting having gone your way,
nothing added under AOB,

you scoop the briefing files
into your overnight valise, leaving
just enough spare time to grab

a magnum from duty-free,
claim your frequent– flier miles,
beat the final boarding call.

                *

You're not quite sure you've met; yet, some
pheromone of officialdom in the air
elicits a half-nod from you as you pass:
your reflex reaction to his comparable suit
and tie; some hunch you may have faced
each other across a departmental table once,
partaken in a joint review group – who knows
what or when? – some confab or delegation
lost in a lifetime's fug of arbitrations, ordinances,
inter-agency liaison, temporising, files.

*

Back from a monitoring mission
    on best practice, you manipulate
the rigid key, snap cobwebs
    sealing the front door,
steal into the cool hall lit
    with a sallow long-life bulb
out of place in daylight,
    an addled firefly.
You punch in the alarm code
    to quell the piercing racket
of the control box,
    drag the mail-impeded door
wide enough to make space
    for your bags, manhandled
just now from the airport cab.

FOUNTAIN

It never rains but it pours.
    Translate into heraldic Latin,
engrave onto the base of this public
    fountain which stores up untold
grudges, sculpted cups running over
    with angry outbursts, intense enough
to wring acidic tears from stone.
    Not a good word can it bring itself
to utter, spitting out vinegary grievances,
    spilling forth the messy details
in the language of the gutter. My God,
    how many sorrows there are
to drown once you get started.

Count your curses, it seems
    to say, *vows broken, illusions lost,*
ambitions thwarted. Let others gush.
    I am the one fountain, unbribeable
with well-wishing coins, that cannot
    be bought off. The truth must out.
Mine is the no-nonsense voice
    for which false hopes will never wash;
in which you hear credence given
    to the fears you keep secreted
in your brain's innermost folds,
    its locked cells, woefully chanting
an unstoppable mantra:

Supposing. Supposing. Suppose . . .

FIFTY O'CLOCK

Clearing out some boxes, the foxed *Guide to Life* comes as a shock. The section devoted to the sensuous mysteries well-fingered in our youth. Can we have spread ourselves so far into its pages since then, slept together through whole chapters? How else might we have reached the years of anticlimax? How can we have arrived so soon at 'Growing Old Gracefully'? What possible relevance does such a chapter hold for the young couple we have, for decades, been?

*

Brokers, I notice, no longer proposition me with slinky proposals, glossy brochures offering to raise the level of my life cover 'without need for medical examination'.

*

First reading glasses pinching my nose,
I peruse the small print of income continuance
plans, tax-efficient pension annuities,
practise the pronunciation of ailments –
reserved exclusively for over fifties –
ending in 'itis', 'osis', 'aemia'.

*

Why the lights all night in the nursing home?
Is someone scared of ghosts?
The ghost of Christmas past or Christmas future?
The ghost in the mirror of the present tense?

*

'I just never thought it would come so soon', my parents' youthful friend, Mary Olive, confessed from her hospice bed.

*

During the halting funeral eulogy, a daughter
recalls her mother's circle of friends,
housewives whose dated names – Kitty, Sadie,
Bridie, Stasia – proclaim their era at an end.

*

Inseparable, my body and I, till death us do part. Death, the bad
company I'll fall in with, last thing my parents would have
expected of me.

*

Ah, but there's everything to play for yet, isn't there? Career shift.
Holiday condo. Early retirement. Isn't there? You falter at a cross-
roads, the stake of a signpost rammed through its heart.

*

And they too passed.
What was confided in low voices
on a homeward journey filtered back to air.
Their car was sold for scrap, for parts.
Cattle in roadside fields were fattened,
slaughtered, quartered, minced, consumed.
Pumps with slender metal taproots
made way for piped water.

*

That I regret everything goes without saying.
What I did. What I didn't.
The time I bought. The time I sold.
Not to have waited. Not to have acted.
To have kept my mouth shut.
To have opened my big mouth.

To have taken it on the jaw.
Not to have turned the other cheek.
To be so weak. So headstrong.
That we didn't meet sooner.
That we met at all.
That I lived.
That I had to unlive.

*

There you are in wedding-day mode, Mother, sporting a rose ('a rose upon a rose', my father rhapsodised): a young woman in love, heart intent on starting a family.

*

They bestowed rosebud hearts on children,
eyes and noses like family heirlooms,
ancestral expressions to which we now
bear helpless witness, each of us a photofit variation.

*

And you really started something, Mother, when you indulged us in creaming off the iron from your blood, siphoning it like red diesel, harvesting your cells, cadging the calcium in your mouth for our own selfish ends. Now cut to this photo of the family reunion where we stuff our faces at a linen-vested table. What an appetite for life you whetted in us.

*

Life was all our ailing neighbour – not yet fifty – asked for.
And she'd snatch as much of it as could be spared.
Enough to see her to old age might do.
Just enough to last a lifetime would suffice.
It was life or nothing as far as she was concerned.
Let others take death lying down.

She was not, quite frankly, the dying type.
Never, ever would she stoop that low.

*

Think, even now, of all the wrong
turnings you will take before
you can call death your own.
All the decisions you will mess up.
All the blunders you will perpetrate.
Future remarks you'll want to retract.
Character flaws that magnify with
every passing year. Betrayals you'll
be in no position to deny.

*

Daydreaming, I imagine my entire life
still stacked in front of me like unspent cash:
as if some outrageous mistake had been made
in calculating my age and I could bring back
my birth cert like a receipt, insisting on a refund.

*

Mother, just the other day I thought of the perfume gift you came
to expect each year, until your fiftieth Christmas. What scent are
you on the trail of since then? Evening primrose spray? Black-
berried essence of belladonna, a nightshade fragrance?

*

[after Hans Verhagen]

A minute later, I noticed your breathing had stopped. The autopsy
recorded secondaries all over, even in the farthest recesses of your
lungs. No wonder you were racked by such agonising spasms. The
miracle was that a ramshackle house proved habitable so long.

FOREVER

Forever some customer happy to sing along with the supermarket muzak, no matter how hackneyed or crass.

Forever the plangent sound of a motorcycle in the early hours, conjuring a world you once had access to.

Forever the young couple shutting the front door, leaving to conjecture what their next move may be.

Forever the van driver slowing down to check a house number against a delivery invoice.

Forever an old boy on a rickety bike with a loyal following of one terrier–type mongrel.

Forever the husband skulking outside the boutique while his wife seeks approval from a mirror.

Forever the kind who believe in God (a little) and horoscopes (a lot) and cannot resist a buy-one-get-one offer.

Forever those with a lump in the throat at every reconciliation scene, the theme music's pathos never failing to work its way straight to the left atrium of the heart.

Forever the cleaning woman tapping the pub window with a coin and the helmeted courier leaning his gob to the intercom.

Forever a caller so long on hold she wonders should she redial and brave the bossy touch-tone menu again.

Forever a youngster hacking the grass with bat or stick in what serves as a green space near the housing estate.

Forever, stopped in her tracks at One Hour Photo, a student smiling indulgently at her recent past.

Forever the secretary sprinting with franked mail to the post office, minutes before the closing curtain of steel shutters falls.

Forever, from an adjacent window, the commentator's animated voice as the ball approaches the goal area and lands *I don't believe it . . . barely wide.*

Forever the widower turning up a Viennese polka on the Sunday morning programme and scribbling *Slovak Radio Symphony Orchestra* on a phone bill.

Forever the girl upending the nearly-empty crisp packet and savouring life to the full, to the last salty cheese-and-onion flavoured crumb.

Forever the old ladies who smile at babies like politicians and suspect the meter reader may not really be the meter reader.

Forever a freckled builder in high-vis jacket swinging his lunch-bag as he clocks in at the chipboard hoarding.

Forever the teenagers who can't pass up a hat display without trying on preposterous headgear in a department store.

Forever the tall schoolboy with pony tail and full-length leather coat. And forever the small one, pate shaved almost bald, nursing a cigarette like a sore finger.

Forever the sort who texts a request for her boyfriend to the lunchtime show – then throws in a greeting to her aunt and uncle, just for the heck.

Forever the thickset woman, dragging a shopping trolley, who pauses to rub a lottery scratch card like Aladdin's lamp.

Forever the exasperated mother – hatchback open, hazards flashing, eyes peeled for the traffic police – while her son, packing the
drum kit, plays it cool.

Forever the laughter fading, a dropped coin spinning to a wobbly
stop.

Forever life heading about its business in places vaguely familiar
like an ex-weatherwoman's face, a New Zealand premier's name.

Forever. And ever. All going well.

EVER AFTER

Whatever construction we put on
the mortification of the flesh by death,
whatever the happy-clappy euphemisms
we choose to shroud its devastation with,

there are few enough consoling glosses
to be put on a body scrapped in
tamped-down clay, trampled underfoot,
so reduced in means as to be human

infill, biodegrading fast, depreciation
setting in unless disposed of smartly.
We joke about it all, fall back
on bad puns, black humour,

wanting to sidestep negative
insinuations, stay true to the living
body, fend off morbidity, sublimate
our dread, stuff the unsettling

dead back into their crumbling boxes,
keep the snuff of their rancid dust from
getting up our noses, install granite
headstones to pin them firmly down.

THERE WAS

there was a house
woodsmoke was part of it
drinking water rinsed in peat
trace elements of cloves and sage
December light was in it
grey as a collared dove

spontaneous gatherings
of rainwater
were funnelled down
the gullies of the sloping lane

above the hooked cooking utensils
on the open hearth
the kitchen chimney made
a look-out post from which
you monitored the sky
that sad-eyed creature
outdoors in all weathers
brushed with mushy cloud

there was a moment
it had a waftage of frankincense
logs came from a toppled trunk
your uncle dragged bodily
from the hilltop forest
like the antlered stag
its mounted head still flaunted in the hall
opposite the mildewed looking-glass
that tarnished everyone alike

antler leaves defended holly beads
the fuchsia bush beside the roughcast wall
had stood the test of eternity

each summer robbing nests
laid-back cuckoos
made their eggs at home
in the forest where your barefoot
father's school carved out
a limestone eyrie among the trees
my god talk about wildflowers mosses fungi ferns
rustlings from undergrowth stirrings from burrows
tracks and pawmarks badger setts fox scents unlikely birds

you gasped a little at whatever
it was you had within your grasp
clutched it as best you could
sensed its closeness as you passed
the rosewood cabinet from which
an illustrated *Christmas Carol*
– with gilded cover blizzard –
had been removed

brothers sister two girl cousins
played with board-games crayons
winds whining outside
answered to a different world
and the mud-clobbered yard
was revealed only to make
the timbered parlour floor
even more secure under your feet
its heat more precious

unthinkable that your parents
would ever need to retrace
the drab miles home
that your uncle might step
out into that faltering day
with hay or mangels for the cattle

and something in the moment
was brighter for the darkness
warmer for the storm putting pressure

on the rowan tree in the rushy field
more reliable for the tiny squared-off
window-panes in which the scene
was compressed into eye-sized segments

the latch rattles in the flagstoned kitchen
a whispered mist of smoke is picked up
a disturbed log sleeping on the job
buds suddenly into orange-squash coloured flames

a dusk chorus of voices
none at cross purposes for once
you know from the tone
everyone is in complete agreement
the details can be thrashed out later
meanwhile tea and lemonade are poured
iced tar-black slices passed around

you are clinging
to the candlelit moment
holding its trusted hand
tightly as a flame
attaches to a wick

shake the day
it might start snowing
like this water globe:
a glass-cocooned nativity
you agitate –
blocked salt cellar –
letting loose its grains
on the stable that could easily
be the rattling zinc-roofed
cattleshed outside

snow lodging
in that yard
would never melt

MIŁOSZ'S RETURN

I searched for it, found it, recognized it.
   – CZESŁAW MIŁOSZ, 'A Meadow'

The field your memory singled out for
special treatment can be located by you still:

the one the sun would always make
an extra fuss about, buff until it gleamed

like a copper pan suspended in the oak-
beamed kitchen of your manor house.

Retrace the well-worn path of memory.
Nothing is beyond recovery. No one has died.

For, as you yourself have prophesied,
The rivers will return to their beginnings . . .

The dead will wake up, not comprehending.
Till everything that happened has unhappened.

Unlatch the gate. Lean against the haystack.
Look where you were taken by her lips.

Where the horse-drawn rake, weeds
stuck between its teeth, was rusting.

Where a cow stood ruminating over
sow thistles or in hock to clover and buttercup.

Where the acquisitive bees made a dash
for the linden grove and light filled in

the gaps between the apple trees.
Where heart-fluttering butterflies clapped wings.

Where green hay, toppled by scythes, soaked up
heat like berries ripening for preserves.

Home in time, you find your bearings there
among sweet calamus and whirring snipe.

SKYWRITING

The sky leaves every possibility wide open,
its wraparound screen receptive to
any scene unfolding on its surface:
constellations fluttering in cosmic gales,
planes plying trade routes across continents,
shooting stars detached like retinas,
sun rays adding decorative motifs.
Primed with a wash of nothingness,
it can stretch its flexible canvas
as far as distance permits,
vanishing point infinitely elusive.

*

Darkness is what mainly marks
these muckraking winter Saturdays
that never quite get off the ground,
becoming bogged down in cloud.
And, at the time of morning when you'd
rather have a lawnmower up and running
or a paint can open like a puree,
torpor permeates your pores,
blackens your soul like the coal lumps

you work up to a heated exchange.
Best to abandon the fight, give up the ghost.
Best to let the darkness have its day.

*

Endlessly pliable, the sky draws out
its substance in every direction, a ductile
metal thinned almost to invisibility,
but tinged at dawn with finger-painted limes,
cornelians and iodines, canned-salmon pinks.
Vein of skimmed-milk blue, font of impermanent
inks, if not clotting into creamy cloud
it soon assumes a pure cerulean
that saturates space without a join or seam,
its uninterrupted stream of consciousness
a testament to life lived outside of time.

*

Light shimmies down this high-rise
art museum to the busy street below,
slipping into any gap that leaves itself
exposed to the benign influence of sun,
dips a flickering toe in the fountain
at the park, coaxes dark trees to lighten up.
The window cleaner of a nearby building pauses
at its 42nd floor, checks his watch, stares earthward,
platform dangling like the basket of an air balloon.
He might be a farmer leaning on a rail fence,
taking stock, squinting across a prospect
of ploughed fields – remoulded drills –
where secreted wheat will be revealed.
Or even, were it day's end, this Edward Hopper
filling station owner, totting his paltry sales
in the frail illumination of his gas pumps:
fir trees plot behind his back to soak in

darkness like carbon dioxide and his
secluded stretch of road runs dangerously
low in light, gauge zeroing in on *empty*.

       *

It must drive you to despair, living always under
leaden skies, a sheltering tourist – transparent
mac over zipped anorak – will propose when
louring clouds conspire with rain; faces give way
to umbrellas navigating down the showery street.
And we agree, as we can hardly not, wet rot
attacking attics, rain entering our bloodstreams.
Yet we have an understanding with the weather:
whenever squalls end and sun returns with
friendly fire, we would forgive it anything.
It resembles Friday evenings then, the grind
of the working week almost worthwhile
for the exhilaration freedom brings by contrast.
And if a rainbow's spray-painted sash is added,
the chemistry between us is a perfect match –
fidelity rewarded, reconciliation complete.

       *

A winter dawn, struggling to shake off
the blacker aspects of the night,
keeps its sleeping inhabitants in the dark.
Sandy beaches take in water: a sleet-chilled
high-salt muddy-coloured mushroom broth.
In lakeside cottages with empty bunk beds
timer switches activate a light bulb rota.
Snow, unseen, rears up on mountains.
What a heroic profile Earth presents,
holding its own against the serried might
of galaxies, the flight of migrating comets,
resisting the tug of anti-particles,
the desolation of black holes.

378

*

True, as friends say cheerily, *it will*
be all the same to you in a thousand years.
But now, right now, it matters greatly
to the small-brained, species-centred,
peer-influenced creature you are.
Joy, glimpsed like a long-tailed comet,
keeps on eluding you: too remote for
the naked eye to know whether that
distant glimmer moves infinitesimally
closer or is spluttering further away.
In either case, it will not cross your
flight path in any foreseeable future.
Meanwhile, taking a dim view of
the present, you come down to earth
with an awful lot of explaining to do.

*

Such an old stalwart, the sun,
always rising to the occasion,
never missing a day, raising crops
of maize to ripeness, rounding melons,
tenderising pears, lending bounce
to black-tipped hooves of lambs,
adding layers of intrigue and silence
to dirt roads wandering off the map.
And, as if that were not bounty enough,
it masters the art of penetrating glass,
brings a glint to every facet of a fruit bowl,
causes the vase of dahlias in the framed
still life to waver: our house elevated
above its station, pitched at the level
of a Dutch interior, lives clarified by light.

*

You can see so much in the dark of night;
even more than that paw-swinging cat does,
marching along its beat, as you watch
raindrop equations repeat to infinity
on the window when you rise at 3 to suss out
some sound you think you may have heard.
You are breaking bad news to yourself – a cold
arctic glow, an aurora borealis of home truths –
with the full disclosure darkness stipulates.
Heartless rains resume thrashing the glass
as the planet continues its orbit into dawn:
one of its travel-sick crew, you find its universal
implications greater than you can grasp,
a yawning enormity kept in check by clouds.

*

I want it to be not just summer but May:
horizons broadening, light expanding by the day.
Not just May but warm, the slightest brush
with sunlight accelerating germination.
Not just warm but bright. Not just bright but blue.
Blue as hectares of bluebells hewn from the air.
Blue as the air itself.

*

Morning incites the sun to make up
for ground lost overnight . . . Light starts
exalting high-rise buildings, spreading
its growth-promoting warmth where
not even hardy weeds subsist, until settling
on a stunted grove of conifers in tubs
at a roof garden's fountain-oozing terrace.
Scaling the stairs of windows, step by step,
it takes hotel personnel by surprise
as they prepare the breakfast buffet
in the Executive Suite: tan cereals,

crustaceous croissants, fanned-out slices
of cooked meats, bowls of dismembered
grapefruits; it seeps into depopulated
office blocks, where workers will teem later,
gannets clinging to a precipitous existence.

*

A glow-in-the-dark night. Radio telescopes
craning to catch reverberations from the universe.
The sky is the one absolute: there is no
gainsaying the truths it tells, pegged out
spaciously in constellations that pinpoint our
locations when we find ourselves at sea;
stars dazzling with the import of stale
news travelling from millennia ago.
Yet, gravitating back in cosmic time,
we know the lure of obscure objects
too: poke about black holes,
explore dark matter for our origins.

*

How dull the world would be without
its shadows. How unjust. Nothing
to attenuate the harsher sentiments
of noon, sun pushing its weight around,
having it all its own way: no second side
to any story; no keeping time with a garden's
limestone sun-dial, nothing to tap the darker
undercurrents, the bass notes, nothing
to restore some balance to the picture.
Grant us more sun so that there may
be shadows in abundance: tenaciously
faithful to every step we take, they
are wrenched from the world only when
we rise above it, jet engines muscling
their way skyward, upwardly mobile,

the plane's earthbound double in
hot pursuit, desperately scrambling
to keep pace, like a waving child
who chases a cousin's departing car.

*

On midwinter day, sun excavates
the entrances of passage tombs,
surveys their corbelled vaults, revives
their spirits with a light touch.
And slabs of weather-beaten stone –
wedged on heathery mountain tops
that offer panoramas of five fertile counties –
carrying boulders like the weight
of the world on granite shoulders
receive a warm overspill of light,
as do these giant incisors – a ring of
standing stones – which form a sun trap.

*

The day is in the clear. Suds of mist
have shifted stains of darkness, purified the air.
More spacious now, spring–cleaned
of detritus, the sky is testing its endurance
to the limit, extending its remit.
April's message sinks in everywhere,
penetrating even to the densest levels
of dowdy brown clay, inaugurating
a flurry of buds and blossoms.
A tortoiseshell comes out of hiding,
wings blinking in the light; in the warm
colours of a day it would be a gross
betrayal to kill off, a squandering
of early promise for a still unravelling
narrative that, so far, has no end in sight.
Refusing to go down without a fight, the sun

will make an exit, stage west, its reds
spreading like wildfire as though everything
remaining had been set alight and the sky
were a backdrop fabricated from flammable
material that had burst into flame.

*

The sun throws light
on this morning's light,
as if a weight of clouds
had lifted from the day
or someone tripped a switch:
even the last flaky scrap
rusting in a ditch breaks
into a captivating shine.

*

No one can look at death or the sun
without being left entirely in the dark.
Nor, with impunity, may the sun
expect to gaze directly at the moon.
Awestruck birds, fallen silent
before totality, know this when
the sun, corona blazing, is deposed.
Blossoms close up shop; nocturnal
moths report for duty; metal-plated
echo-sounding bats might strike out
any moment. A suspenseful chill
creeps across the gawking crowds.
Keeping sparks of hope alive, starlight
gouges air-holes in the untimely night.

*

The sun, in shining form, raises office
morale, hints at a day that has been

scrubbed down, sand-blasted like a sooty
building, smartened with a facelift.
To the tip of my tongue comes the old
chestnut about a stretch being noticeable . . .
But my desk pad's *November* interrupts
with a reminder that the year must contract
further, keep its pact with darkness, that
– contrary to appearances – this buoyant
example of dayhood is limping into port.

*

Streamlined blues as far as the eye
can see. Which is not very far.
Only as far as the next smokescreen
of cloud, or the sunset you are warned,
on pain of blindness, to turn aside from.
Whatever truth lies at the back of that beyond
stays strictly classified, out of bounds: your
frontier is a sky awash with frothy constellations;
sun and moon like eyes in an old master portrait
that follow you inscrutably around a room.

*

Reiterating whatever claim it makes,
a *sotto voce* repetition, rain plays out
a reverie-inducing music on the glass
harmonica of the kitchen's window pane.
But, peeling open the back door
for a rain check, you hear the liquid
swishing grow insistent as a whip;
sibilant drips insinuate their way
between tightly-packed leaves which,
gorging on these waters, never
quite reach saturation point.
Hard to imagine that sweetness
and light might yet triumph,

a freshly perfumed day resurface,
put on airs of mellowness,
a rose-tinted sun assume the contours
of a mountain range, your gable wall.

*

Stillest of Sundays in the village.
You leap ashore into a light
finely spun as fishing line.
The lake comes to, with little
fits and starts: sun makes a play
for its impressionable surface,
rays splashing out in all directions.
Decked in sandals, shorts,
you amble down to check
if anyone's awake to rustle up
some breakfast egg and bacon
at the Lakeview Café's mess.

*

Heat abrades the layers of cloud.
Token fronds of cumulus remaining
are an ornamental garnish, setting off
the sun, trapping twilit juices later
the way swordfish takes its flavour
from a bayleaf and basil marinade.
A pinch of stars will serve as seasoning.
Moon lights up from a stub of sun.

*

A rainbow is frescoed
on the back wall of the sky:
a sky that will digest its iridescence,
wash it down with rain.

*

What a show the sun puts on,
performing like a star,
raining spotlight beams,
cutting out behind a cloud
before – stunt pilot –
revving up its light again.
Or watch its sleight of hand,
its stagy way of conjuring
a coruscating day from mist,
holding it in abeyance,
under wraps – a slow burner –
until the timing is exactly right
(fields hazy about their parts,
birds shuffling in the wings);
then, with a rising degree
of intensity, it blends tar's
redolence with the usual
fragrances – petunia, rose,
mown hay – and refreshes
spellbinding memories
of when there was no
limit to the sky and our
horizons knew no bounds.

*

Moonlight colludes with churchyard yews
to sketch a spectral scene. Weathered headstones,
brought to life, seem to lean back with
brash attitude: a goth band's glowering
entourage on an album-cover photo shoot.
Eldritch beams slip in between the bedroom
curtains, a stalactite sliver of shivery light,
cold as the loner's shot of midnight gin
nipped from the mini-bar of a cheap hotel
on which the darkness confers stars.

*

Come sunset these evenings,
cloud banks – firmly shut till then –
open like clockwork, as if
operated by a time lock.
The golden coin which spills out
is donated too late to save
the day; shops closing,
commuters flocking underground.
No time remains to catch
these last-minute offers of light.

*

Through old elastic-stockinged
aspens with the shakes, I glimpse
the sky in pristine nick as if toxic
smoke had never wafted its way,
planes had never scrawled graffiti
contrails on its glass. Those mountain
peaks, plastered with newly-minted snow,
that could be the illustration on a tin
of breath fresheners will be haloed
at sunset with a violet otherworldly rim.

*

Not a blot on the sky's escutcheon.
Not a cloud on the sea's horizon.
Sea and sky are indivisible here,
invisibly threaded together, blue to blue,
the seam that separates them
barely traceable by the eye.
Then *sunset and evening star*.
Darkness enters cagily, goes against
our wishes, over our heads, flecks
of paradisal plumage showing

through the closing bars of sky.
The day peters out, having, for one day
only, made its countrywide appearance.
Twilight and evening bell,
And after that the dark . . .

                *

Lavish with light, sagging under its own
proliferating weight, the harvest moon
staggers above a mountain, heaves
itself up, hacks through darkness, finding
room for manoeuvre at the apex of the sky,
challenging the sun's monopoly, skimming
off a wattage of its purest energy, sloshing
about in cloud, filtering like blue gaslight
through glass. Mezzotint lakes, enamelled
rivers glinting with a fish-scale silver,
flaking trees, antique hand-coloured
gardens: a world engraved in steel.
Other nights, the moon behaves more
intimately, lowering its sights: a lamp
suspended above a table in a family-run
bistro known only to a lucky few.

                *

I dream a sky cobbled with bombers,
armour-plated with parked planes,
fuselages nose-to-tail; a tongued
and grooved planetary roof
proofed against sun's infiltration.

                *

The pale winter sun is trying to take off
into the wild blue yonder, but its light
lacks staying power; evening – seeking

closure – soon calls it a day.
The one gaping hole still leaking low-level
light, weak as a butane-fuelled cooking ring
on a windy picnic site, is patched over
quickly, airbrushed from the record,
and a united front of darkness presented:
tight-lipped, admitting no dissent; leaving
the starkest possible options to creatures
retorting with feeble reading lamps
and watchful halogens; challenging
frantic eyes to identify a single
resistant pocket, a last defiant reserve.

*

Winter 1957. Stars strung out like fairy lights.
We stood our garden's ground until the Sputnik
satellite came round to our ways: a sidereal
blip, *a one-eyed yellow idol* of technology.
All across the island, shivering families warred
against the cold; pyjamas under gaberdines,
we lined the astral route, waving the flashy
object onward, rewarded with a cursory wink.
Eyes drawn to dizzy heights of stars,
I tried to join their puzzling dots.

*

Late autumn light, bronze as beech leaves,
terminates at my office desk, aggrandising
my memos, gilding the journeyman prose
of my draft Chairman's speech, making
copperplate of briefing papers on compliance
costs, leaning across my coffinwood press,
weakly stooping at an awkward angle,
casting the room in sepia, dispensing
with my presence, pensioning me off.

As your transatlantic flight nears home, clouds
surround the coastline, tidemarks around a bath.
Vacation over too soon, worries pester you again.
The welcome is subdued, scumbled sunlight less
than overwhelming in its warmth when you descend
– backpack, tee-shirt, trainers – from the dishevelled cabin
to the tarmac smarting from an outburst of recent rain.

*

The afternoon lapses into the background
as its shimmering surface holds sway,
making the still moment a mirage of itself,
baking it into memory, an infrangible clay.
Draped across stone steps, sun glorifies
the torpid gravel, shows up a whitewashed
courtyard, imbues a hedge with light
entwined so ardently with every leaf
you must avert your dazzled eyes.
A wasp's narcotic soundtrack amplifies.
It is all beyond belief.

*

We've lived under a cloud all winter,
uniformly grey, like small print
setting out warranty restrictions.
Now a shiny new day dawns,
luminous as ice in a champagne bucket.
Ozone's sunscreen melting, will we
weary of displays of solar might?:
fearing its heat monotonously
bearing down, invading our
space, always butting in,
hogging every conversation,
making us sweat it out,

casting a stifling shadow
on our lives, febrile brains
fantasising about sleet and snow,
olden days when skies pencilled in
a fence of charcoal cloud
and a mild sun beamed benignly
through random slats, rays
dusting rain-irrigated crops.

*

Abandoning the peat-scented heat in which
fireside chairs nested, we blunder towards the car
parked where the farmyard light runs out
and night sets about its work in earnest.
A lamp's beam would only bounce off
the solid black substance which engulfs us,
increase our sense of inconsequence when
up against colossal odds of time and space.
Spreading wind-borne rumours, pine trees
taunt with the doom-laden prophecies
of graveyard yews. A few low-grade stars:
too far away to comfort or shed light.

*

Whatever pious upward-gazing
eyes once saw in the sky's reredos
has become a blur, the apocalyptic
light of dusk – wines, divine golds,
daubs of ceremonial purples:
colours mixed in the sun's image
like the abstract canvases we stand
in awe of at a gallery's sanctuary
as though waiting for the heavens
to open and the veils of our temples
to be rent with intensity of vision.

*

These wintry evenings, the moon – pale
undertaker – shows up with indecent haste,
ushering away the day's remains as soon
as the sun shows signs of wasting, turning cold.
Trees and hedges reduced to squiggles, a rough
sketch, it's back to the drawing board for nature.
In fairness, the vigilant moon keeps its flame
discreetly burning into dawn when the irruption
of a thrush, finding its voice again, lends a certain
splendour to the morning: a wake-up call,
ruffling the feathers of the incoming day, fluffing
them up like the clay in this newly-harrowed land.

*

For as long as the sun can hold its
dominating role, there will be beauty
of a kind: the kind that turns the tide
of rain, trapped on a flat warehouse roof,
into calm seas dipped in syrupy light,
putting the musty word *refulgent* through
its paces, its meaning given a new gloss.
Mosses invade a rooftop overflow tank
like sea lettuce wading a rockpool;
and the ballcock makes a striped beach ball
drifting distantly away under the dreamy
no–cloud sky of an essay on school hols.

*

Summers after work, we drive out to take
the light, burrowing through gilt–edged
tree tunnels, emerging to fields and hedges
shown to best advantage in the evening sun,
delighting in a realm of pure contingency
where every vital detail is left to chance,

light freely associating with gradient of hill
and radiance of rock, arranging serendipitous
meetings of stocky sheep and elongating
shadows, sweeping over obsolete machines
in ramshackle farmyards, permeating lanes.
Sun visors down like knights,
we fend off winter for another day.

*

Having tapped in the alarm code,
like clearing passport control,
I linger at my open doorway,
standing in the sun's light,
blocking its path, knocking
a man-size dent in its rays
while shamelessly poaching
whatever heat I get away with.
What was it I needed to attend to
urgently as soon as I came home?
Immobilised by light, I find my
place in the sun, transported by
this unexpected stroke of luck.

*

Nights don't come much blacker
than this, backup lighting of moon
and stars having failed to generate.
Every trace of life obliterated, you are
up against the ends of the earth.

*

Somewhere the rush of spring water.
Somewhere the excavator-yellow of furze bushes.
A laburnum resurgence sighted through a pergola.
Unimpeded light – every pore translucent – recalling

an age when the sun looked indulgently on a world
in its prime, a planet slanted in favour of its rays
yet unable to absorb so much illumination at one time.

*

While your mother furls the blind, pulsating
sun sneaks in behind her to your sickroom,
underlines the mid-morning peculiarity
of a day off school, an uncanny stillness.
Chest of drawers and wardrobe reverberate
with light as the thermometer advances
a further notch, like a child's height chart.
She settles the bedclothes crisply,
straightens the candlewick quilt, bolsters
starched pillows and leaves you,
with an aftertaste of cough potion,
drowsing in her shadow; woozily paging
your favourite comic; doused in tonic light.

*

January: the zealous moon outshines
everything for miles, out on its own
despite a full complement of stars.
By morning, though, it is a burnt-out
case; a car's frosted windshield;
the ceiling cobweb a brush with
the wing of a migrant goose would
sweep away; a plaster death-mask.
Now jets are sketching trails
in vapour, their lines the shortest
distances between two cities.
To no great avail, a wintry sun –
splinter of ice in its heart – makes
a stolid showing above a fresh,
unyielding pelt of settled snow.

*

An Indian summer in late September
stretches the definition of the season
well beyond what's strictly reasonable,
conceding the latitude everyone – no matter
what their age – relaxing at those pavement café
tables pleads for secretly when the appellation
'young' is doled out casually in conversation.
The sun enjoys its final fling, a last fine careless
rapture, burning its midday oil, as a throbbing
love song hovers above an open sports car.
Living for the present, putting all thoughts
of a rainy day on hold, friends catch the waiter's
eye for a latte top-up or a half-carafe of red.

*

Enhancing the landscape like a soft-focus lens,
a winter mist restores the world this early morning
to its pastoral phase, harmonising clashing colours,
breaking down barriers between field and road
and forest, laminating mountains, sealing in their
freshness, our landfill waste and quarried devastation
vaporised, industrial estates proving biodegradable.
Even the power cables – straight as potato drills –
might be the threads binding the whole narrative
web together, spinning out the seasonal cycle
for a further 1,001 days or however long it can –
without sagging or faltering – still be credibly sustained.

*

To hold a waxed orange is to play with fire,
to watch a blazing torch annihilate the darkness,
lending you the night vision of a marmalade cat.
Best of all possible worlds, its fleece-lined inner
skin is warm even to the eye; it worships light without

395

the swivelling sunflower's anxious scouring of the sky.
Remove one citrus grove from the picture and you
cave in to dark forces, extinguish brightest hopes.

*

Clouds in tatters. The sky fragmented,
shattered dramatically into a million
wads of colour. A thin veneer of cumuli
appears for all the world to be an inverted
beach, tropical sands at sunset,
the kind of resort which travel
brochures invariably dub *unspoilt*.
And though it's morning here, not night,
cold not hot – trees redefined by mist,
delicately nuanced hills, brittle,
vitreous, icy grass – the sky paints
a different picture, totally over-the-top,
laying on molten reds with a palette knife.
The day is dead. Long live the day.
Things hang in the balance for a minute,
the sun itself unsure how the near future
might pan out, but already scheming
to leave early, abandon this morning's
potential, slink away at the first sign
of evening's narrower horizon kicking in
to cut off the last escape hatch that remains.

*

A rainbow tacked on to the sky –
fridge magnet, temporary tattoo,
crèche logo – has a way of prompting
primitive responses, adding a dash
of complication to the world,
redolent of those incongruities
we do our best to explain away
through open and shut laws

of cosmology which keep reopening;
doors of perception that bang on
in the draughty outbacks of infinity,
the awkward gaps between the stars.

*

Though winter starts to clamp down
on the light, enforcing a curfew earlier
every night, yet sun salvages something
of its former power, however tentatively,
on crisp December days, its clarity
cutting no ice, but slicing through
the human clutter nonetheless:
making its mark as a bright patch
perking up some aftermath
to the freshness of organic salad leaves.
On the overshadowed lawn, its calling card
is a fluorescent beam that leads
the whole way to the garden wall
and seems to touch its red brick with
inklings of a realm to which it offers
wider access, operating outside of time's
laws, moonlighting on eternity's behalf.

*

What I remember of the place is light:
its plenitude; how fairly it was distributed
across wheat-thatched fields given the run
of the country without the impediment
of a single hindering hedge;
brilliance so profuse that sunflowers
could not decide which way to turn.
Fluctuating butterflies, light on their feet,
fanned themselves against the summer
heat; bees rounded on lavender spikes
like harvest mice gnawing corn;

and, in a dusty lane under cover
of staggeringly leafy plane trees,
old men stooped to deal out metal spheres.
When sun had sunk to dusk level,
voices resounded from pavement cafés,
nectarine-screened courtyards, shuttered houses.
Sounds – wine glass chimes, clangs
of cutlery on plates, animated conversations
– jolted me back from reverie in my *pension*:
words impacting on each other
like the tiny metal dents left in lethargic
afternoons when *boules* collide.

*

Tailgated by stars, the long-haul plane loses
its battle against the dark: passengers too on
autopilot, cabin lights are dimmed, gibberish
drones through slippage of in-flight headphones.
Yet, all this time, resistance mounts; overwhelming
any final judgement, a rim of light – glimmer
of optimism – appears from nowhere, the sky
running ahead of bleary eyes as breakfast trays
are served, stars brushed away like crumbs.

*

Playing a disappearing trick
on the freeze-framed, heat-stilled day,
Seurat's paint becomes so light
it evaporates into its own haze,
atomises, breaks up like an
out-of-range phone conversation;
stippled grains that could be
tossed around on any breeze:
flecks of coastal sand,
unseasonable motes of snow.

*

Desiccated, dry-as-dust, powder-puff fields.
Scorched earth. There is change in the air,
some shift in the balance of planetary power:
trees strain at the leash of hurricanes, ground
battles deplete plant and insect stockpiles.
The tide turns in the sea's favour:
oceans burst their banks, glaciers snap,
icecaps retreat, meltwaters run like pus.
The world is too much in the sun.
Now the heat is on, threatening meltdown.
We who seized on the spark of promise
in drowned peat, mined coal-seams
to stoke up neon signs, squeezed mileage
allowances from refined petroleum, leave
our carbon footprints on the sands of time,
anoint machines with oils: driving a hard bargain;
wanting the sun, moon and stars; sure our
fossil-fuelled journeys through congested
dusks will lead as ever to a renovated dawn.

*

Think of a number. Double it.
Multiply that, for argument's sake,
by some astronomical figure to find
the rate at which the universe
is speeding into pieces or how many
depleted stars are concentrated
into ravenous black holes.
Round up the answer with your
calculating mind as you try to come
to terms with zeroes lined up to infinity:
so many light years for truth to dawn,
so many theories of dark matter,
so many millennia until night falls
on our universe and everything

on earth comes down to nothing –
like nothing on earth you could
imagine in a billion years.

       *

Difficult to second-guess what might
happen next, what climate of fear
we have coming to us in the future.
But, over today's horizon, May
appears in perfect working order,
seen in the best possible light;
bringing out the colour in furze bushes,
granting leaves a seasonal reprieve.
Butterflies contrive a soft landing
on extravagant polyanthus.
Grain shoots are gaining ground.
Sprays of rowan disperse scent.
And a still-gentle sun caresses
the brow of the hill: a cow
licking her newborn calf.

Dear Life

(2012)

God made everything out of nothing,
but the nothingness shows through.

— PAUL VALÉRY

YESTERDAY

Been there.
Done that.

Digested the three
requisite meals.

Reacted with
appropriate outrage

to whatever headlined
controversies there were.

The dead took no hand,
act or part.

The children of the future
made no demands.

Its like will not
be seen again.

Those of us alive then
had the whole world

to ourselves.
The whole livelong day.

SUB

And if, from the get-go, life were touted
like a magazine subscription, would you –
knowing what you do now – sign up?

Take the six-month trial ('Money back if not satisfied')?
Tick the 'Yes, please' box?
The 'Rush me' one with the 'Bill me later' option?

Or would you sit on your calloused hands,
refusing all inducements, declining
the introductory gifts, the easy terms
available to new subscribers?
Sit there, lend your name to nothing?

                    *

That warm morning, saved like a lock
of ungreying hair, when you dragged
a stiff kitchen chair to the garden,
the gold-embossed blue cover
of your school library classic
matching the hyacinth-blue wrapper
of the Cadbury's chocolate bar
you'd stocked for later pleasure.

That blackbird whose voice
was recognisable from the old
monastic poem penned
in the margin of a vellum page.

That observant lake: logging every detail,
poring over every movement,
taking an impress of the morning
like the credit card of a hotel guest
at the check-in desk.

That moment in summer when
butterflies re-enter your orbit:
package tourists bounding
through Arrivals in Hawaiian shirts.
The dipstick iridescence of a dragonfly.

*

You know well you'd end up
pretending to hover over the boxes
before ticking 'Send no further offers'
or the one starkly marked 'No, thanks'.
Then get on with your life.

FABRICATIONS

God is dead to the world.

But he still keeps up
          appearances. Day after
day he sets out his stall.
          Today, his special is

a sun-melt served on
          a fragrant bed of
moist cut-grass; yesterday,
          a misty-eyed moon,

a blister pack of stars.
          Lakes and mountains
are standard stock;
          flowers and birds

in season. The avocado,
          shining knight, and the
tightly-swathed cabbage
          remain evergreens.

Odd years, for novelty,
          he tweaks the weather
patterns, brings forward
          spring by weeks, lets

the crocus's petal-
          pronged attack on
frozen ground begin
          ahead of schedule:

softening air's frosty
        disposition; making good
the winter's blemishes.
        Special effects – flash floods,

meteor showers clashing
        overhead, the cradle cap
of a lunar eclipse – are reserved
        for visionary interludes.

Not that it matters;
        nothing is sacred anymore;
no one much takes him
        at his word, buys his

version of the story, seeks
        corroboration of his
claims; the steeple's beak
        no longer nourishes its flock.

People idly browse his wares,
        knock back samples
of coconut milk, add Gruyère
        to a quiche, test the texture

of the beach sand with bare feet,
        before resorting to the soft
option of a recliner: a pew from
        which to worship the sun's heat.

Blowing hot or cold
        as mood or precedent
dictates, he offers further
        cryptic clues – a flatfish

sporting two left eyes,
        a tree that moults fur catkins,
an orchid mimicking a fly,
        a blackbird whose bill

is toucan orange, a baby battling
        with acute leukaemia,
a cow resting among buttercups
        like a whale awash in plankton.

But few make the link,
        speculate enough
to track these fabrications
        back to source.

He starts from scratch each day
        with new creations: drafting
a summer dawn, he permits
        the sun – only minimally

resisted by the mist, a token
        skirmish – to assume control,
making for profligate horizons,
        lofty skies, beyond which

other universes stack up,
        dangled in suspense,
the way a mountain lake
        is cupped in sandstone hands.

And every pulsing star will live
        according to his lights,
individually illumined,
        nimbus visible to the eye.

AT REST

Even the most burdened of businessmen –
time is money merchants – are out for
the count, paying the price for switching off
in favour of the weightless state of sleep
by giving up each night's potential output
gratis, like the takings of a benefit gig.

Happy as the night is long, dreamers
revert to a primitive stance and – working
components flipped to standby mode –
heave steady breaths like sighs of relief,
snort the addictive air. Slack penises relax
at half mast, a complete flop, breasts level off.

Equality officers, hedge-fund speculators,
lap dancers, rubber tappers lay down
their lives, defenceless against the night's
inexorable threats, naked or attired in flannel
bedwear, stripped of rank. Can evolution
not dispense with this primeval throwback?

Why – buttressed with labour-saving devices
though their existences may be – are the most
upright citizens brought to the brink of collapse
at the tail-end of every day; nothing less
than this comatose opt-out between duvets,
sheets meeting human recuperation needs?

And they regain consciousness reluctantly,
never as refreshed as they'd envisaged,
the startled faces in the bathroom glass
unshaved, unmade-up, unreconciled,
moon-pale and drawn as ever, sleep
always failing to put off the evil day.

SPARE US

Spare us the spring.
Spare us its garish light.
Spare us the nerve-thumping
rhythms of hopping balls:
empty vessels, sterile leather eggs.

Spare us the false optimism,
the short-term vision, the hint
that winter has been dealt a fatal blow,
that days will keep on stretching,
an economy in boom.

Spare us the emotion of
the choked-up lawnmower
champing at resurgent grass.

And spare us, no less, the need
for wonder: it demands
too much suspension of belief.

Spare us our jaundiced view
of daffodils, those clichéd ingénues
that wizen limply into spineless stalks.

Spare us the shivering snowdrops,
paling quickly to insignificance,
their holier-than-thou aura
melting like Communion hosts.

Spare us the scare tactics
of invading dandelions,
that urine splash from which
no clump of grass,
no roadside verge is safe.

Lump in the leaves – it will be left to us
to pick up their pieces, rummage
through their trash when the tree market
crashes and stocks are in freefall.

And spare us lilacs, scent so over-ripe
suspicion of some cover-up is strong.

Spare us the lambs – bouncing
with complete abandon, needing
no counsel of a *carpe diem* nature,
peeking from the milk-white fleece
of their mothers' blanket coverage,
or savouring mint-green grass
– on whom we pin dark,
raddle-marked declarations of intent.

Spare us the ardent couples
conferring at the paint store, torn
conspiratorially between Dewberry Frost
emulsion and velvet-finish Moonlight Bay.

Spare us the bees raiding every flower in sight,
leaving no anther pocket unturned.
And the tantrum-throwing wasps,
in venomous mood, headbutting glass.

Spare us the spurned bird, egg on its face,
its singsong persistence in soliciting a mate,
its loutish whistling at wing-batting females.

And spare us the dawn chorus
that outwears its welcome
like a loquacious breakfast guest.

Spare us, therefore, the spring,
its fake sincerity, its unethical

marketing strategies, its deceptive
pledges, its built-in obsolescence,
its weeds breeding like flies.

CANUTE

I rush to bring this incoming seawater to heel

to check a new wave of aggression
          warn formally against excessive force
decree that the ocean should sign and seal –
          with its inimitable blue flourish – a binding protocol
on the territorial limits of its influence

I venture to take the waters by storm
          restraining their worst instincts
for conquest the destructive tendency they'd shown
          in pulverising strands with centuries
of foaming foul-mouthed pounding

the time has come to put a marker down
          stand firm against this restless
viscous trembling mess – too long pandered to –
          that slithers past my boundary walls
with brine-borne contraband

meltwater clear though my demands are
          insurgent waves still pillage
mustering superior forces for invasion
          I will maintain my singleminded vigil
curb spillage that seeks more than its own level

and spells bad tidings for whatever dry land may remain

THE SUNDAY GAME

How alive, how excitable
     they were back then,
when they congregated
     in the neighbour's kitchen
for the Sunday game:
     the one neighbour with TV.

Every spot is occupied: painted form,
     squat milking stool, squeaky
Morris Minor seat, with vinyl trim,
     reincarnated as a sofa.
They get stuck in: loud wheezy cheers,
     blunt denunciations of the ref . . .

Tension so immense that if
     a Cathay Pacific jumbo chanced
to touch down on the dung-plated
     sun-saturated farmyard
not one would cast a living
     glance in its direction.

Except, that is, the woman of
     the house: she lifts the kettle off
the hob again, fills it from a shaded
     bucket, the summer-blistered
hall door open to all comers.
     No questions asked.

COMPO

Be absolutely apoplectic.
Fuming mad.
Lobby. Picket. Hector.
Threaten to bring your case
to the highest tribunal in the land.
Demand a proper compensation package.
Counselling. A confidential help-line.
Throw a tantrum. Go ballistic.
Let them know what rage is.
Insist on full transparency. Accountability.
It's just not good enough in this day and age.
Independent experts have shown.
Leading consultants proved.
Hold out for answers for however long it needs.
Draw the line.
Give dog's abuse.
Call for the politicians to do something.
Get off their fat arses for once.
There's simply no excuse.
It should all have been foreseen in the upper echelons.
They haven't heard the last.
No way.
Someone has to take the rap.
You're fed up to the teeth.
Won't stand their crap one minute longer.
Heads must roll.

LAST STAND

God gets nothing right these days,
our ways no longer his ways.
Growing in number, boldness,
his antagonists, planning his overthrow,
refuse to let him stand on ceremony.

Preaching the gospel of human autonomy,
cosmologists supply creation
with a rational basis, a credible pedigree,
a back story, obviate the need for
divine intervention, miracle solutions.

Those consecrated to his cause
were cheated of their lives,
wasting their sweet intentions
on the desert fathers' airs.

Those who feared his might
recoiled from a mere figment
of their warped imaginations.

Brown-robed monks, tonsured heads
crammed with nonsense about eternity,
who spewed out orisons in concert,
were simply amusing themselves,
plainchanting inanely like
their enclosed communities of bees.

Calligraphic scribes, living by
his vision, wringing colour from
his precious stones for pigment,
hanging on to every facet of his word,
illuminating his script, observing
his declarations to the letter,
were no better than doodlers:

wet–day children amused
with a colouring book.

Nuns in wind–chastened mountain
convents, averting eyes from the world,
were victims of a confidence trickster;
virgins of whom he took advantage shamelessly.

The faithful, intoning rosaries in lakeside
retreat houses – bequeathed in his honour
by pious, misguided devotees – were left
addressing high, drystone, whitewashed walls.

His time has come to do the decent thing:
throw in the blood–soaked towel, abdicate
his throne, bow out finally, allowing the will
of the long-suffering majority to prevail.

Impossible to pin down, he has fallen
as silent as the infinite spaces
that rendered Pascal mute:
gaps unplugged in the universe.
Silent as the contemplative order
sedated in the terminal ward.
Silent as the tongues of dusty shoes
dumbfounded in the Holocaust Museum.

His era has ended.
Truly free at last
to pursue the good life
without his spoilsport
interference – not cast
as baddie always,
stigmatised with guilt,
browbeaten to confess –
you are absolved of every sin.
Now let thy earthly will be done.

TABLET X

[Gilgamesh]

Life, ruthless boss, lays us off
without protective notice.
Contracts strictly short-term.
Not one position permanent.

Uprooted from whatever
plot we try to make our
own, we are tossed away
like brittle reeds: there

one second, then – *snap*
– downgraded to the playthings
of a random breeze.
The personable young woman

amassing a high-achiever CV,
defying talk of a glass ceiling;
the raring-to-go young man,
beginning to hit his stride:

they lose ground in time,
caught in a downward slide
of degeneration and decline,
net contributors no longer.

*

And yet we flail about –
signing up for reiki treatments,
touting for new business,
doctoring mortgage forms,

labouring over garage
conversion plans, testing

missiles, feathering nests,
threatening neighbours with the full rigour –

when all the indications are
we are not long for this world:
waste water; sluice gate
froth thrown overboard.

Our mayfly existence –
one-day wonder – is done with
in a flutter, the current
registering no loss, ironing

out its ripples like a girl
smoothing a wrinkled skirt.
Death is the very spit
of life, its flip side: see

how alike they are –
those dead and those
asleep – when the former
repose on the mortuary slab.

Your survival is at
the pleasure of the gods,
their whim, your itinerary
plotted right to the final stop.

They it was who sanctioned
your first gasp of breath.
As for when you may
anticipate your last

and let death have its day,
their lips are sealed like
coffin lids, the whited
sepulchres of mighty kings.

TASKMASTERS

Now that your nose is to the cornerstone,
you'll stay the course, top off each block
with slops of mortar, bring down the trowel's
iron discipline like a ton of bricks.
And soon you're in the swing of things,
absorbed by what you'd dreaded,
content as someone settling in a train,
aromatic latte in hand, newspaper
and glossy mag secured underarm,
moist caesar salad sandwich in reserve
behind protective cellophane –
an emergency lever encased in glass.

*

Spring's surge of hormonal urgency
has long abated as you succumb
to ennui, wondering what you'd
ever seen in that hyperactive season.
Winter's scorched-earth policy takes hold
with a vengeance now, killing off everything
unable to fight back through hardy networks
of roots, brutal bare-knuckle thorns.
Snow flaking from damp walls of cloud,
the ascendant moon assuming pole position,
you abandon every pretence at outdoor
chores, build up defences from
the stockade of logs – the past year's
hatchet jobs – you'd laid in for
the open fireplace of your tied cottage.
You might decide to sketch out plans
for next summer's borders, browse
online catalogues of exotic shrubs.
But chances are you'll just lounge there
on the leather couch, tap into a glass

of home brew or boil the kettle for a warm-up
snorter of hot whiskey, deplete your stocks
of heather honey, lemons, cloves.

*

Oh for the gift of eptitude. No task too big or small or awkward.
As nifty with a reciprocating saw as with a humble bradawl.
Adept at fitting unfamiliar widgets instinctively in place.
No ceiling, joist, masonry or quarry tile an impediment.
Marking out a rebated joint one day, knuckling down
to a cavity tray the next; checking the leak from a valve
spindle, then flush-mounting a socket outlet nearby.
Keeping the show on the road, the jets in the air,
the world's motor lubricated, its axis oiled; waving
aside the clients' plaudits, though their bafflement
is absolute when that guiding hand withdraws.
But by then their lives are set to rights: piped water
sourced again, heat coursing through radiators, the car's
smutty engine blasting off with rejuvenated smoothness.

*

Then wrapping up a job, settling the tools in
the metal box, folding paint-drooled drop-cloths,
snapping the padlock back on the garden shed,
hosing down your splattered boots, changing
into a fabric-softened cotton polo shirt.
Even clicking the cap on the felt-tip, after
you sign off on the planning application.
Filing invoices, certificates, receipts
once the online tax form is completed
and the *Send* button flicked with relief.
Unwonted moments when all the pieces
cohere, loose ends tie up, quandaries resolve.

HEAD OFFICE

Gingham boxers. Toiletries.
Off-duty jeans. Workout tee-shirt, shorts.
Tablet loaded with the files
the showdown with the local unions
will require; stats to back up sobering
disclosures; an update on rebranding plans;
the latest on outsourcing routine maintenance.

How do they find the time to pack?
When does their schedule permit
a window in which they can be measured
for those slim-fit, lilac-striped shirts
matched with jacquard silk ties;
the smart, hand-crafted suits
no one would confuse with
scruffy off-the-peg stuff
middle managers luxuriate in:
chainstore shirts with buttoned
cuffs, half-pressed concertinaed
trousers sweeping the ground?

And when do they snatch the chance
to top up that stand-out tan – keepsake
of some beachfront villa break – that glows
in defiance of all rumours of low market
expectations, negative consumer sentiment?

It's that hour of evening when they
touch down at the airport in time to dine
with a joint venture partner, make a start
on the interim trading statement, review
next day's arrangements, text home, fire off
an ass-kicking circular to marketing staff.

Stand well back. Here one comes, shooing away
the taxi change, grabbing the wheeled
bag in one firm hand, the other ensuring
the cellphone's unbroken flow, then – ignoring
the bellhop's proffered cart – breezing past
the top-hat-doffing doorman to the Carrara
marble lobby and the check-in desk where –
the still-vocal mobile shouldered now –
a gold card is extracted from the ID wallet's clutch.

SYNOPSIS

Life passes at a breakneck rate.
Brisk as text messages.
Time only for the executive summary.
The Dummies' Guide.
The podcast highlights.

The quick synopsis.
The cursory look.
The celeb gossip.
The abridged audiobook.
The no-frill stats. The FAQs.

Reading on a need-to-know basis.
Tweets of Breaking Sports News.
The World at a Glance
in the commuter freesheet.
History a volley of bullet points.

EXHIBITION

How would you like him done
as he roasts on his spit, taking the brunt
of the afternoon heat, skewers
gouging his hands and feet?

How exactly do you like him served?
Rare? – lance-pierced, oozing
maroon juices. Flambéed so fiercely
that no blush of butchery remains?

Do you take illicit pleasure in seeing him
finally nailed down – a bird of paradise;
an exotic death's-head moth,
arms outstretched like spindly wings?

Are you not altogether sorry to watch him,
rigid as a board with fear, tasting
his own medicine, sampling
the pain he added as standard –

with no convincing apologia –
to the human package deal?
Can you bear to catch him squirming,
bursting at the thoracic seams,

flesh vented with gashes, flensed,
the fractured laths of his rib cage
glued with blood as, subdued by
a centurion, he lies in his bed of nails?

Do you favour a script, like
a suicide note, above his head,
sending him up as *King of the Jews*?
Or would you let the scene

speak for itself, as a motley crew
of gawkers, spear-toting soldiers,
and his own blue-gowned
retinue sink to their knees?

Ought he to sleepwalk the plank
into the unknown? Or make his
escape like a contortionist,
reprieved nepotistically

by a *deus ex machina*?
Should you let him go hang,
exercising his free will to embrace
his plan with open arms?

Or, man to man, must you talk him
out of his grotesque death,
grant him your pardon,
commute his sentence to life?

AUTUMN

after Rainer Maria Rilke

Yielding to their frigid nature,
the weeks turn hard as frost.

The dayglo summer-registered liner
drifting serenely past – blue sky

an unflappable flag of convenience –
faces into choppy waters laced with ice.

Wrap the granite sundial in velvet
shadow. Let loose the winds:

release them back into the wild,
awarding them the freedom

of the planet, room for manoeuvre
under porous windows, doors.

Let the word on the grapevine
speak of essences: glutinous

fruit whose case is pressed
into red wine, condensing

summer's exuberance in a cask.
Those without a home will

never put down roots now,
building hopes on flimsy cardboard,

taking cold comfort from a bridge's
solid roof; it is too late in life's

season to contemplate a fresh start.
And the lonely – drafting lengthy,

unsent letters – adjourn sleep;
or walk the streets in no

particular direction, damp leaves
dogging their feet at every step.

REVENUE CUSTOMS

I   *Choir*

Let's hear it for the Revenue Choir, always
in place for the Tuesday night rehearsals,
putting a brave face on their way of life
irrespective of the vagaries of compliance rates,
lending grace notes to their line of work
whose clientele is never less than rancorous.

Listen as – after a shaky start – they bond
together in one voice, forging a harmony that
brings rapport between the contralto from
Large Cases and the bass from Prosecutions,
striking a note the Tax Credits expert
seconds, adding his full-throated support.

Give them a big hand, ladies and gentlemen,
whether at the Christmas concert, raising
the roof in aid of the homeless – who eke out
a life below poverty line, tax threshold –
or singing the praises of Handel and Bach
at the annual Mass for deceased staff.

II   *Museum*

Sometimes at end of day, filing
your papers away, exiting from
spreadsheets, flagging tomorrow's
priorities on your electronic diary.

Sometimes at end of day, when
the office eases into off-duty mode
and unfinished business – tricky
queries, constituency lobbying,
Ombudsman appeals – is put on hold:

network records backed-up,
plastic water pitcher communing
with its cooler, the row of corporate logos
watchful on the open-plan PCs.

Sometimes, at times like these,
they come to mind: old friends
and colleagues; bosses who were
sticklers for detail; dexterous drafters
of sub-sections, pluggers of loopholes;
custodians of the frosted public hatches;
income tax staff inured to tonguelashes;
larger-than-life characters – long dead –
who live on in these museum rooms.

Officers whose squashed initials
left their marks on carbon-copy letters
in archived files, who ruled these
marbled-papered daybooks now on show.
Staff who served at prefab border stations
or made landside seizures
of contraband at airport exit channels.

And sometimes at end of day,
the silence probes so deep
it proves an audit of official lives,
the years from shyly signing
entry papers in the Personnel Branch
to the long-service presentation by the Board.

Years showcased here, impressed in wax,
crystallised in glass, enshrined in paper,
pewter, brass: the past saved for the future,
like a budget surplus; not excised from
the record, but salvaged like scorched ledgers
from our war-torched Custom House.

III *Retirement*

I lost command of the integrated taxation system,
reconstructions and amalgamations legislation,
CGT multipliers, consanguinity reliefs. And there
petered out the susurrus of washroom gossip,

corridor banter, quick rejoinders capping my remarks.
Gone too the ecstasy of Friday evenings
every worker knows, the chastening
diminuendo that crept up on Sunday nights.

I forfeited my rightful place at the tea-break table.
An *I'm Boss* mug expectorating on the draining board.
The *Man United* one Tipp-Exed with a name.
A plastic milk container on which *Stats* is scrawled.

And I waived my advance access to the tax
defaulters list; confidential briefings on
exchequer trends; end-of-year appraisals;
clashes over heating levels, window openings.

Ten minutes fast, to trick me into rushing for
the morning bus, my hall clock was turned back
at last and could start living in the present,
its fidgety hands biding their time, not ushering

in the future any sooner than they strictly must.
My weary briefcase, facing redundancy from
leather fatigue, was relieved of further burdens.
I watched it – *I shall miss thee, Ariel* – wriggle from my grip.

After forty years, I could nearly hold the place
in my affections, look back lovingly at my
metal coat rack, take my last swig of the view
down the corridor's narrow undercroft

almost ruefully, leaving my office gutted –
cabinets in bits, cut-up desk borne
solemnly to a skip – creating space
for my successor to accommodate.

STILL

I know my type.
And I'm not impressed.
Throwbacks to an earlier age.
Set in our ways.
Getting more retro-looking every year.

Our dress code is old hat.
Our interest in networking sites is zilch.
Creatures of habit, we still insist
on written confirmations,
hard-copy documents.

Still hanker after printouts,
passbooks, cheques when
all about us bank online.
Still look to a wristwatch for the time.
Peruse the smudgy broadsheets for our news.

Spoilers of the nation's
vibrant image, its youthful
gung-ho status, here on
sufferance, surviving
past our die-before-date,

we fool no one with
our claims to feel
first rate, thank God.
Not a bother. Tip-top shape.
Touch coffin wood.

OUR FATHER

And we said unto God
'We adore you.'
                    Stony silence.
                    Cold shoulder.

And we added unto God
'We worship you.'
                    Another brush-off.
                    Further snubbing.

So, upping the ante
even more, we laid it on,
tried 'glorify' for size,
put 'venerate' to the test,
went all out, stretching
in sheer desperation
to our nuclear option,
proffering our ace card:
the heart-on-sleeve
one intimating 'love'.
                    Not a crumb of comfort
                    from stale manna
                    was lobbed back; not a
                    tacit acknowledgement,
                    a form letter.

Changing our tune then,
we picked up the old refrain:
'Our Father who art in heaven . . .'
                    Though we put his own encomium
                    where our mouths are,
                    took it verbatim from
                    his book, this goodwill
                    gesture was made in vain.

'You alone are the most high'
we ventured next, relying
on this flattering strategy
to win us a reprieve.

>Yet every bid for conversation
>openers foundered:
>he was all take,
>no give – aloof, withdrawn,
>lacking social graces,
>a dead-loss at small talk,
>autistic in the distance
>he maintained.

His more needy hangers-on
hoped to read some esoteric
meaning in his silence.
'He moves in mysterious ways'
sufficed as formula
to mollify the docile types.
'The meaning is in the waiting'
a Welsh sceptic ventured.
'What does not reply is
the answer to prayer'
an English scribbler opined.

'Not my will, but thine be done'
boosted the next test rocket
we launched into his space
– more in hope than
expectation by that stage.

>And, true to form, not once
>did he engage, not once
>repent his stand-off.
>As though some feud
>among our families raged.

One millennium succeeded
another, without a thaw in this
cold war between the worlds;
no rapprochement of any
moment was forthcoming.

We were left no option but
to put the best interpretation
that we could on whatever
message was conveyed
by the attention-grabbing
voicemail he recorded
on day one: an opening
gambit that came out
of nowhere, bang
in the middle of nothing,
kicking up so vast a racket
we detect its background
music to this day, still treat it
as our sacred hymnal,
our foundational text,
a murmur from his bleeding
heart, as we peruse
the small print of atoms,
molecules, nanoparticles,
ruminate on lurid
supernova illustrations,
the illuminated manuscripts
of galaxies, over which lovers
pore in the dark nights
of their infatuated souls.

VALENTINE

Pure gravy. And don't forget it.
— RAYMOND CARVER

Back in hospital on this fateful date,
but to no complications for once,
I am discharged in good time to light
a candle on the kitchen table, decant
your Valentine's glass of sparkling wine,
sear the steak, sauté the onions, bake
potatoes till their paunchy waistcoats loosen,
launch the gravy boat on its salt voyage,
let mushrooms set sail on melting butter.

Life comes up trumps tonight:
a benchmark moment that we hope
to replicate; a precedent to ease us
through the testing times ahead;
a recipe for disaster aversion.
We note how simple its ingredients are,
yet how infrequently they coincide
in a single season, rare as love
enduring at millionth sight.

We rehearse its elements to
ourselves, like blessings counted,
rounding them up the way friends,
plotting a surprise party, will begin
accumulating mixers, napkins, dips for canapés . . .
Or as a hopeless man, laying down
furtive plans, might jealously
hoard pills, weedkiller, rope.

TESTS

What matters in this heartland
is the impression my chest
makes on the recording
angel's x-ray plate.

I am the colour of my sputum.
The composition of my mid-flow urine.
The density of my bones, made
irrefutably known through MRI.

The scrapings of blood that open
the floodgates to analysis
of my most revealing traits,
spill my deepest secrets.

     *

Death begins to seem a feasible
proposition, a viable option.
I start to look the part, meet the job spec:
age; constitution; medical track record.

Everything proceeds apace:
I might be an executive shortlisted
for a company directorship,
the hot tip in the race for CEO.

I am ready to throw my hat
into the ring, fill my parents' shoes,
follow in a family tradition that
goes back as far as can be traced.

FAIR GAME

The elephant in the room
is sick of being ignored,
presumed too thick-skinned
to have feelings of its own.

It raises its trunk in protest
like a megaphone: a corrugated
tube to amplify its message,
trumpet its urgency.

But the hall threatens to erupt.
Who allowed this cretin entry?
How did a beast so monstrous
squeeze into this conference space?

Should Security not have seized
its cutthroat tusks outside?
This ghastly animal must be sent
packing, dumped in the nearest jungle.

Get this elephant out of the room.
A show of hands will be enough to lend
the motion force: *Let there be no free*
speech for outlandish species here.

THE POWER AND THE GLORY

God's coffers have run low,
now that so many litigants sue
for restitution, demand redress.

He stands charged with misdeeds
of the utmost gravity: he let his garden
run to seed, neglected to purge it of bad

apples, failed to flush them from his ranks
for gross depravity, ignored equality legislation,
displayed no modicum of *noblesse oblige*,

never delivered on the commitments
set out, chapter and verse, in his
gold-edged, calfskin-bound manifestos.

Instigator of a terror campaign,
dating from time immemorial,
he inflicted death on every creature

he had brought to life: a massacre
of innocents, a planetary genocide.
His actions come back to haunt him now.

His record is open to criminal inquisition,
his underworld connections questioned.
His own judgement day has arrived.

We were hungry, but you didn't deign
to break our fast, his lapsed followers
chant; we were thirsty, they croak,

yet not a bead of water rinsed our throats.
We went down on our knees
and pleaded with you – to no avail:

we were expected to survive on a wing
and a prayer, thrive on parables, beatitudes,
pious aspirations, mystifying apercus;

promissory notes that might be
redeemed at some unspecified
time, some arbitrary last day.

You were all talk, never practised what you
preached, disinherited the meek, hinted at
a second coming, to keep us permanently tractable.

You have been top dog too long,
corrupted by your absolute power,
too habituated to the perks of high office,

at odds with the assumptions of a democratic
age when even a god should mix and mingle
more, prove a dab hand at crisis management,

speak in tongues lay people understand,
cut the arcane jargon of theology, cease
talking down, citing scripture for every purpose,

meting out the silent treatment to those
brave souls who challenge your behaviour.
No wonder your fan base dwindles

to a handful, your poll ratings plummet
to an all-time low: congregations, voting
with their feet, desert your sinking barque.

Enough of your prima donna stuff.
Enough of your cult of personality.
Enough of your craving for acclaim.

Enough of lapping up our worship.
Enough of tripping on our sycophantic hymns.
Enough of fishing for our compliments.

Enough of your divine right to rule.
Enough of foisting benign interpretations
on your unconscionable behaviour.

Enough of your surveillance of our minds, while
purporting to have fitted mankind with free will,
your graven image covering a multitude of sins.

PECKING ORDER

Numbers in decline,
        dawn choruses manage
with more modest forces
        like authentic performances of Bach.

     *

A one-for-sorrow magpie,
        rough diamond, on the grass.
And two greenfinches:
        consolation enough.

     *

How dainty the wren's
working parts must be.

How elfin the furnace
that keeps its heart warm.

How miniature the brain-chip
which triggers its alarm.

     *

Drop everything.
The blackbird – jewel on
the crown of the chimney cowl –
must be granted a fair hearing,
afforded the last word.

NOT THE DEAD

It is not the dead who haunt us.
There is no further damage they can do.
We have seen them to death's door.

Made sure they had expired.
Double-checked their pulse.
Tested them for livor mortis, breath.

Turned them over to embalmers
who stitched their lips.
Left them deaf and dumb.

Burned them to a cinder.
Buried them up
to their oxters in muck.

It is the not-yet-born
we are up against.
They will be the first to forget us.

Strike down our judgements
as null and void.
Rewrite our history.

Consign us to the past.
Find solutions to what baffled us.
Put us down to experience.

Outlast us.

TIME ENOUGH

The tally of years
added up so rapidly
it appeared I had
been short–changed,
tricked by sleight
of hand, fallen victim
to false bookkeeping.

Yet when I checked
my records, each
and every year had
been accounted for,
down to the last day,
and could be audited
against old diary entries
(client briefings,
dental check-ups,
parent-teacher meetings,
wedding anniversaries),
verified with credit
card statements
(multi-trip insurance,
antibiotics, concert bookings,
mobile top-ups).

And, although
nagging doubts
remained – an
inkling that I had
been ripped off
in some way,
given short shrift,
made to live at an
accelerated pace,

rushed through
my routines with
unseemly haste –
nothing could be proved,
no hard and fast
statistics adduced.

I had, it seems,
unknown to me,
been living my
life to the full.

THE BARK

The bark knows more than we do.
It is sticking to its story, yapping all night
with a conviction very like the truth,
a credible witness statement.

That bark goes back a long way: it is
on the trail of Odysseus's tail-flagged
homecoming, as the dying Argos tries
to raise his standard to its former mastery.

Replicated in fleabitten city slums,
reiterated on remotest farms, it spreads
rumour in the night hours, alarming
those who lie awake enumerating fears,

assuring them their troubles will
not pass, their heartaches, pains,
will not last one day less than a dog's
lifespan converted into human years.

Barks call us into question, pitch their
message at a level we can apprehend only
too well: they speak our inner language,
adopt the idiolect we use in self-address.

Days that demand a snarling riposte,
canines exposed. And days that fetch up
nowhere much to growl about.

Yet, faithful to its calling, the bark
remains on high alert at all times,
never lets its guard down.

THE FINGER

Allow us
this much,

at least,
as keepsake,

father – your
legacy to

a world
you snubbed,

stubbed out
so abruptly:

your cigarette-
stained

index finger
daubed

in its sad
marinade

must still
remain in clay,

stuck in its
accusatory groove,

tanned by
your nervous

chain-smoker's
fumes, the way

an oak coffin
is treated with

a wood preservative
until fully cured.

THE LONG CORRIDOR

It was late when we chanced on the seminary.

Dark and wet and late. Windy, cold, forlorn.
Lights low. Not a soul to be seen, no candle
burning at either end of the long corridor.

The silence was the midnight ash sifting,
the ember-shifting stir in a presbytery grate.
The silence of pre-dawn meditation.

The incredulous silence that follows accusation
when the chilling message filters down the waxed
corridors of ears and a full confession is warranted.

                    *

Processing against the currents of empty space,

we contemplate the scrubbed, smiling
Ordination Day faces on framed photographs,
numbers dwindling towards millennial zeroes.

Portrayed along the hall in holy oils, set forever
in their pious ways, prelates robed in princely satins,
Sunday best, are taken by surprise;

men at ease with talk of *magisterium*,
fides divina, who believed – in all
good faith – they served a sacred mission.

      *

Bare ruined choirs, labourers too few,
the seminaries drift nearer the abyss;
and in deconsecrated buildings, converted

to hotels, couples immerse themselves in
whirlpool spa, jacuzzi, or mortify the flesh
with weights and treadmills in the gym.

God is well and truly dead and buried,
his name no longer raised in polite company.
Mystery solved. Case closed.

      *

High time, therefore, to leave the long corridor
– its wimpled lilies, its festering anemones –
to its own destiny, sad relic of another age.

Not the faintest ray, not the dimmest glimmer
of light, shines at the end of its tunnel
vision, not a glint of the infinite can be divined.

BLASTS

How come the winds of childhood
blow so fiercely, so insistently,
    still spill out their tales of woe?
You'd have thought they might
    have piped down long ago,
found someplace else to settle,
    something else to whine about,
given it a rest, stopped moving
    heaven and earth to underscore
their message, let off whatever
    head of steam had built up,
then made away for calmer latitudes.
    Instead, they regroup with new force,
roughing you up, calling your bluff,
    activating body searches,
triggering flashbacks, memory attacks
    that shatter your defences,
leave your self-esteem in tatters,
    bring your ramparts crashing down.
Just when you think those winds
    are sealed away with childish
things, kept under lock and key,
    sent to their rooms in deep
disgrace, placed under curfew,
    they drift downstairs and,
spoiling for a fight, recommence
    their bluster: dredging up old
horrors, insinuating blame,
    taunting you with backchat,
leaking secrets, blasting out
    transgressions from the past,
chanting schoolyard names.

SAY BUT THE WORD

You eat your ill-judged
      words in the early
hours, take them back,

retract them one by one,
      try to erase the memory,
remove all trace,

arrive at more benign
      interpretations:
some form of words

to set your stressed-out
      mind at rest,
broker a truce with

your unyielding self,
      allow you draft terms
you could sleep on,

leaving the record blank
      as the crumpled sheets
you toss between.

    *

Say the word 'Future':
      you despatch it to the past.

Say the word 'Silence':
      you undo it.

Say the word 'Nothing':
      you make something of it.

      [*after Wisława Szymborska*]

*

Phone home urgently.
     The power of simple words.
You never forget.

     *

So many of the things
     we go in fear of most
may never happen.

We fear them all the more
     the more they keep
not happening.

     *

Where there's life
there's hope.

Hope and despair.

Despair because
we can but hope.

A WORD

To set up house and home, share
bed and board, with a near-stranger
seems an improbable thing to do,
not least for loners like ourselves:

covetors of our own private space;
slow burners, not given – except
in irony – to extravagant endearments
and never to the demonstrativeness of

Valentine's Day deliveries to your workplace,
red-ribboned frivolities and padded cards.
Yet, by now, our understanding runs
so deep, we'd recognise each other

in our sleep and are sensitive
to the merest tonal fluctuations,
minuscule variations in mood,
permanently on the alert for the unsaid.

We charge summer sale bargains
to the same credit card; find ample
accommodation under one double sheet,
neither party yanking it too far

towards their own side; the porch's
long-life bulb aglow in winter, agog for
the arrival of whoever is the later home
to narrate the day's adventures;

communication so close we split
our colds between us equally, share
viruses like a joint bank account, a
comprehensive policy with 'named driver'.

So here we are, all these years later:
old-stagers of the kind we'd have been
quick to ridicule once, deride as
a couple too set in their ways,

presiding in near-silence over breakfast –
adjusting the coffee plunger, buttering
crunchy toast – with nothing at all
between them needing a word.

IMAGO

Somebody made in the image of a god granted us the benefit of his protection racket.

Someone answering to the name 'God' undertook, on the strictest possible conditions, to keep us from harm's way.

Some force, for which the word 'god' must suffice, stormed into town, promising the sun, moon and stars.

Some man of godlike stature gave us to believe there was nothing on earth – or heaven – we could not achieve.

Somebody purporting to be a god was ready to cut a deal on a time-share in eternity.

Some man with godly presence, adopting multiple aliases, turned up around the world, instilling hope and terror in the locals.

Some character claiming to be god's representative on earth, his sole agent, his authorised spokesman, snapped up votaries the way cash-for-gold shops amass their precious metals.

Some showman, up to his god-like tricks, on tour for a limited run only, mesmerised audiences with his antics: sea-striding, lacing tap water with best vintage, then genetically modifying the wine into his blood.

Some charismatic man, having stepped out of nowhere, relegated earth to a transit camp, dangled the prospect of permanent residency in his kingdom.

Some smooth talker, blessed with god-like confidence, trotted out his one-stop response to every mystery, the same pat explanation for every baffling facet of creation.

Some philanthropic figure who would pass for a god, basking in his offshore haven, backed by unlimited assets, was prepared to stand surety, procure eternal remission for good behaviour.

Someone omniscient enough to be a god pledged a further coming; but – time-span winding down, lamp oil running low – we fear we have been stood up, palmed off with this mystifying no-show.

HOW OLD THE YEAR

Summer's frivolousness, its *joie de vivre*,
its live-for-the-day impulsiveness,
gives way to darker moods.

The last of the bees, scoffing dregs
of nectar – shoppers with their
snouts in end-of-season bargain

troughs – have left the scene.
Swallows, like tax exiles, pack
for more lenient regimes.

Elderberries crushed for wine
are the broken blood vessels
in an ageing face.

Apples fatten into jams and jellies,
chestnuts in polished casing
are hauled over smoky coals.

Something chill begins to stalk
the land, proves itself a force still.
There is no going back now: too late

to stop the rot, resurface corroded
leaves, conserve them like the copper
fittings from some listed building.

An uncanny charge remains in
the space discarded by the songbird.
Condensation draws a veil across the glass.

You scratch about for things to do, change
the filter on the wintering lawnmower,
measure for extra shelving in the utility room.

The sun settles at a modest level,
its light on a dimmer switch, enters a less
frenzied phase, simmers in its own juices

like comfort food, a mutton and veg
concoction, stewing in a slow cooker,
for your homecoming from the wind-chilled dark.

Stars proliferate: sesame seeds
sprinkled at night on a bowl of oatmeal
set in readiness for a quick breakfast.

It is the time of lowered expectations,
long, unnerving silences, vitality slumps.
Night-class websites prompt old memories

of back-to-school resumptions, the tactile
pleasure of fresh textbooks, the rousing
whiff of newness wafting from unsullied pages.

How old and stiff the year looks, slowing
noticeably, showing its age, summer's
laughter lines wrinkling its rigid face.

Even the mightiest trees are ruffled: shaken
by the force of muscle-flexing gales, they drag
on their reluctant shadows, clinging for support.

Though chastened, less intense, the light can
still surprise, stepping unscathed from a great
weight of cloud; raising the day's stakes,

it comes down on the side of a field,
catches it unawares, places a possessive
finger on its ploughed-up ground,

offers no explanation for why this
should be the favoured one, allowed its
moment of pre-eminence in the sun.

THERE IS NO REASON

There is no reason they can tell
why this life should not go on for ever.
The unflagging adults bang about
already in the kitchen where the flypaper
is scored with victories over evil
and the sausage-spiced air
they could slice with that breadknife
sinking its serrated teeth
into a buttermilk-based raisin loaf
hisses as the frying pan's palm is greased
with newly-churned doubloons of gold.

Friesian cows top up with marginal grass
on rambling journeys to the milking
parlour's lactic whitewashed walls.
A stippled calf is on the loose
like a stray Dalmatian pup.
Frantic hens scour the yard
for something they never mislaid.
The chubby sow, slumped
in an armpit of mud, wallows
shamelessly in stained pink
nakedness, the full concatenation
of her tits on show.

Each day's routine is foreknown always.
Which field needs a fallow season. Which rotation.
When the seed potatoes should be planted.
When to risk the first nick in the meadow.
When the time is ripe for the combine
to make quick work of the corn.

Wisdom is a given, like the lush lime soil.
Like the climate which – for all their perennial whining –
gets it right on the whole, increasing (or not)

precipitation to the requisite extent,
turning up (or down) the volume of the sun
by the most appropriate degrees,
its tour de force their toast if it
delivers archetypal summer days,
hot on each other's heels, burning
with zeal to alchemise their crops.

Though not of this world, they know
full well each rood and perch they've
been allotted: its high points, its weak spots,
every vagary of its behaviour.

The last rounds of haycocks, raking in
the heat, sundried like sandcastles,
must be rushed away to the safe
haven of the barn in case the fragile
weather shatters into smithereens of rain.
Cattle – methodically grazing meadows,
not missing out on a single juicy shoot –
will be drenched against liver fluke and husk.

Wake up, children.
Get dressed. Fast.
Haven't you noticed it's morning?
A once-off morning, far too good to miss.
The sun has been casting about for ages,
raring to shadow your adventures all day long.

Be seated on the timber form
while your honey-sweetened oatmeal
cools and home-cured bacon
blossoms rosily on the pan.

THE FALL

The backyard wall
stands guard between me
and the cemetery
on the other side.

My garden haven
is a riot of colour,
red-hot pokers stoked
like flaming swords.

The far side is devoid
of life, headstones drab
as concrete slabs
of high-rise flats;

a living death: freedom
of expression is withheld,
travel rights suppressed;
scarcities abound.

Tenacious as a border
guard's Alsatian,
ivy sinks its vicious
teeth into the wall:

its fall will force
a regime change,
unite me with
that darker side.

BEST PRACTICE

Dear God!
Oh man!
How did a being of your supreme intelligence
get bogged down in our affairs,
dragged to our mundane level,
entangled in our fate?

Was there an element
of repentance in your actions?
Having botched our prototypes,
betrayed our cosseted first parents,
placed temptation in their way,
and – with apple tree as plant –
acted as agent provocateur,
laid a honeytrap for Adam,
did a guilty conscience
bring you down to earth,
shocked that creatures
made in your own image
proved so fallible?

Were you hoping
to amend our ways,
ameliorate our faults,
attempt a product recall,
make ad hoc conversions
to our fallen natures,
patch up our shortcomings,
adapt us to best practice,
tweak our hardwiring,
energise our lives with love –
like some new biofuel – in lieu
of our more toxic kinds of power,
high-octane club and dagger hatreds,
our machete and Kalashnikov aggression?

You went to incredible lengths
to become one of us: stressing
how intensely you felt our pain,
knew what we endured daily.
But how convincingly did
you play this snivelling role?
Were you not badly miscast
in humble guise, as you tried
to flaunt your bona fides,
flourish your common humanity,
while – a populist president with
a Liechtenstein bank stash –
the best seat in your father's mansion
was reserved for you alone,
who never shared our fear
of the unknown, who were spared
our insecurity of tenure?

Spoiled rotten by your privileged lineage,
born with an apostle spoon in your mouth,
you failed to rein in your snobbier traits,
your petulant behaviour, incensed by
those who questioned your credentials,
stamping your sandalled foot, letting
us go to hell if we didn't live strictly
by your book; willing to forgive us,
turn the other cheek, provided of course
we surrendered on your terms,
meekly adhered to the dictates
you set in stone, threw ourselves
at your mercy, adopted your norms,
respected your dress code,
conformed to your sexual constraints,
conceded your hierarchy of sins.

Your coming among us was
a madcap charade, a reckless
prank allowed to go too far.

You planned your death
as the perfect crime,
expecting others to take the rap,
get caught in the act,
while you washed your hands
of guilt, though the perpetrators
were mere scapegoats,
more sinned against than sinning:
dupes who followed your orders,
fleshed out your script,
gave credence to your actions.
And then, to crown it all, weren't
you sighted three days later
like a life insurance fraudster
born again with a new identity?

Espousing peace and sword,
you were street angel
and house devil personified.
You charged your father
with forsaking you, yet lent
your imprimatur to his brand,
established your cross
as a global logo, promoting
the family firm, and obligingly
fulfilled a plethora of prophecies,
checking them off, balancing
the two books to marshal
their testaments into synch.

You wanted things
both ways at once.
To play lion and lamb.
To be God and man.

And were never
more vulnerable,
never more

lovably human,
than in that
dithering spirit.

MEMOIR

It has been
absolutely

fascinating
being me.

A unique
privilege.

Now my
whole life

lies ahead
of you.

No thanks
at all are

called for,
I assure you.

The pleasure
is all mine.

PAPER TRAIL

Once, money had credibility. Its word was its bond.
The story it told was backed up by casket-shaped gold bullion
interred in cold, calculating vaults of central banks.

Once, money added up, was secure in its identity, knew
exactly what it stood for. It had standing: was seed capital,
buying power, providence, a healthy reserve for future needs.

The love of money was the root of evil. Yet thrift was virtuous.
Saving was good for the soul. The poor would always be with you.
You gave to God and Caesar, took whatever credit you were due.

Prudence was guaranteed. Fixed returns on principal assured.
Old money was deferred to, its ancestry traced to slavery,
hard labour, patented inventions, plantation estates.

The money trail led to the bank's rock-solid door: time locks,
safe deposits, a manager preaching restraint, making you pay
for your excesses, demanding deeds to underwrite his trust.

Then the bottom line turned notional; losses, gains
proved mere statistics, collateral for loans a default mode
consigned to timorous, wimpish, bygone times.

Labyrinthine instruments were trafficked on
global exchanges in the blink of a cursor's eye,
quicker than a bullish broker could roar 'Buy!'

Every big deal was a bonus for the Lamborghini-owning trader
playing the markets who (such heady discretion, such adrenalin!),
with a click of the finger, could drive his pedimented institution
    to the wall.

Now where does the paper trail – demented treasure hunt –
lead? When you follow the money, you are directed down
a dirt road that denies you purchase on its slippery surface.

You are on your own. Press onward? Abandon route?
Who knows? The silence, like a bubble, tightens hold.
Some miscalculation made has led you down this path.

STOCKS

while stocks fail
like blighted crops

your best investment
for a steady yield

a return guaranteed each year
is a field of grain

ears braided
like a pony's mane

sheaves of frantic grasses
easily swayed

but calmer when
a dose of drowsy

poppy blossoms
is dispensed

or risk a flutter
on a herd

of butter-sculpted
cows grazing

near a stream
from which foam

rises to the top
like cream:

crush market
forces with

a cloven hoof
a cheddar wheel

SNOW

Snow has sentimentalised the world,
      left it sugar-coated, a baked Alaska
conjured from the palest of vanilla ice creams,
      the purest of swan's egg whites,
its mushy, too-sweet-to-be-wholesome look
      topped with a confection of candied trees –
bare-branched candelabras – holly waxing
      eloquent with berries in a citric winter dusk.

In denial about whatever smacks of negativity,
      it stops death in its tracks, adopts a hard
line on burials, sets up road blocks, brings runways
      to a standstill, placing travel plans on ice,
permitting no escape from its airbrushed vision,
      plotting to frustrate communications
networks, keep bad news in abeyance, seal
      the mouth of every outlet, stifle all dissent.

Its powder washes whiter than any rival's,
      even the field-blanching moon's,
obliterates earth's lumpy surfaces, smoothes
      its awkward bumps, insists simplicity is truth.
Too good to last, too huge a con-job
      to sustain, too false a facade
to maintain beyond one season, snow's
      hour of reckoning comes, its defences

crumble like a pomegranate meringue
      gateau, churning mucky sludge,
a filthy vinegar of meltwater under which
      the world it wished away can be defrosted,
dust itself off, when spring's no-nonsense air
      prevails: its new twig broom will sweep
all vestiges of slush before it, letting life resume
      its complex, messy, necessary routines.

DEAR LIFE

you should be the love of my life,
my soulmate, the entire
raison d'être of my existence.

I have devoted my whole life
to your cause, doing my utmost
to stay in your good books,

keep on your right side, humour
you with guff about how truly
wonderful you are: a miracle;

the nest egg in which
I sank my hopes,
invested my life's savings.

     *

Impulsive, prone to whim,
more than capable of turning
against me without just rationale,

you have proved a difficult match.
Yet there are times, life, when we
seem sublimely partnered and I yield

to mawkish talk: losing the run
of myself, I start to blab about us
sharing the remainder of our days.

     *

Life gives
        us something
to live for:
        we will do
whatever it takes
        to make it last.
Kill in just wars
        for its survival.
Wolf fast-food
        during half-time breaks.
Wash down
        chemical cocktails,
as prescribed.
        Soak up
hospital radiation.
        Prey on kidneys
at roadside pile-ups.
        Take heart
from anything
        that might
conceivably grant it
        a new lease.
We would give
        a right hand
to prolong it.
        Cannot imagine
living without it.

        *

And we go to
        the ends of the earth
to further life's ideals,
        build on overgrazed
savannah blades,
        lop down

forest canopies,
        dole out supplies
of nylon tents
        to famine refugees,
purify our sewage,
        drink recycled piss,
having issued
        lesser species with
notice to quit,
        driven them underground,
sent them scurrying
        into oblivion,
stuffed them for
        museum displays,
glad to see the tail end
        of their ruddy butts,
their toxic fangs,
        their shitty scuts,
regretting only the loss
        of ivory supplies,
aphrodisiacal rhino horns.

        *

Life is a full-time role,
its terms and conditions
as tricky to get your
mind around as rules

of foreign grammars:
mastering its usages with
native speaker fluency
requires constant practice.

And it goes beyond a joke
as you grow to comprehend
the full extent of the
obligations laid at your door:

Save the planet. Cut back
on plastic packaging.
Shield your children
from chatroom predators.

Buy fairtrade fruit.
Love thy neighbour:
rein in your impulse
to beat him to a pulp.

Refrain from counterfeit
designer fashions,
defamation. Indulge all
things in moderation:

sex, embezzlement, booze.

*

Tossed together out of stellar stuff,
deposited on a hostile planet, left
to fend for our perishable selves,

pick up the entire tab – the total
cost of living – as though the onus
fell entirely on our shoulders,

we reap and sow for our survival –
runner beans, asparagus, mango,
whatever current climatic conditions

allow – plant tea on terraced hills
steam-cleaned in a brew of pristine
mist, try to make sense of our plight,

look to the star-crossed sky at night
for leads, trace the sparkle in an eye
to the cosmic soot and sand wedged

between the constellations, then track
the orbit of our ancestry down to earth,
crack open the fossil record where

an ur-parent slithers out of its allotted
habitat, worms its way from the sea
on thin, fin-like transparent props:

gasping like a transatlantic wave
collapsing at its final landing place,
it transmogrifies into our futures here,

equips us to cap oil spills, propagate
GM crops, foil teenage cybercrime, cope
with information overload, age-old disease.

*

Poorly adapted to the hazards
of the world, we don crash helmets
to soften impacts, our torsos
strapped to car seats for safekeeping,
heat borrowed from bedclothes,
sweaters, woodchip stoves,
always privileging our own lives,
keeping our digestive juices
flowing at any cost, even as
our prime is well behind us,
time stiffening its arthritic resolve
as we cling to dwindling existences
by walking frames, lean on
the acquiescing shoulders
of crook-handled canes,
help just a panic-button away
so that we can fend off
the death from which the breezy
medics shelter us, although it

goes on festering under our
noses, our cataract-blurred eyes.

*

No disrespect to death, but it meddles
too much with the living, ordering them about,
tormenting the life out of the able-bodied,
lodging bullet-sized tumours in soft tissue,
flooring the unwary with an underhand attack,
its one-track mind focussed on ambushing
its victims, picking them off like a serial killer
waging a personal vendetta, its bony finger
beckoning the unsuspecting baby
to its cot death, insisting the hour
of reckoning has come for the military chief
and the grief counsellor, diverting people
from whatever plans they've made, subverting
their potential to its own monomaniacal aims,
blowing them off course as though they had
sold their bodies in some diabolical pact
and the moment of truth – payback time –
had come to pass, undermining their
confidence in the future, dictating their fate,
altering conditions of service in mid-contract,
suffering life to carry on without them.

*

And after your parents'
Big Bang, here you stand;
you can do no other: too remote
a creation to be fathomed
even by yourself, but emitting
distant signals that attest
positively to your existence.
It is no easy station to be
assigned: inhabiting your own

474

space, knowing you will
collapse in on yourself,
and conscious, mean time,
of the dark matter you contain,
the dark energy that rages
in your sphere, the infernos
seething beneath the crust of skin
that constitute your very core.

*

Incapable of grasping a fraction
of the scientific data – the latest
takes on leptons, quantum
theory, gravitational entropy –
so much of which remains
above our heads, generating
more heat than light, we feel
weighed down with its gravity,
prefer to be left in the dark,
reduce the mesmerising
revelations to a human scale,
happily distracted by more
mundane stuff, try to reconstruct
the case for our pre-eminent
status as a species, recall
the whys and wherefores
of our special destiny,
making up rules as we go along
that harden into rituals
and laws, become elevated
to dogmas, superstitions,
myths, our assumptions
adopted as immutable truths,
our nobler and our baser traits
fractured into warring factions,
throwing body and soul into
the fray, one half living for

the dwindling day, the other
laying claim to notions of eternity.

*

Finally, I cracked life's code, bored straight into the nuclear core of its mystery. But having no paper to hand, I seized a newly-fallen autumn leaf, sketched my findings on its palm, not reckoning with the pilfering wind that snatched it from my grasp. Leaves swirl around my feet now in a crinkled tin-foil din. Thousands of leaves. A sybil's mixed signals, they shift positions, shuffle their decks like tarot packs, gyrate suggestively. I go on my knees in search. Keep on drawing blanks.

*

Thanks a heap, parents.
Your role in brokering my life proved vital:
you gave me heart and kidneys,
kitted me out with all the parts
I needed to assemble a full
working specimen of humanity.
Without your selfless organ donations,
how could I have known
how 'loneliness' is spelled,
gained insider knowledge of euphoria,
experienced the piquancy of mixed
emotions (pride in my children's
progress, say, allied to despair
of the future), learned to mow grass,
cook *al dente* pasta, etch a message
on train window condensation,
wait in a frigid church porch for
the hearse to emanate through rain,
report to Radiology
in my tartan dressing gown?
Muchas gracias, parents.
You were far too kind.

Where would I be without you?
You shouldn't have.

＊

Nothing is beyond our understanding.
We will unravel all the secrets
of the universe for sure, tease out
the machinations that set the whole
shebang in perpetual motion, gave rise
to spiral galaxies, planetary rings,
antimatter, moonstruck oceans.

We launch telescopes to screen
archival footage: old clips replay
the initial flint sparks of existence;
capture the razzmatazz that marked
creation's opening phase, firework
displays that touched off the inaugural
torches: eternal flames.

Everything is under control:
curvaceous as planetary spheres,
the nicely-rounded figures
(distances, light years) are reeled off
confidently by cosmologists,
backed up by dusty ranks
of blackboard calculations.

Yet it can be lonesome this
far out on evolution's path:
no ultimate destination agreed;
no ecstatic ending guaranteed;
no Yggdrasil, no Dantean dark
wood in sight, for shelter on
this exposed stretch of road.

And miles to go. And miles to go.

*

You know full well the struggle
nought availeth, know you are
duped, lulled into a stupor
by so much willing diversion:
drown your winter sorrows in
a steaming chowder, follow
the squabbles at the bird feeder,
relive your hour of glory on reality TV,
the ace goal that changed the fortunes
of your street league team . . .
Nothing whatsoever you have
done, won, accomplished – your
personal best – will add up when
your final balance sheet is filed,
no matter how persuasively you
spoke on some Toastmasters motion,
how sportingly you stayed the course
in the mothers' egg and spoon race.
Whether you were decorated by some
pretender deemed to be your king,
or did time in the sex offenders' wing,
you will not escape with your life,
despite taking the necessary steps
to pass on the essence of this venture –
doomed as it is – to future generations,
initiate them in your doubtful ways.

*

It's good on the whole
to be bypassed by life,
not thrust into the limelight
or the firing line, but not
forgotten either; dropped in on
intermittently – an ivied
abbey accessed through

a plashy field; an obscure
website registering a few hits.

     *

Demand for human life is soaring.
Projections for the coming decades
forecast unprecedented growth,
the scale so great, migration
of souls so commonplace, no one
can keep an accurate track.

Ganging up on hegemonic death,
our numbers must surpass
the skull–count of the all–time dead.
It only takes a few minutes to make
a man, a late 'Dream Song' maintains,
laying it on the line, but exaggerating

the case, when less than seconds –
teenage haste, spontaneous urge –
will do the needful consummately.
End–result the same in terms of hungers
to feed, feelings not to hurt, bereavement
counselling to dispense, convictions to appeal.

     *

Where did it go, that life
I once held firmly in my
grasp, heart fluttering
in eagerness, suspense;

fluttering like a bird
trapped between palms
before striking out for freedom
and wide open skies?

*

You have reached the postscript stage,
left just enough room on the thin-skinned
page to allow you set the record straight
(that one moral collapse, that single lapse
of judgement scarring you for life),
put the best construction possible
on your past, lend your behaviour
a more favourable slant, avail of this
breathing space to deflect attention
from your gaffes, spare your blushes,
permit some, at least, of your redeeming
features to be credited, before – too late –
you fizzle out into ellipses and your
life is designated a done deal.

*

Dear death,
we were destined
to meet sooner or later.
Now I've come to be
your understudy,
monitoring my regress
towards your ends.

Dear friends, you owe
a debt of gratitude to me.
There was a need,
statistically speaking,
for this diagnosis
to be pinned on
somebody, like blame.

So be glad it was *my*
name that was called,
my number that was

up, that it is to me
it falls to satisfy
the quota. And let this
be my legacy to you:

I saved your lives.

      *

When the results
came through,
I was no less alive.

Alive enough to know
the score. As alive
as the woman giving birth

in the top-floor ward.
As alive as the wailing
outcome of her labours.

As alive as the partisan
young man sniping at a
US convoy; the teenage DJ

deafening neighbours;
the broker notching up
another killing on utilities.

To buy a pair of shoes
was an act of faith
in my own prospects.

When I paid a bill,
my spending too
boosted consumer trends.

My referendum vote
counted just as much
as anyone's.

This was life
more or less
as I had known it.

I caught an inkling of resistance
from the corner
of the mirror's eye.

And when my stomach
grumbled, it was for
life itself it hungered.

ADMISSIONS

Before you do down life again,
badmouth a world that never lives up
to its billing, recall how glorious it seemed,
your unwillingness to let go, that evening
you were driven to Admissions.

Every shabby sight you passed
gleamed with some ameliorating
feature, mustering enough initiative
to demonstrate its best case scenario.
Your own scrawny excuse for a lawn –

one part weed to two parts moss –
glowed with previously unsuspected
zest; the day's remaining light was fraying
at the edges as the sun signed off on
the horizon's dotted line: a virtuosic chef,

concocting dishes from leftovers,
drizzling pigment, tossing in whatever
mix of clashing tinctures lay unused.
How carefree everyone appeared as
they flashed momentarily into view

along your painful route: tourists perusing
the early-bird menu, a buggy-wheeling
mother cutting through church grounds,
hoodies ganging up against the counter
in the steamy comfort of the takeaway.

That you fell for the world's seductive looks
that evening in the psychedelic dusk
is not to be denied; how some confidence –
insider information you had withheld until then –
was let slip: *and he saw that it was good.*

NOCTURNE OP. 2

A sad air's best for night as you mope about
the house, closing windows, checking doors.
Slow, cumulative strokes of the violin bow,
the most ruminative notes that can be coaxed
from the cello, nocturnes unlocked by black piano keys.

Strains that are trained directly on the heart
when its resistance sinks, like temperatures,
to a day's-end low: music that tells of how
things stand in the troubled world you now have
in your hands to potter about in on your own.

Music of the kind whose fearful darkness would
unnerve you as a child, but whose darkness
seems the very point, this late night here; a slow
movement's stark conclusions ringing sadly true.

Update

(2014)

THE ROCKS

The rocks are determined
to spend each second well.
They calculate on a geologic
scale the time they can still

reckon on, and have no
expectation of escaping
the sun's blowout, predicted
in a mere five billion years.

Stoically, they hold their nerve,
adapt calmly to their limited prospects,
expand or contract as each
season's heat or cold demands.

Intent on making the best
of things, they treat each day
as though it were the last, use
their time enjoyably while they may.

They will be dust long enough.

TICKING THE BOXES

Tick the relevant boxes
in this census form tonight
if you are still in the land
of the living at that time.
You must remain
in suspense until then.

You have all morning still.
You have all afternoon long.
One continuous hour.
A whole six minutes.
Twenty-eight precious seconds left.
Three.
Two.
One.

In which to lose your job.
Your citizenship.
Your house.
Your spouse.
Your child.
Your mind.
Your sight.
Your faith.
Your life.

Count on absolutely nothing yet.

STREETWISE

Do I what?
Of course. Of course.
I know him all too well.
We keep on bumping into one another,
me and that agitated man –
semblance, soul brother –
who mutters to himself at all hours
as he roams the streets,
comfortless in his own skin,
clearly a seasoned hand
at the contrition game,
in the advanced stages
of self-reprimand,
driven to taking disadvantage
of himself, vandalising his mind,
attempting a citizen's self-arrest,
staging a public show trial,
engaging in *ad hominem* accusations,
adducing self-incriminating evidence.

Settling old scores,
he practises own goals
compulsively, penalty kicks,
has them down to an art
as fine as the sword on which
a broken man will fall.

A middle of the night waker,
no doubt, tireless in his rigorous
self-appraisal; unable to mediate
a peace in the protracted stand-off
between self and self, hostilities
raging on both sides of his divide.
He is his own worst enemy.

Then the silent treatment begins:
no longer on speaking terms with himself,
he serves a barring order on his person,
wondering which – if any – of his selves
he should seek custody of.

Even in seemingly quietist phases,
his somnambulist's gait
gives his game away.
Scratched eyes. Contorted face.
How, without forewarning,
he lashes out suddenly,
lunging at some nobody
down a solitary dead-end.

BIG APPLE

bistros buffets
burger joints
brasseries
eat all you can
low-cal
fat-free
supersize
jumbo
triple scoop
club
dagwood
drive-thru
take-out
chrome-trim vintage diners
glinting through the night

greasy spoons
members-only clubs
farm-fresh wild tenderised
macrobiotic organic vegan green
fillet of supreme of cream of
puree prime-cut lean
tear and share
house specials
catch of the day
belly dancer singing waiter karaoke cabaret
delis where money can buy you anything
milk and honey
manna and ambrosia
house-smoked peppery pastrami
with asiago cheese on rye
spicy cilantro-marinated swordfish
cedar-wrapped ginger squash salmon
McDonald's Pizza Hut Dunkin Donuts KFC

O brave New World
that offers such abundance
O land of the free the obese the anorexic the bulimic
the morning-after lycra-clad joggers
strapped to heart monitors pedometers
protein drinks in holsters

spring sunshine reinvigorates the lunchtime park
at which office workers unlatch sushi boxes
fork tuna salads from their screwtop plastic bowls

lunch is a legitimate business expense
for the executives who don their Gucci specs
to scrutinise the wine list
in the Michelin-starred penthouse
while the bowtied sommelier
keeps his discreet counsel
until vouchsafed a peremptory nod

so much unfailing comfort to avail of
at the food bar where singles
ladle ready-meals for dinner
curried wheatberry salad lemon mint
citrus kamut chicken enchilada
orzo with olives edamame succotash
such a glut that surplus tons
are slopped out nightly into trash bins

next stop the gym
to work off excess cals
manipulate weights at muzak tempo
hasten to the treadmill's measured destination
man – like galley slaves – the rowing machines
resolve to test the latest low-carb diet
no greater terror to war against
than the sight of the accusatory
bathroom scales gaining ground
advancing like the hands
of the doomsday nuclear clock

halal kosher fast food slow
peeled prepared cleaned
julienned dressed sliced diced
seasoned stuffed marinated
traceable sustainable fairtrade
squeezed plucked rolled boned
smoked crowned skewered rotisseried
halved quartered drawn BBQ-ed
skimmed raw fortified with vitamins iron
microwavable suitable for freezing just add water

a people content to live with blueberry smoothies
bircher muesli soaked overnight in yoghurt
leek and pea risotto with grilled calamari
dreamy cream-filled cupcakes
chocolate malted crunch hand-scooped ice cream shake

prime T-bone onion rings hash browns
tempura-battered Chicken McNuggets
chinese cabbage tofu soup

wars fought in their names
are tucked safely out of sight
like the faceless illegals
who pick on asparagus tips
bow low in heat
to rows of big-hearted lettuces
frilled as the bathing costume of a paddling child
cooling off blissfully in her backyard pool

no need at all to soil your hands
unless they smudge on Belgian chocolate muffins
contract a tincture of the sticky spare-rib sauce

no antibiotic no growth hormone no gluten
no added sugar sodium no artificial flavours
no dairy no transfats no synthetic colours
no emulsifiers no bad carbs no MSG no 'E's

no issues no sweat
nothing whatsoever to fret about
worry yourself sick over
health inspectorate
food and drugs administration
biodegradable packaging
carbon write-offs making reparation
for refrigerated truck deliveries
guilty air miles
peace and plenty
and lots lots more where all that came from
everything *everything* to go

ESCAPISM

Even without these shoes, they would have tramped home happily on bare soles: a ragged army in triumphal march, so much did they miss their little shtetls.

Even without these metal prostheses, even without these crutches, they would eventually have limped to the finishing lines of their village squares, where dogs still kept expectant vigils, chickens picked their broody way through cobbles.

Even without their bales of hair, the houseproud women would have beamed as brightly as the full moon's candid stare through newly-fitted window panes.

Even without these suitcases, they would have gladly sent themselves packing, to rebuild the ghettoes with fired brick, secure the picket boundaries around their intimate Jerusalems.

Even without their teeth, they would have eaten heartily, treated each mushy dish as a Passover feast.

Even without these glasses, they would have tracked their way back by blind instinct, recited the joyful hallel psalms by rote.

Even without these canisters of gas, they would have died in the fullness of time, reunited with their bedside children, buried with full honours by grown sons.

Auschwitz Museum

And when, inevitably, the liquidator moves in, pushes you aside, convenes a meeting of your fretful creditors, you must seize the initiative at once, get your PR team cracking on communiqués for immediate release, putting a positive spin on your actions.

Learn to say you fell victim to a global downturn, stiff competition from the East, soaring labour costs, crippling taxation, unfavourable exchange rates, excessive regulation and compliance requirements – red tape gone mad – not to mention insufficient vigilance of cowboy operators, cack-handed official crackdowns on the black economy. Reel off, too, some spiel about decline in discretionary spending, shifting tastes, migration online of your dwindling customer base, the market flooded with cheap counterfeits. Slip in climate change. Commodity price hikes. The unreliability of raw material supplies from war zones.

Save face. Persuade acquaintances you've flourished in adversity. Bang on about a learning curve, the premium you place now on your cherished family and friends, enjoying quality time with your partner, assisting your kids with school assignments, life-work balance perfectly in sync.

Lay it on the line about your struggle, day and night, to save the business, slaving only for the taxman in the end, crippled by bank interest, the cash-flow tap turned off, ineligible for further subsidies or grants. Reference the effects of chronic stress. The health toll.

Or, with a mischievous smirk, shoot the breeze with drinking pals about the liabilities you've parked, jettisoned for others to worry over. And, lest debt collecting agencies or Revenue investigators home in uncomfortably close, you've made sure to shred sensitive records, stash vulnerable assets offshore.

Publicly, speak of failure as a badge of courage; at least you had the guts to try. Quote that witty quip you heard at Rotary: '... something ... something ... fail again better'.

It never hurts – voice quaking with emotion – to bullshit about some cod addiction: alcohol, online gambling, say. Depression hits the spot too. Steer well clear of cocaine. If more desperate measures are called for, be seen to sign into a clinic; play along with counselling until the storm has safely passed.

Always stonewall awkward questioners by reference to legal proceedings pending. You are precluded from comments that might prejudice the outcome of a trial. Your thoughts at this time are with your loyal staff.

And, needless to add, in cases tainted with a hint of impropriety, allegations of hanky-panky carry-on with employees, you must take the tried-and-trusted route of an ancillary statement from your spouse, a carefully-slanted declaration of the standing-by-you kind, the sort that pleads for privacy at this – what's the phrase again? – this *difficult time* for you and your family.

Express regret only insofar as absolutely necessary; even then, confine remorse within the narrowest parameters, lest you come across as wimpish, weak. Vaguely allude to possible new ventures in the pipeline. A clean slate. Maintain an option on name-checking God.

THEN

Hard though I know
you find this to believe,
I was actually alive once.
Alive. And well enough,
at least, to play my part.

I too faced heartaches, disappointments,
embarrassments and vanities
not all that unlike yours, kept up
with the pressing issues of the day,
registered weather's moodiness

on my skin, brooded on the big
life–and–death questions when
I indulged my more reflective traits.
And if it's any consolation,
it feels no less strange to me now

to conceive that I was truly
such a creature once,
and had some small say in how
the world – as it stood at that
time – conducted its affairs.

That my birth would not make
a blind bit of difference,
in the final analysis, does not
negate my life, and counts
for precious little against

the surges of unbounded joy
I felt, on better days, imagining
my highest hopes were still fulfillable.
There was everything to live for then.
It was all before me.

BORN FREE

We have been rumbled, unmasked,
shown up for what we really are,
reduced to our blood-and-water essence,
confirmed to be a cocktail of amino
acid sequences, interacting proteins,
myosin, insulin, enzymes and all
the well-documented elements
that serve as our nerve-wired contrivance,
our millennia-aged behaviour
still dictated by the same old trite
devices, manipulated by their primitive
bag of hackneyed tricks.

We are standard models, economy stock,
our systems equipped with similar
connective tissue, acting out –
to the last chromosomal cue –
the genome's encoded script,
not one among us capable of reasoning
for himself, every thought emerging
from the regulation synapses, every task
we undertake a reflex to some hoary
neural stimulus, a kneejerk reaction
to primal cognitive commands.

What gets you down is not your son's
accidental death, your acrimonious divorce,
but your crying need for a top-up of serotonin.
Blood sugar and hormone levels determine
the vicissitudes of your daily moods.
Prayers and swear words issue through
likeminded channels of brain tissue;
an equivalent succession of cortex processes
heralds an act of magnanimity or rape.
No better than the sum of our corporeal

parts, it seems, our heartfelt professions
of love are revealed to be the cunning ruse
of androgens to achieve their devious goals.

Plot as commonplace as the monotonous course
our oxygenated blood constantly adopts, we are
an open book, exposed to the close-reading
of a microscopic eye: a crow's intrusive scrutiny
of a hedgehog's gory entrails, its inside story.

AMOK

You feed your inner demon
with the prime cuts of your life,

fatten it, a hand-raised hog,
throw it your juiciest scraps,

let it run loose among
your private grounds.

*

Sniffing around whatever
chestnuts you've concealed,

it unearths secreted kernels,
starts squealing indiscreetly

on you, brings pungent
truffles to the surface.

*

Exposing your most tender
roots, it wallows in the mud

it stirs up, proves capable
of making it stick.

Your heart is in its mouth now,
your future in its cloven hooves.

TODODAY

Distance is the soul of beauty.
— SIMONE WEIL

How will this seemingly off-the-rack day
eventually stack up? A day that does
its routine duty, and is pulling out
the stops now for the usual grand finale,
as the sun, voyage terminating, discharges
runny colours like ship's bilge.

Will this day survive the test of time?
Will we live to see it notch up classic rating,
like a novel – posthumously acclaimed –
that had suffered multiple rejections,
a reappraised basement painting
newly accorded old master status?

Could this day – so humdrum it seems
forgettable – become numbered among
our very best: free of crisis, a vindication
of the quiet life; belated recognition for
an understated Sunday that shunned
the limelight, yet may still withstand scrutiny?

Might what appeared, in its own day,
to have made a modest splash, at most,
seem nearly faultless in a retrospective light,
redeem the reputation days gain for adversity,
shine sublimely in past tense, display
an unsuspected aptitude for happiness?

TRUCE

I have no idea what came over me.
It was so totally out of character.

Stand-offish – hostile even – though
I'd learned to be, I embraced myself
unwarily for once, renewed acquaintance,
blurted out a few supportive words,
enquired if I might help with anything,
plumped my pillow, dabbed my forehead,
gave me as much encouragement as I could.

I just cannot for the life of me imagine
what sparked off that rapprochement.
But I was glad we had laid down our arms.
It was exactly like old times, when me and I
were constant comrades, trusted buddies:
at ease in our own presence,
able to bear the other's company, enjoy
a no-holds-barred, heart-to-heart confab.

It was as if I recognised
this final chance for what it was.
As if I'd had some tip-off
about not seeing myself again.

NEW YEAR PARTY

By landslide vote
we drive the old year out,
unanimously pass
motions of no confidence.

It had been granted an entire year
to fulfil its promise, only to renege
on its mandate, plague the world
sadistically with tribulation.

The new year's manifesto
is progressive, forward looking.
Now we may turn a fresh leaf,
happy that winter's recession
will give way to steady growth,
longer, balmier, user-friendly days.

We take to the streets:
rabid supporters of the New Year
party, cheering its inauguration,
determined to renew its mandate
annually from now on.

Let the midnight countdown begin.
High time the bells chimed
with our boisterous rejoicing,
lent ringing endorsement
to our future prospects,
while last year's absolute ruler
is banished: Disgraced.
Outdated. Past it. History.

COMEDY

We have worked through most of life's
set-pieces now, assumed the roles of mewling
infant, truant student, canteen-fed breadwinner,
toothless, treble-voiced old codger.

Our 'exeunt all' phase is advancing:
the finale where the circling actors
dance their hearts out and the spirited
veterans earn a special round of cheers.

The wise old couple, the pair who
spared the king's abandoned child,
rise to the occasion, kicking up their heels,
ceasing for the moment to act their age.

                *

Lower the curtain while the going is
still good, and all the world's this stage,
while, fresh from solemn vows, the starry-eyed
newlyweds take their prolonged bows.

Nothing ill will happen while the dancing
lasts, while the enchanted audience claps time
to galliards and the tambourine-jingling
jester leads the rhythmic yelps and hups.

Bring down the curtain quickly, like a vinyl
privacy screen around a hospice bed.
Make no further scenes. Give no intimation
of what, ever after, takes place next.

THE MAIN EVENT

We frittered away so much of life
organising our lives –
scraping a minimal wage,
meeting household outgoings,
grappling with family demands –
we lost track of whatever it was
we were supposed to be alive for.

There was something about life
that resisted living, put itself on
the long finger continually,
lent precedence to the mundane tasks
that needed immediate attention,
so that we never quite got to the point.

Outmanoeuvred at every step,
hampered in our efforts to participate,
frustrated like snubbed customers,
closing time drinkers who failed
to catch the barman's eye,

we missed out on the main event,
rising each day to find
what diversions were lined up
that would delay us ever longer
from making life's acquaintance.

BREVIARY

Summer

The pickaxe plop
of a lobbed–back shot
all summer from
the tennis club.

*

Dinner

a woman in kitchen mitts
pounces like a boxer

summons her tardy
children from the garden

challenges them
to step inside

*

Blackrock Clinic

You take a turn:
the second left
after Ben Inagh Park.

*

Postcard from Tiberias

Sun brings out
the Sea of Galilee
in pure azure.

On a clear day
        you can see
God from here.

        *

1959

Best of all treats for the feverish
young patient: luminescent grapes,
pearls of great price for which
straitened parents sacrificed.

Fork out for a bunch in Bertie's
and he'd automatically enquire
'Who's sick?', then fling
an extra fistful in the bag.

Get Well gesture.
Corporal work of mercy.
Cure for whatever ails you.
Just what the doctor ordered.

        *

Magpies

Magpies curse you from a height,
fly off with scoffing sounds
when their protection racket is disturbed.

        *

House of the Dead

A day of ashen silence,
an icy chapel of rest.

Below leafless trees
with skeletal nests,

'wreaths of smoke'
heave from

a grief-choked
chimney breast.

*

The Accident

Had you spent a split second less at A.
Had you delayed an extra minute at B.

Had you hesitated before entering C.
Had you been a tad more cautious at D.

Had you bided your time at E.
Had you changed your mind before settling on F.

Had you clawed that accidental moment back.
Had you been given – A to Z – your life to live all over again.

*

Floods

Water under the bridge
flows from the tears of those
who cried their eyes out
over spilt milk.

*

End of Term

students at
the University of Life
we await our final grades

still ignorant
of how we
were appraised

no wiser
as to who it was
that set the tests

in the dark
about what
marks success

*

Taking Your Life

I know where
        you are
coming from.

But not where
        you will take
your only life.

*

Honoris Causa

Your last honorary degree
        will be an R.I.P.
conferred posthumously.

FAME

The bells your
name once rang
no longer toll,
their clappers
fallen silent.

FLIES

The flies of today
are no longer the flies of yore
— RAYMOND QUENEAU

No, they don't make flies
        like they used to anymore:
big bruisers with limber wings,
        fidgety legs kicking
germs in your face,
        capable of dismembering
a brace of roadkill rodents
        in a single, sated morning,
swarming to the crash scene
        like emergency services,
or slurping a drunk's
        hurtled spillage
while still appetisingly warm.
        Exemplary team workers,
they set contentedly about
        their tasks, humming
at their toil, rebuffing
        the distraction of

a baton-wielding fly conductor
        when they made landfall
on a butcher's luscious bloodbath,
        hygienically dispensed
with a load of roadside crap,
        or pressed a viral gift
on some unsuspecting
        beneficiary's kitchen.
Such hefty specimens
        there were in olden times,
a far cry from the scrawny
        pushovers of today.
A pleasure to behold:
        strapping, brassy chaps
with healthy all-you-can-eat
        mentalities, hatched out
on squelchy cowpats,
        flexing wrestlers' pecs
before a round or two
        of jousting with
pavement café diners,
        then cooling off in
soothing sirloin juices,
        backstroking a few lengths
in the deep end of a wound.
        We miss them bitterly
when summer comes,
        how they swooped down
like clouds of sticky heat,
        creating a lively buzz,
always good for a laugh,
        hassling cattle, battling
campsite picnickers,
        making a pass at lovers
supine in a fragrant hayfield,
        teasing listless sheep.
So unlike the gutless types
        in circulation nowadays,

prim, figure–conscious snobs,
     all skinny limbs, manicured nails;
failing to meet their quotas
     in the salmonella department,
remiss about dysentery dispersal,
     tolerating deficiencies
in cholera dissemination,
     proffering pesticide-based
excuses for their lack of breeding,
     a flyweight disgrace
to their species, betraying
     the heritage of brave forebears:
gallant freedom fighters,
     front-line combatants
against oppression by flypapers,
     spiderwebs and sprays.
Conscientious messengers,
     they conveyed first-hand
news of fashionable
     pathogens to die for,
gorgeous wings as glossy
     as a corpse's suppurations,
a pony's running sores.

LUNCHTIME

And yet, for all that you are
technically dead for decades,
certified as such in public records,
I know otherwise.
Only today I watched you
venture out in your paisley-patterned
crossover apron, elastic stockings,

bearing the good tidings
of your straw shopping bag
past the box hedge, wasp-pocked
orchard, heavy-lidded rose beds,
tenebrous sheds of sows,
suckler cows, deep-litter hens,
then face the full glare

of the unsparing sun
in light-headed meadows
basking on grass mats,
to find that the hay-saving men
are gagging for a sup of 'tay',
tongues 'hanging out
with the drought'.

And here you are,
now and forever,
unpacking the vacuum flask,
the luncheon meat sandwiches,
the newly-baked caraway cake,
the sugar-studded rhubarb pie,
the enamel mugs,

giving the lie to those
who gave you up for dead.

THE GOOD OLD DAYS

'The music of what happens', said great Fionn,
'that is the finest music in the world.'
— THE FENIAN CYCLE

And did his warriors not go on
to ask Fionn what the saddest music is?

I catch an old-style sing-song from
my Alzheimer neighbour's house.

She is home for Christmas,
her family have gathered in her name.

They chat about times past,
look back on her behalf to happy days.

Maybe Fionn's response was, 'The music
of yearning: that is the saddest music in the world.'

They press on with their reminiscing,
then launch into a further bygone number.

They do this in remembrance of her.

OBIT

Like all the mothers round the town,
ours was shamelessly immodest
when it came to talking up her children:
their roles in carol concerts, school plays;
their end-of-term reports; their drollery,
their funny deeds; the glorious careers
they would be guaranteed.

Now is our chance to do her
proud, in turn, show her to full
advantage, keep her memory alive.
How best to set about the task?
We can't very well mention her
prowess with soda bread; it had
to be savoured – steaming hot,
nut-flavoured, streaming
buttery rivulets – to be believed.
And her pièces de résistance –
the sherry trifle after Sunday lunch,
the flawless cherry cakes in which
the fruit never clustered at the base –
were scarcely the stuff of newspapers,
even those where anything local goes.

Where did this leave her? Or us?
We checked the previous issue's
obits for 'housewife' write-ups.
All were reportedly of 'quiet,
unassuming disposition' – one
with a weakness for bingo; this other
'generously lent her time' to Tidy Towns.

What accomplishments might we
attribute to our own housewife,
unless her vigour with the washboard

figured, unless the ill–afforded treats
she brought us from her headscarved
expeditions to the town, our welcomes home
from school to chops and gravy
dinners, warranted attention?
How she kept her lipsticked dignity
without tap water, bathroom, fridge . . .

The page glares back accusingly at us,
blank except for her name, young age,
Valentine's date of death, details
of her 'surviving' husband, children.

Was she an outright failure, therefore,
in the eyes of the world? Had it
no need of further word of her?

Were there no noteworthy deeds to set her
apart from the other 'greatly missed'
mothers in the obit columns?

Had she left no mark whatever
worthy of a record? Miscalculated
so badly as to come to nothing?

Was there no good word we could put in for her?
No persuasive case to be made in her favour?
Could she, our comforter of the afflicted,
have disappeared without a trace?

MEMO TO A PAINTER

Why put so opulent a gloss on the picture
when the unvarnished truth stares you in the face?

Is it not all a bit rich? Why not shame the devil,
tell the story straight, stick to the honest-to-god facts?

Don't fall into the trap of doting parents,
who idolise their babies as some golden calf.

Desist from gilding the lily, over-egging the tempera,
laying a false god before your gallery worshippers.

Every figure witnessed through the stable's
wormy frame was truly humble,

except of course for those slumming visitors
you admit: star-struck kings with gift-wrapped

frankincense and myrrh – odours of sanctity
to offset the noxious fumes of ox and ass –

who kept their distance
from the unkempt shepherds,

the great unwashed whose offering
would morph into a sacrificial lamb,

its horns snagged on the barbed wire
of a crown of thorns.

NOTE: *Adoration of the Magi* ('style of Pieter Coecke van Aelst',
1502–1550), National Gallery of Ireland, depicts the nativity in
elegant surroundings, without the stable or its animals.

We Irish, born into that ancient sect
But thrown upon this filthy modern tide...

— W. B. YEATS

How well I remember the early
Twenty Tens, when the Euro-agony
dragged on, chronic depression,
through each recessionary week.

Chancellor Merkel, stern matriarch,
single parent of the EU family,
incredulous at her spendthrift
adolescent dependents,

topped up their pocket money
with Deutschland's life support.
Year by financial year, the credit rating
agencies downgraded Member States,

their loss of boomtime ostentation
as rapid as the toppling
of Arab dictators in those days
of Twitter-fuelled civil coups.

Anti-austerity riots in profligate Spain.
The creaky Greek administration
feeling the heat from workers, hot under
their while collars about abolished perks.

Dissolute Berlusconi jilted in Italy.
Ireland no longer idolising
chummily-named remittance men
it once plied lovingly with landslide polls.

Any gathering of friends could count
on chit-chat punctuated with
'bailouts', 'quantitative easing',
'negative equity', 'debt forgiveness'.

Cries of 'Burn the Bondholders'
went up, like howls for immolation
at the stake: the witch hunt redivivus.
Wall Street occupied. St Paul's Cathedral

grounds monopolised by anti-capitalists:
new scourge of the money changers.
Deep-pile Celtic Tiger fur recycled
as a threadbare hair shirt.

                *

We Irish – engulfed in this
filthy tide, protesting our innocence
of every charge – felt confident
of rescue in our hour of need.

Someone was bound
to hasten to our aid;
if not Mother EU, then
our Yankee cousins –

whose ancestors, buried
alive in coffin ships,
fled from famine –
would not see us starve,

Olympic-class charmers that
we are: great *craic*, laid-back,
chancers perhaps – but always
of the most lovable kind;

salt of the earth, adored by everyone,
distinguished by our fetching
snotgreen football kit, toast
of the world in replica Irish bars,

a rebel ballad never far
from our lips, feet responding
in jigtime when a fiddle
strikes the right note.

HOPE ETERNAL

From time to time, the ageing couple
talk of making funeral plans.
But the subject somehow changes.

Now here they are, this Easter,
envisioning the future:
how their savings
may be gobbled up
by eldercare fees,
home monitoring costs,
exorbitant hospital bills.

They warm then to their topic.
Extol medical advances.
Anticipate a further surge
in life expectancy.
Determine to keep fit and well.
Be only as old as they feel.
Maximise the active years ahead.

Hearing them enthuse
you could believe
that someone had
assured them of eternal life.
That they had already
risen from the dead.

GRACE BEFORE MEALS

For what we are about to digest, dear Lord,
our heartfelt thanks. Though you exacted
a hefty price, demanded your pound
of muscular flesh, the sweat and blood

of our furrowed brow, at least you made
due recompense, acknowledged services
accomplished, set blackberries on their marks
for your starting gun, rendered peppers

and tomatoes incandescent, sent apple
blossoms into overdrive, triggered the 'germinate'
function in arable lands, released
pollinators from your strategic bee reserve:

greyhounds darting from a trap.
Let us envision, as we fill voracious plates,
sower, seed, and every food-chain link
to our laden dinner table, from loam-turning

worm to home-delivery grocery bagger,
and not forgetting rain and sun that act
as guarantors that grains, herbs, fruits
and brassica will fulfil their growth potential.

Whether airlifted in burlap sacks imprinted
with a UN logo, slow-cooked as dinner stews
by working couples, picked over on first dates,
or flatbread-wrapped in sidewalk kebab carts,

let us proclaim our thanks for whatever vital
sustenance the philanthropic earth has spared us.
May these compliments to the celestial chef
not fall by the wayside, nor land on barren ground.

GALLERY NUDE

For God's sake,
throw on a dab of paint.
Try to look half-decent.

Take yourself in hand.
Make yourself respectable.
Brush yourself down.

Duck behind the sofa.
Grab that scumbled curtain.
Improvise a fig leaf.

Salvage whatever dignity
you can. You are an
open house, vulnerable

to public scrutiny,
every crevice on full show,
all your flaws laid bare.

Avoid a scandal.
Run for cover.
Wrap up before you start

attracting gawkers.
Let the arty crowd direct
their eyes elsewhere.

IRISH ART AUCTION: THE OLD SCHOOL

Labourers in these milk-and-honey
hayfields neither toil nor spin
but idly while the time away
in spick-and-span landscapes.

Thatched cottages wag a welcoming
tail of smoke. Sunset blazes
a trail to where currachs, lugged
ashore, recover land legs.

These painters adopt
a retrospective line on beauty spots,
return them to the drawing board,
backdate scenic views,

eliminate disfigurement by buildings,
restore fouled lakes to their
pristine state, let them make
a counterpart of sky, match it

cloud for cloud, recast impasto
mountains in watercolour,
soften them up to float
as delicately as leaves.

Drystone walls, plaid-shawled colleens,
hens at large in blossoming orchards,
headstrong horse fairs, donkey creels of peat,
neat villages with window boxes, tea rooms,

lion-mouthed water spouts,
are grist to their riverside mills.
Vistas of little fields mimic
antique Tiffany lampshades.

The sea, though, still holds pride
of place, best-loved of all motifs:
pouted lips of breaking waves,
sheer cliffhangers that, unscathed

from transatlantic journeys,
snap shut on lonesome strands.
And here a pauper's barefoot daughter
tramps a road resurfaced with fresh snows.

Here a flock of plush swans poses.
And, lest old acquaintance be forgot,
a leather-hided ancient, quayside seadog,
puts memories in his pipe and smokes them.

REUNION

With scant regard for privacy,
my parents butt in on my dreams,
cut across my reveries,
abuse my hospitality,
presume on my indulgence
of their unwarranted rebukes,
treat me as a child.

Have they lost all track of time?
Forgotten that we
severed our connection
forty years back?
Are they even conscious
they are dead?

Should I gently break
the bad news, inform them
of their whereabouts,
beg them to keep
to their side of my bed?

4.12

Sleep drops me off
half-way, leaving me
to cope for myself,
complete the journey
into morning under my
own steam, grope back
through clammy blankets
of compacted dark
to the dream house
of childhood I have
just mislaid the key to.

Which way to turn now?
Could that barking mad
racket have been unleashed
by the toy dog
– the miniature collie,
prodigal pet from
the corn flakes packet –
I needed to complete
my full collector's set
of canine breeds?

Arrived at long last,
its agitated scratch
leaves its mark on
what used to be
the front door of
what, once upon
a time, was home.

RED ADMIRAL HIBERNATING

Wings shut for winter business,
the butterfly has come to rest
at our guest-room window ledge:
a striped deckchair stacked away,

folded on the hinges of its wings,
to be dusted off when the sun,
resuscitated, has returned to summer form.
A social butterfly, it lives in quivery

expectation of the next big garden party,
the flower-to-flower flirtation; the ecstasy
of wafting on the trampoline of July heat:
frisky, jittery, shadowboxing, run off its sticky feet.

The very prospect drives a surge of blood
through its piping, illuminates its flight deck,
excitement cramping its juiced-up
abdomen: butterflies-in-the-tummy stuff.

Do not disturb. Tread lightly on its
dreams of buddleia. Home is the sailor.
Home and dry. A Red Sea admiral
returned from voyaging, having

breasted the petalled foam, ridden
the crest of heather waves, triumphed
over predatory enemies, the piratical
rivalry of nectar-guzzling honey bees.

PETITION

With all due deference, Lord,
and whatever kowtowing
your reverence calls for,
we ask for full disclosure
of your strategy, humbly take you
to task for allowing our agony
in your once-paradisal garden
to drag on interminably.
May we appeal for leniency,
touch your bleeding heart,
implore you to weed out
our surplus-to-requirements tribulations.

Restore their rightful memories to Alzheimer patients,
steady the trembling Parkinson's elders,
lift depressives from their vicious torpor,
allow despairing MS victims to step up
nimbly from adjustable beds,
throw off incontinence sheets,
evacuate adapted bathrooms,
dispose of motorised wheelchairs as scrap.

Admit us backstage, permit us access
to your patents, blueprints, R & D,
all the revelations you've denied us,
how you've left us clueless about
the remedy for cancer, groping
for the antidotes to Ebola and flu.

Can we – susceptible to road rage, embezzlement,
ethnic cleansing, schadenfreude –
really be created in your image and likeness?
Or is this your dirty secret: you are no better
than ourselves, no more the Chosen One,
the Great Supreme Commander,

than Kim Jong-il or Chairman Mao,
and – though just as befuddled as
the rest of us about how something
came of nothing – happy to take credit
where not due, brook no dissent,
instigate a crackdown on protestors?

Accept a fault-on-both-sides settlement.
Desist from visiting the sins of our first parents
on us, hellbent though you remain
on vengeance for a fall from grace,
a catastrophic lapse of judgement
that took place aeons before our time.
Good Lord, get over it.
Soften your intransigent stance.
Let the fruits of redemption
be made accessible, tasted wholly:
the perks of your breathtaking escapade,
your daredevil suspense story,
your born-again plotline
of death and resurrection;
a three-day wonder that exerts
a mesmerising grip on our imaginations still,
a fascination that translates
into big-budget films, church fêtes,
cult followings, inhuman civil wars.

CHRISTMAS IDYLL

And after a duvet-wrapped
lie-in, to find all the standard
props reliably in place: a silver pot
of hot-shot coffee miniaturising
the log fire blaze; exotic chocolates
from a son's adopted country;
mince pies; mulled wine; vintage
TV comedy; fried breakfast –
everything permitted for a day,
all dietary restrictions lifted.

There too, in the rarely-inhabited
sitting room, carols, crackers, balloons,
shimmering tinsel garlands, a card-
sprouting tree aglow with excitement,
sharing the delight of those whose
gifts it nurtures like laid eggs.
No tension in the air yet. No old
resentments flaring yet among
the children, each on best behaviour,
home with studded boyfriends, urbane,
designer-attired young wives.

How precious they must look from
the empty street, framed picture-perfect
between chintzy curtains, untouched
by suffering, immune from pain,
luxuriating in an otherworldly Thursday
that segues to a dreamy Sunday.

Only the clock-watching woman
coaxing the stove in the lonely
flagstoned kitchen – fretting over
dinner preparations, rinsing sprouts,
basting turkey, struggling to recover

a duck pâté gone wrong –
maintains a foothold in real time.

Stepping out to bin the forcemeat
waste, add roast potato peelings
to the compost heap, she is assailed
by melancholic winds, whipped
by hail, chilled by a dark killjoy air
that – refusing even a single
day's remission – threatens
to rough up this stage set,
snuff out the frivolous fairy lights,
abolish the nonsense
of a goodwill season,
pour cold water on the fire,
bring down the whole house
of glitzy greeting cards,
drown out the ethereal boy treble's
tidings of *comfort and joy*,
comfort and joy, expose a raw
world incapable of betterment:
our dusty futures hanging on
the prospects of a small blue
planetary bauble in a glittering,
infinitely expanding universe.

UPDATE

God, I still miss you some days,
fondly recall our happier times.
You used to take me into
your confidence, while I
fessed up to my transgressions,
owned up to grievous flaws.
And, granted absolution, I would
ascend to cloud nine,
mind on higher things,
ears only for your voice that conversed,
not in our inarticulate vernacular
but through lapidary Latin,
plainchant, exultant motet.
I recall the wet cathedral evenings
when your fair-weather friends
had absented themselves,
and we settled down by the fire
of the votive candle shrine
for a heart-to-heart confab,
our conversation never flagging.

What a good listener you always were
to me, God. I so wish we had not quarrelled,
gone our separate ways, making
too big an issue of the Jesuitical
distinctions that divided us, failing
to see eye-to-eye on articles of faith.

I still watch out for news of you,
gossip column tattle, and – an obsessive
divorcee – track your movements, eager
to learn which lovers take my place,
what types you hang about with these days,
what you're up to elsewhere
as you expand your horizons,

establishing new branches of your empire,
propagating universes by the second.

And you must feel a loneliness
close to empty nest syndrome
now that so many of your
erstwhile acolytes have flown the coop,
escaped your cage, questioned
your discretion, no longer prepared
to submit to your rough justice,
remain prisoners of your conscience.

God, how much I miss the comfort food
of your home-baked communion host.
And hush. The megaphones roped
to the telegraph poles relay around
the town your May procession:
The blue-gowned Child of Mary
women join with the choir.
The petal-strewing schoolgirls,
the banner-carrying sodality men,
and the canopy-bearing deacons
– custodians of the fragile Marian shrine
buoyant on its wildflower-brimming float –
break into song, give 'full-throated' voice
to the humming fecundity of early summer.

The year, refurbished, kitted out afresh,
is soaking up warm pastel colours,
reaching perfect pitch, oozing
through rejuvenated fields
a slow sempiternal note.

BEDTIME

No smoke without fire: ash droppings,
flashing cigarette morse from the other
brass bed, give my uncle's whereabouts away.

He is plotting his tomorrows before sleep:
install tripods for peas, weed the mangolds,
turn further hay for winter's feeding frenzy.

The small sash window, crouching under dapper
thatch, is open wide, scouting for a breath of air,
our tartan Foxford blankets thrown overboard.

Day's over-eager light does not know when
to stop: I can still speedread wallpaper rosebuds,
bear witness to the holy pictures' apparitions.

A Beauty of Bath apple ferment overwhelms
the back room, where pheasants slump from
doors in autumn, and vital supplies are stored:

plump beer-bellied Guinness bottles and Time ale
for visitors; Corcoran's orangeade; selection boxes
of Lemon's Pure Sweets for grandchildren;

jelly and custard leftovers; canned mandarin oranges
and fruit cocktail; Goodall's salad cream; beetroot-red
sandwich meat; skinless sausages; flaking grinder loaves..

Little flutterings and scurryings from the farmyard.
Then everything settles again. I wake to a grainy smell –
the boiling vat of layers' mash – dinging churns,

uncles up, about in overalls, and singing, from their milking
stools, 'Lipstick on Your Collar', or 'Achin' Breakin' Heart',
to boost the friesians' creamy yield.

INDEX OF TITLES

The index includes (in italics) the titles of all poems grouped under the 'Breviary' headings, but not titled sections of other poems.